# Trauma and Meaning-Making

# Inter-Disciplinary Press

## Publishing Advisory Board

*Inter-Disciplinary Press* is a part of *Inter-Disciplinary.Net*
A Global Network for Dynamic Research and Publishing

**2016**

# Trauma and Meaning Making

Edited by

## Danielle Schaub and Elspeth McInnes

Inter-Disciplinary Press

Oxford, United Kingdom

The *Inter-Disciplinary Press* is part of *Inter-Disciplinary.Net* – a global network for research and publishing. The *Inter-Disciplinary Press* aims to promote and encourage the kind of work which is collaborative, innovative, imaginative, and which provides an exemplar for inter-disciplinary and multi-disciplinary publishing.

British Library Cataloguing in Publication Data. A catalogue record for this book is available from the British Library.

Inter-Disciplinary Press, Priory House, 149B Wroslyn Road, Freeland, Oxfordshire. OX29 8HR, United Kingdom.
+44 (0)1993 882087

ISBN: 978-1-84888-455-7
First published in the United Kingdom in Paperback format in 2016. First Edition.

# Table of Contents

**Introduction**                                                                vii
*Danielle Schaub and Elspeth McInnes*

**Part 1    Publics and Trauma**

Recording Death, Confronting Trauma, Ascribing Guilt:            3
Four Palestinian Web Memorials
*Jeanne Ellen Clark*

*The Memorial to the Murdered Jews of Europe* and Its           21
Associations with Vicarious Trauma
*Mark Callaghan*

Gaining Agency in Response to Trauma: The Role of Physical       41
and Virtual Memorials
*Catherine Ann Collins and AnnaMaria Mencarelli*

**Part 2    Representing Trauma**

Images of Suffering: Trauma and Homer's Troy                     73
in Euripides' *Hecuba*
*Lisa B. Hughes*

'Split in two chronologically': Loss and Dis/Orientation of the  93
Emotional and Geographic Exile in Nancy Huston's *Losing North*
*Danielle Schaub*

'Stigmatized body in pain...what?...who?...no!...she!'           123
Samuel Beckett's *Not I*
*Svetlana Antropova*

**Part 3    Trauma Spaces and Places**

Representing a Trauma Space and Rendering the Real of the        143
Spanish Civil War in Carlos Saura's *La caza*
*Jeremy Kasten*

Towards Narrating Trauma: The Impact of the Civil War in         159
Former Yugoslavia
*Emina Hadziosmanovic and Nigel Hunt*

From Accomplice to Victim: Catholic Church, Spanish Civil    181
War and Collective Memory
*Mireno Berrettini*

**Part 4**     **Post-Traumatic Recovery and Growth**

Developing Trauma-Informed Pedagogy in a Classroom with    209
6-8 Year Old Children
*Elspeth McInnes, Alexandra Diamond and Victoria Whitington*

Trauma and Growth: The Psychology of Self-Actualisation    231
and Positive Post-Traumatic Processes
*Peter Bray*

# Introduction: Trauma and Meaning Making

## Danielle Schaub and Elspeth McInnes

Humans cannot escape trauma. Mortality implies that injury, sickness and death will at some point mark the lives of individuals, families, communities and nations, forcing humans to confront their darkest fears and agonies of pain and loss. With no one spared from the experience of trauma at one or another stage in life, one cannot downplay the importance of confronting the questions that haunt beings after traumatic experiences and continue the search for insight into and comprehension of trauma and the human condition. In his various writings on trauma that largely focus on Holocaust memory, Dominick LaCapra explains that the victims of trauma suffer from a fragmented identity formation. Possessed by the calamitous event, those who have suffered trauma relive the incident of the past compulsively in the present. They see the signs of the primal scene elsewhere when representations trigger it, collapsing past and present and entrapping the self within a kind of zero time. The traumatic event may not even have been experienced directly, but by a parent, so that children may bear the burdens of distorted memory and experience an inability to directly remember trauma and recollect it in order to move on. In *Writing History, Writing Trauma*, LaCapra focuses on the healing process, noting that events may remain so imbued with traumatic power that individuals cannot represent the harrowing moment to themselves, that they cannot integrate the event into their narratives. An experience becomes momentous when it seems to fissure one's rationale of identity, relationships and existence. It becomes catastrophic when it disintegrates the stories through which one narrates oneself into being, functioning like a black hole into which meaning collapses. The disorientation can cause an anaesthetising feeling, so that even if the historical event is recalled, it is revived in an emotionally-deadened manner that belies the explosive emotions relocated – mislocated – elsewhere.

Ubiquitous, trauma arrives in each life as a complete shock. Each person who experiences trauma, directly or vicariously, undergoes a unique personal event not readily equated with another's experience even when it derives from the same source. Personal antecedents, previous events, the singular perspectives and perceptions of different individuals, the range of options and resources available to them — all shape how human beings experience trauma and how it affects them over time. Some events, such as war or natural disaster, traumatise whole populations, yet each individual constructs a different story of it based on their personal make-up. Coming to terms with traumatising events, as an individual or a population, involves a process of meaning making, 'making sense' of what happened. As social and learning beings use their memories of experiences to inform future actions and orientations, understanding what has happened in a traumatic event provides them with a guide to avoid or prevent such events, or rather to best minimise harm from such an event in the future. How people fashion, recall and give voice to what has happened entirely depends on the complication from the disruptive impacts of trauma on memory. Survival of the traumatic event may indeed depend on suppressing the memories of the experience. Alternatively, trauma survivors can also experience intrusive flashbacks to the event, forcing them to repeatedly re-live the experience. Helping people understand the traumatic experience and their response/s to it as a guide to the future, processes of meaning-making include therapy, creative arts, reflection and shifts in identity and the self in relation to the world. By no means mutually exclusive, these different processes may be engaged simultaneously or sequentially, individually and privately or collectively and publicly.

*Trauma and Meaning Making* draws together articles focusing on the diverse approaches of individuals and collectivities in response to trauma — whether individual and private and/or collective and public — in their attempt at 'making sense' of events by definition overwhelming and at times incomprehensible. The collection of essays results from the interactive efforts of researchers in different fields and different parts of the world that previously met at the Third Global Conference on 'Trauma: Theory and Practice' organised by the Inter-Disciplinary.Net in Lisbon, Portugal. The conference allowed specialists of multiple fields, such as semiologists, historians, psychologists, psychiatrists, therapists, social workers, writers, performers, literary critics, economists and more, to share their approaches and insights into trauma so as to benefit from the interaction. At the outset, we invited some researchers to submit their research and deepen knowledge in the field through dialoguing with one another. The fifth in the series, this book covers various current approaches to the field. With their substantial expansion of their findings they contribute to furthering knowledge about ways to make sense of traumatic experiences. In their own fashions, they have examined parameters of different contexts and disciplines through their own expertise, contributing wider knowledge in the process.

Public responses to trauma can include formal state acknowledgement defining the event, its causes and consequences, and framing understandings of 'the victims'. Alternatively, people affected by a traumatic event may themselves make spontaneous public gestures and encourage collective responses. The first section of this collection on 'Publics and Trauma' explores these variations and underscores how the private experience of trauma may lead to public commemoration, enabling identification and interpretation beyond the directly traumatised. Jeanne Ellen Clark's chapter examines Internet renditions of the conflict between Israel and Palestine from the perspectives of Palestinians as well as responses to them. Her examination of four different Internet sites that commemorate the suffering of children through photographs throws light on varying patterns of response, including victimhood, demonisation of the other side, resistance, violence, and more. Mark Callaghan deconstructs the making of the Berlin Holocaust Memorial and the complexities of creating a national memorial for a national crime. His description of the non-representational memorial clarifies how commemorative sites may lead to vicarious trauma, not by informing the public about the specifics of the traumatic ordeal, but by allowing them to experience how it must have felt, and how survivors must live with the unspeakable. Closing the section on Publics and Trauma, Catherine Ann Collins and AnnaMaria Mencarelli investigate the actions of ordinary citizens in their public responses to tragic events, such as missing children and road deaths, as each contributes to a publicly generated memorial as both a commemoration and an expression of grief. Discussing how pilgrimage to memorials leads to working through grief as well as minimisation of the trauma, they also point out the problematic stagnation of the missing in the past through photographic representations and their alterations.

Among the numerous complexities of representing trauma, the capacity to 'speak the unspeakable' affords multiple reflections, not only because of the horrors this may invoke, but also because of the numerous physiological responses to trauma. While happening, traumatic events cause the reduction of blood flow to the cerebral cortex as the body mobilises for survival. Survivors may comment on their literal inability to speak at the time of the event. Also as part of its survival mechanisms, the body may shut down receptors in the brain that enable the formation of memory. These physiological processes mean that recalling or giving voice to what has happened becomes difficult, with disrupted memories and/or intrusive, overwhelming flashbacks. In Section Two on 'Representing Trauma', Lisa B. Hughes analyses the texts of Ancient Greek writers and their depictions of trauma in narratives of war, sacrifice and conflict. She examines Euripides' play *Hecuba* in relation to Homer's Iliad, focusing on the art of representing trauma for an audience as a source of working through individual and collective trauma as well as of encouraging civic conduct. Danielle Schaub focuses on the textual markers of Nancy Huston's essay *Losing North* that cue the readers to identify how narratives of disastrous events embed. As she engages in psychoanalytical and textual scrutiny of phenomena resulting from exile in unconscious response to childhood trauma, she highlights how by addressing the very erasure of the traumatic source, the text allows the readers to revisit their own traumas and the traces these have left, and in so doing, negotiate meaning for their own experiences. Svetlana Antropova concludes the section with an analysis of Samuel Beckett's short play *Not I* and the dramatic markers of trauma in his works. Her close reading of the stylistically alienating devices and stage direction borne of the identity loss resulting from sexual abuse emphasises how spectators and readers alike live the obsessive re-telling through the senses as if the trauma inscribes itself on their bodies.

Traumatic events take place in geographic spaces. Wars across territories confront populations in war zones with the destruction of people, property and routine, converting their daily lives into survival. After the conflict has ended the scars remain in geographic space on the psyches of those who have survived. Sights, sounds, smells that trigger reminders of the harrowing events can catapult survivors into re-experiencing them. The question arises whether survivors should leave the place of destruction or stay and work to recover and rebuild. Section Three on 'Trauma Places and Spaces' considers how populations relate to the war zone after the conflict has passed. Jeremy Kasten inspects the locale of Castile in Spain as a 'trauma space' and an enduring symbol of loss and disorientation emergent from the Spanish Civil War. His focus on the spatial characteristics of trauma — the place where it happened, the place that contains traces of it, the place that shapes and fashions memory of it — enables a discussion of the repressive denial prevalent in Spain of psychological wounds left by the Spanish Civil War in Castile. Emina Hadziosmanovic and Nigel Hunt review, through the lens of space, the differences between survivors of the Bosnian War who have stayed in Bosnia and those displaced as refugees in the United Kingdom. Her chapter shows that the multiple responses to displacement largely depend on location and its particulars. Mireno Berrettini tackles institutional memories of trauma with special attention to the approach of the Catholic Church to the Spanish Civil War. His chapter examines how the political positioning of the Catholic Church in the war period has played out in narrative constructions about twentieth-century Spanish political cleavages. Discrediting the Republican, and hailing the Nationalist, perspective, the Church wove a picture that left an imprint on memory, affecting the psychological, political and religious landscape.

Living through a traumatic experience almost always changes how individuals and collectivities view themselves, their world and their relationship to it. As mortal beings, humans go about their daily lives with expectations that they will not suffer catastrophes and that their routines and habits will continue much as they did before. 'Everyday' traumatic events which change people's lives, sometimes forever, include receiving a diagnosis of serious illness, facing a family death, emerging from a road accident, experiencing a house fire, suffering family violence or a street assault. On a larger scale, terrorism, war and natural disasters affect loss, death and destruction across populations and territories, shattering the rhythms of daily life and erasing spaces and relationships. Such sudden and radical shifts prevent any easy return to the understandings and attitudes formed before the event, requiring individuals and communities to create new ways of understanding their world and their place in it. Section Four on 'Post-Traumatic Recovery and Growth' examines the possibilities and processes of such changes. Elspeth McInnes, Alexandra Diamond and Victoria Whitington engage with issues of recovery, in this instance with special emphasis on inclusive practices in classrooms to assist children exposed to chronic stress or trauma. Chronically stressed and traumatized children can struggle in school as trauma affects receptive learning states. They present a case study of interventions in a primary school class that successfully assisted children in difficulty. Finally, Peter Bray explores the concept of post-traumatic growth and the ways in which some survivors come to see their world anew in a deeper and more profound way, sometimes even realising the beneficial changes occurring while trying to tackle, or come to terms with, the challenging experience. Without disregarding the disabling psychological wounds inflicted, he evidences the positive transformations that may ensue by examining multiple approaches to the phenomenon that recognise the potential growth paradoxically afforded.

The collection highlights multiple practices of meaning making after traumatic events, continuing the exploration of trauma in the lives of individuals and communities. In doing so, it demonstrates some of the diversity and complexities faced when responding to trauma. Questions canvassed include what has happened and where, who holds responsibility for it, who has fallen victim, how and who speaks about it, how one remembers it as victim or onlooker, what determines if and how one remembers it, what effects it affords, if one can heal from it and how. As a response to trauma, meaning making consists both in a personal journey to finding a new way to exist and live in a world shattered by trauma and in public politics locating and defining what has happened. In both perspectives, the collection evaluates the impact achieved by naming the victim/s thus the right of the victim/s to suffer from its aftermath or refusing to recognise the traumatic event and thus the right of the victim/s to respond to it. The researchers examine these topics through a range of paradigms and techniques that invite the reader to consider anew the specificities of context and relationship in the negotiation of post-traumatic survival. By attending to how one 'makes sense of' traumatic events, this volume will enable readers to draw links between practices grounded in diverse disciplines encompassing creative arts, textual analysis, public and collective communication, psychology and psychotherapy, memory and memorial.

Never written in isolation, books result from all sorts of interaction, particularly in the case of collected essays. The publication of such a book involves the talents and commitment of various individuals beyond those whose names appear on the title page, and we would like to express our gratitude to them. First, we would like to thank the contributors for their willingness to share their expertise and patient acceptance of editorial queries and/or suggestions; they have made our work enjoyable, for their subjects and argumentation have enriched us. Next, we wish to thank Peter Bray, our Project Leader, for his warm support in the early stages of this project and later. Thirdly, we owe gratitude to Inter-Disciplinary.Net and more particularly to Lisa Howard and Ana Borlescu, their encouragement and prompt answers to all our queries during the editorial process. Finally, we wish to acknowledge the generous support and good nature of our partners and/or children, who cheerfully accommodated the time required by the collaborative editorial work and decisions involved in producing this book.

# Part 1

# Publics and Trauma

# Recording Death, Confronting Trauma, Ascribing Guilt: Four Palestinian Web Memorials

*Jeanne Ellen Clark*

**Abstract**

Vernacular and official memorials provide outlets for a traumatized community to share their loss and vent their grief. The identity of both the mourned victim and the mourning community are expressed in the form and content of these memorials. Official war memorials may function to convey a political message within the presentation of the traumatic memory: whether to support those who died for national policy, or to present the consequences of enemy action. Registering the deaths of children in the Israeli/Palestinian conflict since 2000, three primary websites (Remember These Children, Fakhoora.org, and the Palestinian Holocaust Museum) participate in the struggle for how to remember the on-going trauma resulting from the Israeli/Palestinian conflict. Established by NGOs rather than government agencies, these memorial sites may serve as a focal point for grief intensified by the innocence of the victims. An earlier site memorializes the disputed, but iconic martyr of the al-Aqsa Intifada: Muhammad al-Dura. All four sites register societal trauma so others may confront that trauma. Pictures of victims and/or testimonies of witnesses to their deaths provide a vivid reality of cost. The sites are designed as an indictment as well as a memorial. This chapter explores the double edge of politicized trauma memory within these sites. Name listing requires an acknowledgement of the degree of loss. Associated witness testimony permits a working through of trauma by the witness and personalizes the victims for the larger community. The form, however, with its ties to Holocaust memorials, while potentially intensifying the guilt associated with the victimizers, complicates the willingness of the larger community to assign that guilt to the descendants of the WWII Holocaust.

**Key Words:** Web memorials, politicized memory, polarizing, commemoration, agency, testimony, trauma, identification, Israel/Palestine, identity, victimage, consilience.

*****

## 1. Memorializing a Contested Past

Memorials to past suffering punctuate the landscape of Israel/Palestine. The Yad Vashem Holocaust Memorial, Herod's fortress at Masada, the rusted out tanks and trucks of past wars intentionally left as markers of those battles, the abandoned villages of Deir Yassin and Kafr Bir'im, the marble monument in Gaza to the nine Turks who died in the raid on the Mavi Marmara—all evoke moments of historical trauma in a contested past over a disputed land. In so doing, all play a part in the narratives of identity of Israelis and Palestinians. Those narratives reflect their traumatized past: the Holocaust, the Nakba, the bloody cost of achieving or retaining the land, deprivation, a loss of respect, of family, or home. The narratives shape the way the contesting parties perceive the world and each other. As Rotberg notes, 'History is the reservoir of resentment, the fount of blame.'[1] Drawing on those narratives in memorializing that contested past can fuel the blame, thus exacerbating the conflict with polarizing discourse that cannot or will not recognize the values and needs of the other. The morals supported by the narratives can become 'fists' and commemoration can turn to 'moral indignation.'[2]

Burke speaks of piety as 'a system builder....a sense of what properly goes with what.'[3] Narratives of identity shape those pieties offering a sense of what to value, what rites to perform, what to reject. These narratives, a lens for communal memory, offer explanations for what one should commemorate, and how one should express that reverence. Bell points to the danger,

> Communal memories act as subtle yet powerful mechanisms for generating a sustaining social solidarity. While such memories can act as a social adhesive they are always contestable, and it is in this realm of conflict, and the complex power relations that underpin and structure it, that the politics of memory is enacted.[4]

## 2. The Martyr-Hero

Khalili's study of the politics of Palestinian national commemoration discusses a shift in the portrayal of the hero-martyr over time, changing from the celebration of the militant *fedayeen* to the memorialization of the innocent victim.[5] She argues that '*what* is valorized, celebrated, and commemorated in different nationalisms reveals a great deal about how that nationalism is formed.'[6] The trauma of the WWII holocaust is a dominating narrative in Israeli national identity along with Masada, resulting in a deeply ingrained pious attention to military strength and national security in a country understood as surrounded by enemies;[7] the Palestinian trauma is expressed as rooted in the events surrounding the formation of the state of Israel—in the displacement of refugees, destruction of villages, and eventually the occupation of the still more land by the new state of Israel.[8]

As Khalili observes,

> Commemoration is almost always staged or 'performed' for a public...and demands reactions from that audience, whether that reaction is...political action...a critique of the present...a demand of 'moral accountability'...or charting a map of the future....particular commemorative practices can be interpreted as engaging a nationalist audience in one setting, and as appealing to international human rights in another.[9]

Khalili examines an early museum memorial exhibit to the first one hundred Palestinians (adult and child) to die as casualties of the al-Aqsa intifada. The exhibit consisted of photographs and artefacts associated with the victims. The objects included empty birdcages, a used coffee cup, work pants, and school notebooks with scrawled sketches—detritus of daily life set to establish the normalcy of the dead.[10] These one hundred individuals were like those viewing the exhibit, but they had been killed/martyred; they had not, however, sought martyrdom. The exhibit established the importance of such victims for Palestinian memory and collective identity. The four following memorial sites continue that commemoration, appealing to familiar pieties as each site directs the memory in diverse ways. While two of the sites foster polarization, the remaining two show the possibility of using commemoration to lead to a 'rhetoric of consilience;' in such discourse, diverse and divergent groups are 'invited' to come together, leaving their separate narratives and memories 'in favour of a common set of values or aspirations.'[11] We begin with polarization and the demonizing of the other through commemoration.

### 3. Al-Dura Memorial Site

On 30 September 2000, the second day of the al-Aqsa *intifada*, twelve-year-old Muhammad al-Dura was filmed, as he died crouched with his father behind a cement barrel, caught in a sudden crossfire between Israelis and Palestinians in Gaza. The images, filmed for French television, played repeatedly on international news. The boy became the quintessential Palestinian victim and the captured stills transformed into civic murals, national stamps, posters, YouTube videos, and sculpture. In the following months and years, the initial image of a boy perceived to be targeted by unfeeling Israeli soldiers was reread as a boy set up for killing by manipulative Palestinian forces, and then as a boy who never really died. The image used as the basis for 'othering' both Israelis and Palestinians justified further violence and hostility. Over ten years later precisely what happened is still disputed, but the power of the image remains.

Not surprisingly, one of the early Palestinian web memorials builds on that image; it offers a shockwave flash presentation dedicated to Muhammad al-Dura.[12] Created by AlSham.net, the shockwave presentation celebrates the boy as a Palestinian martyr and serves as an online eulogy enhancing his status as the perfect victim for the cause. For twenty-seven seconds the viewer watches quick cuts and close ups with graphic manipulation. The basic images and four still shots excerpted from the video footage. Shifts between the stills and close ups of the faces within the stills create movement. Suddenly graphic gun sights appear and disappear overlaid on the boy's head. In an extended use of a still shot of the wide-eyed screaming father facing the camera while the crying boy burrows into his father's back, a sight settles on Mohammed's forehead and a graphic depiction of a bullet hole oozing bright red blood appears. The image shifts to another still with the slumped father and limp child. Dripping computer-generated blood covers the screen. The blood fades out, the bodies reappear and the boy's body apparently rises in the air, his body then graphically wrapped in a Palestinian flag like a martyr on a bier. Other images on the screen fade out and a light comes up behind the wrapped boy. A message of promise and continuation, directed to his mother, then appears on the screen,

> Don't cry, mother, Rami will live forever in our conscious [sic], His cry for help in the last minutes will echo forever in the minds of every free Arab to remind us of the cruelty of our enemy. His bleeding wounds will remind [sic] open in our hearts until the giant wakes up and the land will be free.[13]

Verbally and visually the site paints Muhammad Rami al-Dura as a Palestinian martyr, a victim in the battle for restoration of the land. He does nothing but cry and die, but that suffices. Visually his role as martyr is enhanced and the pain of the witnessing audience is sharpened by the computer-generated blood, which would remind the Palestinian audience of the unwashed body of the martyr. The generated gun sights intensify the sense of al-Dura as an innocent victim of an evil force, for surely only an evil force would intentionally target (as the graphic gun sights blatantly suggest) an unarmed child. The shockwave flash presentation manipulates familiar stills from the news video to formalize al-Dura's death as the perfect victim, the apparently unblemished lamb of the al-Aqsa intifada. The presentation focuses the horror of the event for the viewer while portraying al-Dura and his father as total innocents.

This memorial site can function only for Palestinian true believers. It uses what Haas terms 'a totalizing rhetoric'[14] that demonizes the other and does not allow ground for mutual recognition. The memorial supports the master narrative of the Palestinians as a traumatized people defending their land; the graphics create an enemy with alien values who does not value the life of a child. The narrative of this trauma 'has to do with self-definition, self-understanding, survival and destiny of the people involved.'[15] The narrative centres on an identity tied to horror and loss, leading to mistrust of a world permeated with such loss. The shockwave memorialization of the al-Dura trauma reinforces the master narrative of victimage by a demonized other. As the presentation contends, such an enemy should be confronted and rejected; this memorial exacerbates rather than alleviating trauma.

### 4. Palestinian Holocaust Memorial Museum

In February 2005, Matan Vilnai, Israeli Deputy Defence Minister, announced on Army Radio that the Palestinians 'will bring upon themselves a bigger *shoah*.'[16] The use of the Hebrew term for catastrophe possibly referred to the Arabic term for catastrophe, *nakba*, used by Palestinians as the name for the events of 1948.

However, *shoah* also frequently points to the holocaust of WWII; a group of pro-Palestinian activists focused on that naming as they announced the development of a new web-based memorial museum to be called the Palestinian Holocaust Memorial Museum. While dedicated to 'all the civilians who lost their lives during the attacks,'[17] it was to focus on children. An announcement in the aftermath of Operation Cast Lead, the Israeli war in Gaza during December 2008-January 2009, said the site would 'feature the photos, names and stories of Palestinian children killed by Israeli forces in the context of a new Holocaust.... Testimonies of the survivors will also be published.'[18] The announcement requested reports of child death with details of their dreams, their hobbies, their photos, and their diaries. The museum, intended to offer a strong sense of the individual, was to be modelled after the Holocaust museum in Washington, D.C. One thirteen-year-old boy, killed by an Israeli missile, is listed as enjoying 'drawing and swimming,' dreaming 'of being a lawyer like his father.'[19] Other reports emphasize the death event and the on-going trauma; a four-month-old girl, shown with a gaping hole in her chest, is described as having been killed by shell fragments that went through her back and 'dispersed parts of her body;' her mother remarks, 'Until now, her toys are still all in place...her lollipop, her bed, her clothes—all are in the same place.'[20] Images, provided by photographers who witnessed Cast Lead,[21] show destroyed homes, dead children wrapped for martyr's funerals, dead children in medical facilities, and occasionally dead children in the rubble of destroyed buildings. In exceptional cases a school photo of the child while alive is used. The scenes are sometimes stark, and shocking. One particularly horrific image shows just the dirty, tousled head of a four-year-old girl emerging from the rubble of her destroyed home.[22] The images stand as evidence of the death of innocents, but they create a highly politicized memory. The dead are consistently listed as martyrs. In several cases the information lines refer to murder rather than death. By late May 2009 Al-Ahram reported that the site had recorded over 500,000 visitors.[23] Sometime in late 2012 or early 2013, the site disappeared and the domain came under the control of GoDaddy.[24] Remnants of the material associated with the site are still available online. While one site with such remnants is professionally laid out with simple typeface, the YouTube video clip showing some of the original site employs a dripping typeface for the title reminiscent of that used in old horror films.[25]

This intentionally provocative memorial proved overtly offensive to many in the international audience. While it might effectively function as a memorial for a group of Palestinian true believers, the form was too confrontational for the content to be easily afforded reverential memory by a larger audience. In explicitly adopting both the terminology of the WWII Shoah and some of the forms used in memorializing that tragedy, while simultaneously and explicitly blaming the descendants of those earlier victims for the deaths in this new horror of war, the site designers would violate the beliefs, the pieties of many in a broader audience.

Laden in pathos, but shocking in its implications, the site would seem to denigrate the original trauma while describing the latter.

Grob and Roth describe the Holocaust as a ghost 'never far from the Middle East arena, contaminating the air breathed by both Israelis and Palestinians.'[26] The Palestinian Holocaust Memorial Museum reflects that contamination. Its development would inevitably feed the memory of long suffered anti-Semitism and reinforce the sense of a nation besieged by its enemies, both in real life and virtual life. The form alone would offend some and the content reinforced the offense. The site would offer a place for memorializing, but would shut out the possibility of consilience.

## 5.  Fakhoora Memorial Site

A third web memorial is structured by the organization, al Fakhoora. Its funding is primarily but not solely Islamic: the Islamic Development Bank, Qatar Red Crescent, U.N. Development Program, Palestinian Medical Relief Society, and Islamic Relief Worldwide. The activities of the organization centre on increasing educational opportunities in Gaza: leadership training, scholarships, improved care for youth with mental health concerns, coordinated online social meetings. At the same time the organization presents itself as a form of memorial; it is named for the United Nations school in Gaza's Jabaliyeh refugee camp where an Israeli tank shell attack in 2009 resulted in forty-three fatalities and one hundred additional victims. The organization proclaims: 'Our campaign symbolizes an outcry against targeting schools during war, and the safekeeping of educational institutions during aggression.'[27] As part of that campaign, al-Fakhoora offers a second specific online memorial to the 352 children who died in Operation Cast Lead in Gaza— mentioned as a disproportionate number of innocent victims, 'one quarter of all fatalities' in that war.[28]

The memorial records the deaths of children ranging in age from two months to seventeen years. The memorial site relies on name lists and reports rather than visual information. Over half of the names (always recorded with the age) hyperlink to pages giving details of the death. These specifics include the location and typically a brief narrative of the death, with some accompanying witness testimonies from a parent, other relative, or friend. These statements constitute a public memorial for the family—a hero/martyr commemoration of a less politicized form that the familiar martyr posters published by families and militant organizations to record the deaths of their hero martyrs. The memorial is structured from information supplied by Defence for Children International. The organization notes the 'extensive research on the ground'[29] by that group as a way of establishing the veracity, the credibility of their recorded names and conditions. While the act of reporting to Defence for Children may have served an immediate trauma witness function for the family or friends, this online vernacular memorial record serves a political function, not uncommon in official war memorials.

This web memorial focuses not on the hero martyrs active in the fight, but on the innocent victims of the fight in which their lives were caught. The site stresses and intensifies that purity, beginning with the opening explanation that this memorial is devoted 'to the innocent children that lost their lives as a result of a conflict they played no part in.'[30] Location, age, or activity of the victim typically establishes the blameless state. Description serves as intensifier, but unlike the related statements associated with the Palestinian Holocaust Memorial Museum, that description does not rely on what might be seen as exaggerated adjectives. The brief accounts seem written to serve as evidence for an international audience of Palestinian loss and trauma.

A broad audience would commonly accept the markers of innocence. Infants and toddlers have the purity of extreme youth. Other victims are described in activities evoking their youth: playing ball with friends, playing marbles, hallucinating about a children's television program. Still others are sleeping or preparing for bed—activities that evoke images of peacefully sleeping children who, in the words of an old familiar children's bedtime prayer, did indeed die before they woke. Other victims are highlighted as dying in the midst of helpful actions: feeding birds on the roof, fetching bread or warm clothes for the family, helping a stranger. Others are portrayed as self-sacrificing, having been killed while trying to protect the family. These markers of innocence are crucial if international viewers of the site are to sympathize and acknowledge the experienced loss and trauma. The details typically reflect values and pieties shared by the international audience and the Palestinian victims. That similarity of substance renders the Palestinians as worthy victims.

One piety employed on several occasions would serve to draw some of the audience in, while distancing others, i.e. reference to religious devotion: a victim might have been killed while at prayer or going to or from prayer. The link of al-Fakhoora to Islam makes the references appropriate, but the linkage of Hamas to militant Islam makes the references risky for a non-Muslim audience.

Diverse strategic details enable the memorial narratives to intensify the sense of trauma for the witnessing audience. Time sometimes becomes a tragic factor with death occurring during a school shift change, in the midst of a ceasefire, near the end of the war, or ironically while running home to report a relative's death. On occasion it gives the sense of preventable death: ambulances are unable to reach the scene so the necessary medical aid cannot be secured in time. There are references to the on-going signs of trauma experienced by the families after the death incident: nightmares, bedwetting, constant crying, and the dispersal of a close-knit extended family that is now homeless and scattered. Horrific injuries are recounted: exposed brains, bodies bleeding out, bodies decapitated, legless, or completely blown to bits with families collecting the pieces to bury. This last is at times made even harsher by the report that they could not find all of the body, or could not collect the body until after its mutilation by tank traffic or scavenging dogs. The vivid and grotesque details create images of death difficult to set aside. The close visitor to the site, one who reads the accounts linked to the names, witnesses the trauma of such deaths, rather than merely skimming a meaningless list of names.

Parental proximity or felt involvement in the death compounds the tragedy and extends the basis for audience identification with the sufferers. War twists universally familiar relationships as a child dies while sitting in a parent's lap, or a parent recognizes the head of a burned corpse 'by my daughter Ala's braids that I had combed myself. I know how I combed her hair. It was my daughter, Ala.'[31] Another parent mourns the death of a child because the parent had allowed the child to play in the street during a ceasefire; no missile strike would be expected and the children had been long cooped up inside. The expressions of parental concern and evidence of parental care are crucial. The celebration of child martyrs elsewhere led to charges that Palestinians intentionally sacrifice their children, implying they do not respect life (such charges play a central part in the controversy over Muhammad al-Dura). Statements of parental care and loss recorded in this site serve to mitigate that belief and to demonstrate a shared pious attitude as to how children should be valued and treated.

Within these accounts Israelis are typically reduced to the mechanical and faceless. It is usually the weapons that kill—drones, tanks, F-16s, missiles, and occasionally the still faceless sniper. On rare occasions the Israeli soldiers are described in face-to-face cruelty: firing on a family walking under a white flag, killing a father and the wounded child he is carrying, targeting a school sheltering 1900 civilians with white phosphorus. One report of a family death notes that the Israeli newspaper Ha'aretz reported the attack as an 'operational mistake' but an officer in the resulting probe asserted, 'We will not apologize for an operation in which only ten of our soldiers lost their lives.'[32] In quoting this statement, the witness requires the attackers to demonize themselves by showing a differing evaluation of human life. Such moments, however, rarely occur in this set of accounts.

The accounts emphasize Palestinian suffering and Palestinian loss. Loss clearly comes from and because of the Israelis, but in distancing the deed from the doer, in typically linking the deadly results to the weapons rather than those using them, the reports allow international readers to focus their attention on the Palestinian victims without directly confronting the culpability of the historically traumatized Israelis. The site makes Palestinian victimage vividly real and the victimising force implicitly clear, but does not hammer the visitor with repeated, explicit accusations of individual Israeli guilt.

The recording of death matters, but a major part of its significance here lies in the ability of that record to sway international public opinion. The personalized record is also set as a sympathetic account with which a non-Palestinian audience might identify. The memorial with its victimage record still available on the web, no longer appears within the site index. The record of past loss would seem less important to the organizers than their on-going activity. With their focus on education, particularly increasing current educational opportunities, and with their desire to 'begin leading the way for a new generation to tackle issues deemed unsolvable by previous generations trapped in a cycle of deconstructive rhetoric,'[33] the site unsurprisingly no longer focuses on the memorial, but on images of the living Gaza and the modern students 'campaigning for the right to education…engaging the community and trailblazing advocacy.'[34] The bulk of the site stresses their social action, their reconstruction efforts, and their social media presence. They want the world to know not just the dead of Palestine, but the living people with 'names, faces and families…dreams, stories and ideas for a better future.'[35] The hosting organization exists as an active response to the victimage they suffered in war—a living memorial with an educational purpose that can enable a positive and peaceful response to a larger political agenda. The dead are not forgotten, but the organization as memorial is morphing commemoration into a new form. The trauma is acknowledged, but the message of the site beyond the memorial increasingly conveys providing care and moving beyond trauma.

## 6. Remember These Children Memorial Site

The final memorial website is tied to three nongovernmental organizations: Americans for Middle East Understanding, The Israeli Committee against House Demolitions, and the American Educational Trust. Targeted at an international audience, particularly, but not exclusively an U.S. audience, the site developed by these three non-Palestinian NGOs explicitly memorializes the deaths of both Israeli and Palestinian children. .

The introduction stresses their focus on 'innocent non-combatants.'[36] The total number of deaths between 29 September 2000, the beginning of the Second (or al-Aqsa) Intifada and 1 May 2012 is noted: 1477 Palestinian and 129 Israeli youths. The children cluster as a suffering group whose deaths are described as 'a waste of human life—of hope and future promise.'[37] As in the al-Fakhoora memorial, the tragic death of the children is brought closer by their extreme youth: 'Even infants and the unborn have not been spared.'[38] For some the intensifying details are familiar activities; they are said to have died 'in the course of what should have been normal childhood pleasures—playing soccer, eating pizza, shopping for candy, or going to and from school.'[39] Others are reported eating a meal or looking out a window, presumably safe at home. This summary treats together Israeli and Palestinian victims, evoking pious references to the innocence of children and the safety wished for them. The memorial consciously constructs them as one group in need of remembrance in this opening. Victims are identified as 'killed' by either Israeli soldiers or Palestinian militants. Sympathy is offered to all the involved families as the site provides needed recognition for all the victims. The introduction offers the unreclaimable lives of the child victims as motivation to ensure there are no more such victims.

Within that context the site distinguishes the Palestinian children while reporting on the many of both nationalities 'suffering psychological trauma'; a Tel Aviv University clinical psychologist claims some fifteen per cent of Palestinian children express a desire to become 'martyrs.' Attributing that wish to the conditions of daily life in which the children live, the psychologist asserts 'This should be a warning not only to Israeli but also to Palestinian society [about] what they are doing to the next generation.'[40] The guilt for the on-going trauma spreads throughout the site and across the national groups, even as the threat of continuing trauma is extended and recounted in the site.

The memorial pages are structured in parallel columns of Israeli and Palestinian victims by days within months from September 2000 through September 2013. This sets up an overt structure of even-handed attention, but it effectively emphasizes the disproportionate number of deaths of Palestinian children. At the beginning of each year the comparative number of deaths is reported; then each death is recorded on the appropriate side. Over the course of almost thirteen years there twenty-four months when no children were killed on either side. There were many additional months when there were no reported Israeli deaths. That pattern creates vast white space in the Israeli column while victim after victim is listed among the Palestinian children. The contrasting black ink of victimage and the white space of freedom from death make their own clear statement. The columns are color-coded for easy view identification. Each month is headed with a flag of the country and the typeface of the names of the victims is keyed to the flags—blue for Israeli victims, green for Palestinian.[41]

The website makes limited, but carefully selected use of images. All of the children are alive in these images. The cover photo of the memorial booklet[42] offered by the sponsoring organizations appears on every page: a crying Palestinian toddler stands in the ruins of a demolished house. The same few selected photos underlay the heading of the dead for each year: five head shots that might be school photos of smiling children at the head of the Israeli column, two similar photos at the head of the Palestinian column. One larger image also underlays the list on the Israeli side, appearing just below the photos of the children we see an Israeli policewoman holding a baby that appears unhurt.[43] We learn elsewhere that this image comes from the scene of a suicide bomb attack.[44] Notably, all of the images show living, apparently uninjured, people. The image focuses on the innocence, the similarity, not the experienced trauma.

The memorial booklet, downloadable from the website, makes much richer use of photos. These images mix grief, normalcy, and tragedy. The opening image shows a Palestinian schoolgirl in Gaza standing next to a desk adorned with flowers and the portrait of another student, a vernacular memorial; the caption explains that the girl in the portrait was dead, shot in the head by Israeli soldiers.

There are twenty-three images on the sixty pages of the booklet. None are graphic death scenes, but three show coffins (two Palestinian and one Israeli). Paired images show Israeli and Palestinian children getting medical aid, and contrasting paired images of normalcy—children from both groups playing on beaches. Seven of the images indicate trauma, although free of blood, with Palestinian children standing in the rubble of homes and other buildings.[45] This destruction stands in for the loss of life. Less grotesque, less apt to shock, it addresses the pious need for a home and security that the international audience could expect to hold. Both the site and the booklet use images to move the audience to empathy and identification, but not to numb the audience with the horror of graphic death.

The death reports themselves offer thumbnail sketches immediately visible to the viewer, not requiring a link. The statements are brief, clearly delineating the nationality and organizational base of the killers—whether Palestinian militants or IDF soldiers, Palestinian suicide bombers or Israeli settlers. In contrast with Fakhoora's focus on weaponry this site clearly references the nationality of the agent behind the missile, the gunfire, or whatever.[46] The parallel structure and naming, with the guilt ascribed to the agent rather than to the weapon seems more justified as even-handed, and thus easier for an international audience to accept.

The summary reports list name, age, hometown, where and how the person was killed, and sometimes offer an explanatory context. That context may lessen the guilt of the killer as when the victim dies while placing a charge or throwing stones. While the violence level of the latter action is often disputed, the action does indicate provocation at the least, thus potential mitigating guilt. Elsewhere context may suggest the death was collateral damage in a targeted assassination or during an incursion. Sometimes context emphasizes the innocence of the victim: 'while shepherding,' 'during a peaceful demonstration,' or when denied medical access at a checkpoint. The quite brief reports do not include the body parts and wound horror so common in the Fakhoora memorial reports. With Remember These Children, the trauma reports focus on the overwhelming numbers of deaths over time, stressing the cost of lives wasted and innocence lost.

While the site does not allow a place for comment or even signatures by site visitors, it does suggest specific responses, thus enabling a sense of some interaction with the memorial and allowing the visitors to become active in the remembrance. The introduction makes the political agenda of the site explicit. The appeal goes from the neutral ('call for an end to the killing of children'), to the more pointed (call for 'a just peace in the region…a fair resolution'), to the explicitly targeted ('You might wish to call for an end to Israel's illegal occupation since 1967 of land acquired by force.'). Almost immediately the site pulls back to what might seem a milder option ('support the deployment of international observers'). The list of possible actions ends with a politically neutral but emotionally charged appeal: 'We are confident that, in your own way, you will want to help save these children whom the world appears to have forsaken.'[47]

On a separate page visitors are asked to 'raise awareness,' 'distribute the remembrance booklet,' 'voice your concerns' to opinion leaders like elected officials and newspaper editors, 'be informed,' and 'support this site.'[48]

Remember These Children affirms the value of each victim and acknowledges the guilt of all the killers. It does not focus on horrific detail, but relies on the established innocence of youth and sometimes on the ordinariness of final activities to reinforce the victimage. The site allows narratives of national loss to remain in play while it ultimately asks the visitors to engage themselves beyond the remembered trauma in actions that might encourage a Palestinian narrative of recovery and redemption alongside the Israeli narrative. As Haas observes,

> New metanarratives can and do emerge, if we are willing to let them…. It is not a question of who is right and who is wrong, but of whether each Grand narrative can finally make a place for the Grand narrative of the other.[49]

How the victims are remembered is contestable. In this case we see extended trauma as a social construct, as Alexander would argue, since a group that has endured a horror has their memories marked 'forever…changing their future identity in fundamental ways.'[50] If the ensuing discourse about that trauma reduces responsibility and agency while demonizing the other, then mistrust may never be overcome. The answer does not lie in repressing or rejecting the presence of trauma, but in a less polarizing memory that allows complexity.

## 7. Commemoration, Identification and Consilience

As she considers commemoration within the Occupied Palestinian Territories, Khalili contends that the focus on the Palestinian as abject victim, deserving aid and sympathy, with an emphasis on the suffering of innocent children, amounts to depoliticising the conflict, removing the agency of resistance from the Palestinian and leaving it with the NGOs and outside forces.[51] Within the range of her protagonists, from guerrilla to martyr, that proves true, but does not establish a complete truth; for it does not give a full picture of the way recent Palestinian memorials to children are shaped, nor of the way they seem to function. Clearly the four sites examined here stress the innocence, the universally pious worthiness, of the child victims. That the sites memorialize children does indeed lessen the sense of Palestinians as violent resisters, but to depict a people as other than violent does not reduce them to passive victimhood, nor does it depoliticize the sites; the demonization of the other in the al-Dura flash shockwave memorial and in the Palestinian Holocaust Memorial Museum is sharply political and clearly polarizing. The other sites achieve a milder tone in different ways. Aspects of the memorials could read as expressions of the core Palestinian piety, *sumud* or steadfastness, in part the need to resist by staying in the land no matter the cost.

The child victims partake in the tragic cost. The memorials show that the children are highly valued, but so is the land. Fakhoora.org retains a detailed commemoration of the costs, but seeks a newer identification with the broader world through a social media presence and work for restoration of health and education; it portrays a positive resistance for the world. Remember These Children emphasizes the costs to two peoples, and in seeking identification at that level, works toward a narrative of consilience—a narrative to achieve peace.

## 8. Reflections on Public and Private Trauma

In each of the three case studies in this unit, a trauma event that had severe private impact has extended into the public as that event is remembered and commemorated, interpreted and reinterpreted. Each case calls us to remember that tragic events, whether as large as the Shoah or as singular as Kyron Horman's disappearance, are initially viewed and then remembered through diverse lenses. The values and identities brought to memorializing shape what we see and do in commemoration, even as values and identities shaped the initial trauma experience and the testimony regarding that experience.

For some in an international audience, the exaggerated graphics of the al-Dura shockwave flash memorial site may seem almost troll-like in their harshness. They take on the tone of intimidation that Eisenman evokes in the Berlin memorial, but where Eisenman's strategy seems appropriate, if fear inducing, in the al-Dura memorial the stridency seems at odds with the grief one expects in mournful remembrance; this amounts to highly politicized remembrance. Similarly, the trolls on the Kyron Horman Facebook memorials in the Collins and Mencarelli study in this volume might seem to be engaging in socio-political criticism of public grieving on the social media. With al-Dura, a private grief is written large and made a harsh public criticism of a demonized other. With Horman, the public expression of grief is infiltrated and undermined as a formalized use of the social media is critiqued. A larger society may rightly question the propriety of either form as the trauma of victims and those involved with them is transmuted into something other, something more political than personal, even as the personal may still be postured.

Mark Callaghan's study in this volume of the Berlin memorial to the Holocaust takes us to another form of politicized remembrance. He reminds us that such memorials are intended 'primarily for the vicarious witness...for those who approach the Holocaust through the experiences of others.' In considering how vicarious trauma can be communicated in this memorial 'without the arguably instructional and overt illustrations' common to such commemorative monuments, Callaghan looks at how the details of the structure itself create experience and focus emotion. On a much smaller virtual stage, Remember These Children uses site structure to encourage almost subconscious recognition of disproportionate losses within that conflict; the site does not rely on harsh images or shocking verbal detail, but on listing within a graphic structure that sets up inevitable comparison. Subtle, carefully structured detail in each case leads the viewer to a heightened experience.

 Each of the cases shows routes to empathetic identification within varied forms of commemoration. Each helps understand how a public possibly lacking personal or direct experience of a trauma event may come, through commemorative sites—whether real or virtual—to a level of understanding, to a substantive identification with the remembered trauma victims and their associates.

## Notes

[1] Robert I. Rotberg, 'Building Legitimacy through Narrative,' *Israeli and Palestinian Narratives of Conflict: History's Double Helix*, ed. Robert I. Rotberg (Indianapolis: Indiana University Press, 2006), 1.
[2] Kenneth Burke, *Permanence and Change: An Anatomy of Purpose*, 3rd ed. (Berkeley: University of California Press, 1984), 192.
[3] Ibid., 74.
[4] Duncan Bell, ed., *Memory, Trauma and World Politics: Reflections on the Relationship between Past and Present* (New York: Palgrave Macmillan, 2010), 5.
[5] Laleh Khalili, *Heroes and Martyrs of Palestine: The Politics of National Commemoration* (Cambridge: Cambridge University Press, 2007), 114-116.
[6] Ibid., 3.
[7] Yael Zerubavel, *Recovered Roots: Collective Memory and the Making of Israeli National Tradition* (Chicago: University of Chicago Press, 1995); Robert Wistrich and David Ohana, eds., *The Shaping of Israeli Identity: Myth, Memory and Trauma* (London: Frank Cass, 1995); Yaron Ezrahi, *Rubber Bullets: Power and Conscience in Modern Israel* (New York: Farrar, Straus and Giroux, 1997).
[8] Nur Masalha, *The Palestine Nakba: Decolonising History, Narrating the Subaltern, Reclaiming Memory* (London: Zed Books, 2012); Ahmad H. Sa'di and Lila Abu-Lughod, eds., *Nakba: Palestine, 1948, and the Claims of Memory* (New York: Columbia University Press, 2007); Phillip L. Hammack, *Narrative and the Politics of Identity* (Oxford: Oxford University Press, 2011).
[9] Khalili, *Heroes and Martyrs of Palestine*, 91.
[10] Ibid., 113-114.
[11] David A. Frank and Mark Lawrence McPhail, 'Barack Obama's Address to the 2004 Democratic National Convention: Trauma, Compromise, Consilience, and the (Im)possibility of Racial Reconciliation,' *Rhetoric and Public Affairs* 8.4 (2005): 572.
[12] 'In Memory of Rami Dura,' *AlSham.net*, viewed 14 October 2013, http://mivy.ovh.org/linfo/15_proche_orient/411_al-dura/ad-images/rami_fichiers/rami.swf.
[13] Ibid.

[14] Peter Haas, 'Moral Visions in Conflict: Israeli and Palestinian Ethics,' *Anguished Hope: Holocaust Scholars Confront the Palestinian-Israeli Conflict*, eds. Leonard Grob and John K. Roth (Grand Rapids: Wm. B. Eerdmans Publishing, 2008), 15.

[15] Ibid., 21.

[16] Rania Khallaf, 'Documenting the Palestinian Holocaust,' *Al-Ahram Weekly Online*, 28 May-3 June 2009, viewed 14 October 2013, http://weekly.ahram.org.eg/2009/949/feature.htm.

[17] Ibid.

[18] Adar Shalev, 'Online Visit to "Palestinian Holocaust Museum",' *ynetnews.com*, 1 April 2009, viewed 14 October 2013, http://www.ynetnews.com/articles/0,7340,L-3649751,00.html.

[19] IslamOnline, 'Palestinian Holocaust Museum,' *Real Holocaust in Gaza* (blog), gaza1, 6 January 2009, viewed 14 October 2013, http://gaza1.wordpress.com/2009/01/06/palestinian-holocaust-museum/.

[20] Ibid.

[21] Khallaf, 'Documenting the Palestinian Holocaust.'

[22] IslamOnline, 'Palestinian Holocaust Memorial Museum (PHMM) HD,' viewed 14 October 2013, https://www.youtube.com/watch?v=FUM6p_dwg9Y&feature=player_embedded#at=171.

[23] Khallaf, 'Documenting the Palestinian Holocaust.'

[24] Palestinianholocaust.net, viewed 14 October 2013, http://palestinianholocaust.net/?nr=0.

[25] IslamOnline, 'Palestinian Holocaust Museum;' IslamOnline, 'Palestinian Holocaust Memorial Museum (PHMM) HD.'

[26] Leonard Grob and John K. Roth, 'Prologue: Haunted by the Holocaust,' *Anguished Hope: Holocaust Scholars Confront the Palestinian-Israeli Conflict*, eds. Leonard Grob and John K. Roth (Grand Rapids: Wm. B. Eerdmans Publishing, 2008), 2.

[27] Al Fakhoora, 'Our Name,' *Fakhoora.org*, viewed 14 October 2013, http://fakhoora.org/node/1651.

[28] Al Fakhoora, 'Memorial,' *Fakhoora.org*, viewed 14 October 2013, http://fakhoora.org/memorial.

[29] Ibid.

[30] Ibid.

[31] Al Fakhoora, 'Memorial: Ala'Khaled Khalil an-Najjar,' *Fakhoora.org*, viewed 14 October 2013, http://fakhoora.org/memorial.

[32] Al Fakhoora, 'Memorial: Areej, Ala, Amani, Khetam, Rab'a Salabil, Sharaf, Qamar, Ali, Yousif and Mohammed ad-Dayeh,' *Fakhoora.org*, viewed 14 October 2013, http://fakhoora.org/memorial.

[33] Al Fakhoora, 'The Campaign,' *Fakhoora.org*, viewed 14 October 2013, http://fakhoora.org/node/1652.
[34] Ibid.
[35] Ibid.
[36] American Educational Trust, 'Remember These Children,' viewed 13 October 2013, http://rememberthesechildren.org/about.html.
[37] Ibid.
[38] Ibid.
[39] Ibid.
[40] Ibid.
[41] Ibid.
[42] American Educational Trust, *Remember These Children*, 3rd ed. (Washington, DC: American Educational Trust, 2007), viewed 13 October 2013, http://rememberthesechildren.org/index.html.
[43] Ibid.
[44] Ibid., 11.
[45] Ibid..
[46] American Educational Trust, 'Remember These Children,' viewed 13 October 2013, http://rememberthesechildren.org/remember2000.html.
[47] American Educational Trust, 'Remember These Children,' viewed 13 October 2013, http://rememberthesechildren.org/about.html.
[48] American Educational Trust, 'Remember These Children,' viewed 13 October 2013, http://rememberthesechildren.org/doyourpart.html.
[49] Haas, 'Moral Visions in Conflict,' 23.
[50] Jeffrey C. Alexander, 'Toward a Theory of Cultural Trauma,' *Cultural Trauma and Collective Identity*, ed. Jeffrey C. Alexander et al. (Berkeley: University of California Press, 2004), 1.
[51] Khalili, *Heroes and Martyrs of Palestine*, 204.

## Bibliography

Alexander, Jeffrey C. 'Toward a Theory of Cultural Trauma.' *Cultural Trauma and Collective Identity*, edited by Jeffrey C. Alexander, Ron Eyerman, Bernhard Giesen, Neil Smelser, and Piotr Sztompka, 1-30. Berkeley: University of California Press, 2004.

Al Fakhoora. 'Memorial.' *Fakhoora.org*. Viewed on 14 October 2013. http://fakhoora.org/memorial.

———. *Fakhoora.org*. Viewed on 14 October 2013. http://fakhoora.org/.

AlSham.net. 'In Memory of Rami Dura.' Viewed on 14 October 2013.
http://mivy.ovh.org/linfo/15_proche_orient/411_al-dura/ad-
images/rami_fichiers/rami.swf.

American Educational Trust. *Remember These Children*, 3rd ed. Washington, D.C.:
American Educational Trust, 2007. Viewed on 13 October 2013.
http://rememberthesechildren.org/index.html.

———. 'Remember These Children.' Viewed on 13 October 2013.
http://rememberthesechildren.org/remember2000.html.

Bell, Duncan, ed. *Memory, Trauma and World Politics: Reflections on the
Relationship between Past and Present.* New York: Palgrave Macmillan, 2010.

Burke, Kenneth. *Permanence and Change: An Anatomy of Purpose*, 3rd ed.
Berkeley: University of California Press, 1984.

Ezrahi, Yaron. *Rubber Bullets: Power and Conscience in Modern Israel.* New
York: Farrar, Straus and Giroux, 1997.

Frank, David A. and Mark Lawrence McPhail. 'Barack Obama's Address to the
2004 Democratic National Convention: Trauma, Compromise, Consilience, and
the (Im)possibility of Racial Reconciliation.' *Rhetoric and Public Affairs* 8.4
(2005): 571-594.

Grob, Leonard and John K. Roth, eds. *Anguished Hope: Holocaust Scholars
Confront the Palestinian-Israeli Conflict.* Grand Rapids: Wm. B. Eerdmans
Publishing, 2008.

Hammack, Phillip L. *Narrative and the Politics of Identity.* Oxford: Oxford
University Press, 2011.

IslamOnline. 'Palestinian Holocaust Museum.' *Real Holocaust in Gaza* (blog).
gaza1, 6 January 2009. Viewed on 14 October 2013.
http://gaza1.wordpress.com/2009/01/06/palestinian-holocaust-museum/.

———. 'Palestinian Holocaust Memorial Museum (PHMM) HD.' Viewed 14
October 2013.
https://www.youtube.com/watch?v=FUM6p_dwg9Y&feature=player_embedded#a
t=171.

Khalili, Laleh. *Heroes and Martyrs of Palestine: The Politics of National Commemoration.* Cambridge: Cambridge University Press, 2007.

Khallaf, Rania. 'Documenting the Palestinian holocaust.' *Al-Ahram Weekly Online,* 28 May-3 June 2009. Viewed on 14 October 2013. http://weekly.ahram.org.eg/2009/949/feature.htm.

Masalha, Nur. *The Palestine Nakba: Decolonising History, Narrating the Subaltern, Reclaiming Memory.* London: Zed Books, 2012.

Palestinianholocaust.net. Viewed on 14 October 2013. http://palestinianholocaust.net/?nr=0.

Rotberg, Robert I. 'Building Legitimacy through Narrative.' *Israeli and Palestinian Narratives of Conflict: History's Double Helix,* edited by Robert I. Rotberg, 1-18. Indianapolis: Indiana University Press, 2006.

Sa'di, Ahmad H. and Lila Abu-Lughod, eds. *Nakba: Palestine, 1948, and the Claims of Memory.* New York: Columbia University Press, 2007.

Shalev, Adar. 'Online Visit to "Palestinian Holocaust Museum".' *ynetnews.com.* 1 April 2009. Viewed on 14 October 2013. http://www.ynetnews.com/articles/0,7340,L-3649751,00.html.

Wistrich, Robert and David Ohana, eds. *The Shaping of Israeli Identity: Myth, Memory and Trauma.* London: Frank Cass, 1995.

Zerubavel, Yael. *Recovered Roots: Collective Memory and the Making of Israeli National Tradition.* Chicago: University of Chicago Press, 1995.

**Jeanne Ellen Clark** teaches rhetoric and media criticism at Willamette University in Salem, Oregon. She has been studying and writing about the Middle East in the media, and particularly Israel/Palestine, for over twenty years, since her years living in East Jerusalem and working as an archaeological research assistant.

# The Memorial to the Murdered Jews of Europe and Its Associations with Vicarious Trauma

## Mark Callaghan

**Abstract**
This chapter concentrates on the issue of creating a unitary memory for a country's heinous past and the complexities of vicarious trauma for both artists and the public alike. As the medical definition of trauma refers not to the injury inflicted but to the blow that inflicted it, not to the state of mind that ensues but to the event that provoked it, my research questions whether designs for the Berlin Holocaust Memorial Competition were more concerned with the blow and the event rather than the injury itself. I contend that Peter Eisenman's winning design does not represent the injury but instead aims to cause the visitor to feel disorientated and therefore reflects the nature of death in the Final Solution–the blow and the event. According to Cathy Caruth traumatic events return to us even though we are vicarious witnesses because trauma itself cannot be fully understood, despite so many artistic attempts to do so. We should therefore consider the effects of trauma-related art, as we may appreciate why Eisenman's design was favoured in the face of so many compelling proposals. Along with analysing Eisenman's winning blueprint, this chapter also examines vicarious trauma in relation to two further submissions for the competition, both leading contenders for selection: Renata Stih and Frieder Schnock's *Bus Stop!* and Daniel Libeskind's *Stone Breath*. Through perusal of these designs we can see further support for the argument that post-reunification Germany was drawn to proposals that expressed their own trauma, a vicarious one.

**Key Words**: Vicarious, empathy, abstraction, memory, representation, innovative, individual, collective.

*****

From 1994-1997 The Berlin Holocaust Memorial Competition received more than 500 proposals from an international field of artists and architects. Designs ran the gamut of taste and aesthetic sensibilities, from the kitsch to the controversial, from the clichéd to the innovative. The winning submission–Peter Eisenman's undulating labyrinthine field of concrete stelae (Image 1)–came to represent Germany's aesthetic choice for the issue of *Vergangenheitsbewältigung*–the German appellation for coming to terms with the past.[1] Eisenman's design, officially titled *The Memorial to the Murdered Jews of Europe*, was selected due to its lack of symbolism, its determination to be non-prescriptive, and as a result, the hope that visitors would interpret the memorial with complete objectivity.[2]

The expanse of grey blocks stands close to the Brandenburg Gate, within sight of the Reichstag, overlooked by the revived Potsdamer Platz, and just a hundred metres from the location of the *Fuhrer Bunker*. This means that a memorial selected primarily for its non-representationality occupies a five-acre plot of Berlin highly symbolic of Germany's temporality, as it succeeds in adding, with notable permanency, a new monumental figure to the city's landscape; one that seems to complete an axis of icons representing Germany's Prussian dynastic history, the country's shameful period of fascism, its confident postmodernist regeneration programme, and now its reunified and self-reflexive present.[3] Thus in the very centre of the new Berlin, there is a national memorial to German crimes against humanity, that ultimate rupture of Western civilization seen by some as emblematic of the twentieth-century as a whole, a curse on the house of modernity that we now inhabit with enormous trepidation.[4]

***Image 1:*** Peter Eisenman's *Memorial to the Murdered Jews of Europe*, Berlin.
© 2013. Image courtesy of Mark Callaghan.

The project to build a national Holocaust memorial coincided with debates concerning reunification, German national identity, the question of assigning guilt, generational differences (that became highlighted by these same debates), and the inescapable issue of *Vergangenheitsbewältigung*, which in many respects is the idiom under which all such discourses belong.[5] I wish, however, to focus on a commonality between the majority of artists, competition jurors, politicians, and the public too: they were all *Nachgeborenen* (the later born), the post-war generations who did not experience the Second World War and faced the continuing problem of being vicarious witnesses to the Fascist era. By looking at three of the competition's most popular submissions, I posit that Germans sought, perhaps unconsciously, for a memorial that relates more to their state of vicarious trauma than a drive to commemorate the murder of six million Jews, still incomprehensible crimes committed by their forebears. As the Holocaust was an event some five decades before, I argue that Germans could only see the atrocities from this distance and so favoured proposals that expressed their own trauma, a vicarious one–a history that repeats what they cannot grasp and one that remains ungraspable even to those who experienced events at first hand; the remnants of a history that Susannah Radstone describes as the 'traceless traces' of memory.[6]

Given that the following case studies differ aesthetically, we should ask what caused their utmost popularity with the *Nachgeborenen*? Do we expect the vicarious witness to be affected viscerally, emotionally, as a primary function of the artwork, rather than understanding the events or even the artwork that has led to this response? Did the eventual selection of Eisenman's design reflect this expectation? Though non-experiential designs were also short-listed for the Berlin competition, the three case studies appraised in this chapter suggest a tendency for Germans to draw closer to the Jewish experience of Nazi Germany by preferring concepts that would relate to Jewish trauma whilst also exemplifying the inaccessibility of those same feelings.

Before addressing these questions further, one could argue that vicarious trauma is not only evidenced by Germany's need to build a national Holocaust memorial, but also by a competition that began with opaque precepts and was at one point disbanded due to lack of consensus: a process that tried, often in vain, to assuage multiple interest groups, and included jury members who did not feel qualified to make judgements on aesthetics.[7] An increasingly complex and disjointed process perhaps suits a nation trying to address its difficult past, a nation still dealing with the effects of its Nazi heritage. Furthermore, whilst *The Memorial to the Murdered Jews of Europe* might sound like a clear dedication to the victims, there was no accord concerning its patronage: some claimed the memorial geared to Germans; others believed in its European dimension; still others saw the memorial as international in scope.[8] However, whether geared to a singular, multiple, or still contested patron, the memorial primarily addresses the vicarious witness, those who did not experience the Nazi era at first hand, those who approach the Holocaust through the experiences of others. Though Germany perpetrated the Holocaust, one might argue that the victims include post-war generation Germans–the *Nachgeborenen*–who continue to deal with the resonating effects of a legacy that must always haunt them. Seen through the lens of contemporary memory culture and trauma theory, the Berlin Holocaust Memorial Competition provides a significant insight into vicarious trauma and how to understand it.

The medical definition of trauma refers not to the injury inflicted but to the blow that inflicted it, not to the state of mind that ensues but to the event that provoked it.[9] Here we might read Eisenman's design as more a representation of the blow and the event than the injury itself. His design does not, for instance, represent the loss of life, or any suggestion of a relationship between the field of stelae and genocide, but instead aims, with varying results, to cause the visitor to feel claustrophobic, due to the close proximity of the blocks, and increasingly disorientated as the viewer walks between the pillars, becoming submerged as the ground descends and the stelae rise (Image: 2). Eisenman wanted this intimidating encounter to transmit an aspect of the Jewish experience. He designed the memorial to reflect a state of anxiety and confusion, as an insight into the experience of others. A specific type of stone was even selected in order to create an echo of people's footsteps, an effect intended to remind the spectator of the approaching sound of Jackboots.[10] The design can therefore present visitors with intense and varied stimuli to hearing, touch and kinesthesia. These physical experiences intended to stimulate emotions pave the way for feeling the purpose of the memorial rather than thinking it.

With these experiential purposes in mind, I argue that Eisenman's model relates to Cathy Caruth's assertion that the enigmatic core of trauma relates to the delay or incompletion of knowing so that the traumatised carry an impossible history with them, or they become themselves symptoms of a history they cannot entirely possess.[11] If the Jewish experience cannot be fully known even to those who lived through the Holocaust, then the selection of Eisenman's design becomes symptomatic of Germany's everlasting position; it signals that the *Nachgeborenen* are trying to comprehend vicariously what even the witnesses could not recall due to the same incompletion of knowing. Eisenman's experiential rendering thus provides an insight into the Jewish plight but also something unreachable and suitably incommensurate to their suffering.

Caruth writes that trauma concerns a 'response, sometimes delayed, to an overwhelming event or set of events, which takes the form of repeated thoughts or behaviours'.[12] Accordingly, traumatic events, such as the Holocaust, return to us even though we witness it vicariously and cannot understand it, despite so many artistic attempts to do so. The predominant view that massive trauma precludes all representation because it temporally destroys the ordinary mechanisms of consciousness and memory implies an encounter inaccessible to understanding and imagery.[13] Whilst this theory suggests, in an Adornean sense, the redundance of art after Auschwitz, the Berlin competition overflowed with abstract proposals, with some artists believing only abstraction suited the subject, the nearest to Adorno's famous aporia.[14] Like all abstract art, Eisenman's design does not try to reproduce the world by depicting empirical reality, but instead tries to push culture forward by resisting the paradigm of Holocaust iconography and semiotics, thus being innovative and arguably Delphic as a result. However Eisenman's proposal differed from the scores of other abstract designs submitted to the competition in that Eisenman aspired to produce an effect,not as opposed to or distinct from thought, but as the means of producing a kind of understanding.[15] To underscore this point, we should remember that whilst we stand in front of abstract artworks, the lack of a depicted image tends to heighten our awareness of materials, of compositional (or anti-compositional) structures, of the process of looking itself.[16] *The Memorial to the Murdered Jews of Europe* emphasises these conditions through interactiveness, as it encourages visitors to walk within the memorial's channels of blocks rather than expecting them to observe the memorial only from a distance, just as when perusing a conventional monument. Eisenman, however, does not try to represent the Holocaust by imagery, or entirely by abstraction, but instead by way of an experience, an experience of course disproportionate to the reality of Jewish suffering but nonetheless one that relates to trauma–the blow and the event.

*Image 2:* Peter Eisenman's *Memorial to the Murdered Jews of Europe*, Berlin. © 2013 Inter-Disciplinary Press. Image courtesy of Mark Callaghan.

The experiential features combine to make Eisenman's design more than a passive viewing experience. Instead, true to its subject, the memorial becomes a striking and incomprehensible event, designed as an ungraspable and recondite encounter not only with the original trauma, enabled because that initial trauma remains equally incomplete, but also, perhaps unwittingly, because of Germany's vicarious position. The memorial still defies narrative construction and exceeds comprehension, which recalls how Marianne Hirsch defines the post-memory experience of the *Nachgeborenen*, something that happened in the past with effects that continue into the present, experiences that they remember only by images and behaviours among which they grew up.[17]

However, though non-representational, Eisenman's design can result in didacticism, particularly if one's time in the field of blocks relates to the objectives of the aforementioned acoustic and experiential features and makes it understood as evoking the Jewish experience. This wider approach to thinking and representation can be contextualised by considering the cultural background to the Berlin Holocaust Memorial Competition, an initiative proposed against a backdrop of both leftfield and mainstream Holocaust culture, including award-winning films such as *Schindler's List* and popular documentaries that evidenced graphic images of the Shoah. Ann Kaplan describes such productions as:

> Placing the viewer in the position of being vicariously traumatised with potentially negative results, as on the one hand the effect may be negative if the impact is so great that the viewer turns away from images instead of learning through them. Whilst on the other hand, a degree of vicarious trauma may shock a viewer into wanting to know more and perhaps to do something about what they have seen.[18]

Due to the memorial's abstraction, combined with its experiential constituents, Eisenman's design both circumvents and relates to Kaplan's assertion regarding visual representation. Though devoid of iconic visual triggers (or representational imagery of any kind, for that matter), the memorial can still shock viewers due to its potentially disorientating effects, which could prompt further enquiries regarding the Jewish experience of Nazi Germany. Instead of representing an appalling image, *The Memorial to the Murdered Jews of Europe* attests to the possibilities of vicarious trauma without the arguably instructional and overt illustrations found in numerous Holocaust-related artworks, regardless of genre, independent of genus.

Eisenman's design only becomes graphic if one uses one's imagination and draws upon a personal stockpile of Holocaust imagery accumulated by encountering the work of other artists, writers, photographers, sculptors, and film-makers. So an insight into the Jewish experience emerges through the experiential effects of Eisenman's work–specifically a sensation of fear or confusion–further supported by our visual knowledge of the Holocaust via more conventional art-forms. Countless works explicitly represent the Jewish experiences, such as Margaret Bourke-White's photographs of stacked corpses at Buchenwald, scenes from *Schindler's List*, or Kenneth Treister's *Holocaust Memorial of the Greater Miami Jewish Foundation,* Miami Beach, unveiled in 1990, with its gargantuan outstretched arm towering over the rubble of a punctured landscape, with the explicit forms of agonising figures joined together as one tortured mass to create the erect limb.

Nevertheless, despite this apparent dependency on the visual history of the Holocaust, I posit that experience-based memorials can produce a more memorable way of remembering–a more active rather than passive role likely to involve the viewer, not only in a connection with the past, but through a bodily experience with the artwork itself, through physiological feelings stimulated by the design's architectural features.

Jill Bennett stresses the repeated argument that trauma resists representation in relation both to psychological process and to aesthetics.[19] Yet despite this continued query against the possibility of visually registering trauma, Germany insisted in exploring and representing its vicarious trauma with the three sponsoring groups (the Federal Republic of Germany, the citizens' action group *Förderkreis* and the State of Berlin) steadfastly pursuing the creation of a national memorial to open up examination of the nation and its difficult past. As the 1994 Competition press release states:

> It is not too late for a monument because the obligation to deliberate and to have a confrontation with historical responsibility for the crimes of the National Socialist Germany is imposed upon us Germans and will not pass away. So it is vital for us to carry the burden of knowledge, to express regret and sorrow as well as benefit from the realization of the past lessons for the present and future (....) The object of this competition is of course difficult because it is not about getting rid of duty and we are not trying to draw a line under the past.[20]

The jury's assessment criterion also reveals that the panel anticipated designs that would relate to vicariousness whilst also drawing emotions from the viewer:

> An essential element of a design is the choice of the means to capture the emotions of people. It is to be noted whether 'reality-based' or symbolic actions are supposed to be 'vicariously' activated or if information and contemplation are placed in a balanced relationship.[21]

The resolve to pursue the creation of a national Holocaust memorial demonstrates Germany's self-effacing post-unification attitude by way of its apparent drive to commemorate the Nazi era. Some scholars, however, might see this production as relating more to the idea of closure than creation, more an illustration of resisting *Vergangenheitsbewältigung* than embracing it. As Marita Sturken states, the concept of an ostensible 'screen memory' usefully contributes to thinking about how a culture remembers, particularly as in contemporary culture, memory originates in photographic images, cinema, and television. Sturken believes that these mnemonic aids also serve as screens, actively blocking out other memories more difficult to represent.[22] This suggests that the creation of a Holocaust artwork, let alone a large, centrally located memorial, might come to represent an entity made up of both an exploration and expression of atrocities whilst also a self-censoring barrier to overly disturbing aspects of the past. In this analysis, then, the selection of Eisenman's design, with its lack of symbolism and only one title sign on the entire five acre site, suggests that Germany commissioned a Holocaust memorial consisting in a duality of commemoration and censorship.

Whilst this point might stand, note that Eisenman's field of blocks does not qualify as a 'screen memory' per se, it does in no way convey the Holocaust through overt representation. Though some visitors misunderstand the memorial, those that appreciate Eisenman's concept will draw close to the emotional effects that stark renderings often produce. The difference, however, lies in these emotions based on the visitors' own sense of disorientation whilst walking within the field of blocks rather than the kind of contemporary visual triggers that Sturken refers to. To date, however, theorists of trauma and memory have paid relatively little attention to visual art. Yet the ways in which an artwork might evoke immediately affective experiences suggests the possibility–for both artist and viewer–of 'being a spectator of one's own feelings', a point evidenced by the reception of Eisenman's design. I do not argue that, through such a process, trauma enters the realm of representation. Rather than reducing itself to a form of representation, such imagery serves to register subjective processes that exceed our capacity to 'represent' them.[23] The extent to which the memorial functions as a 'screen memory' does, however, return to the analysis when one considers the aforementioned reliance on the visual history of the Holocaust, and how, without images of the atrocities, Eisenman's abstract design might open up our memories of the Holocaust accumulated through contemporary culture. Eisenman's rows of concrete stelae therefore qualify as a national monument that both hinders and encourages representation of Germany's difficult past.

Whilst an engagement with Eisenman's brooding blocks can transform a passive participant into an active explorer of meaning, or perhaps even epiphany, the notion of creating an architectural experience as a simulacrum of Holocaust experiences does, however, fail to connect with some visitors, as the design often activates playful rather than the reflective and the fearful responses that Eisenman conceived of. For instance, people often leap from block to block, or hide from friends amongst the maze. In some respects, had Eisenman's original intentions for the design succeeded in captivating more visitors, it would have been arguably more inappropriate than the sight of such levity, as even the most uncomfortable of spaces would be incommensurate to the suffering experienced by the victims of the Holocaust. Either way, both responses risk trivializing the horrific events. Eisenman does recognise that 'the enormity and horrors of the Holocaust are such that any attempt to represent it by traditional means is inevitably inadequate'.[24] His memorial thus neither has a focal point, nor images of suffering, nor symbols of hope; but it does not suggest either that the field offers a perfect solution. Anyone who would argue such a point has overlooked the memorial's full reception. Additionally, if we consider issues of vicarious traumatisation through the work of Joshua Hirsch and Janet Walker, we can appreciate the value of this endeavour to portray collective trauma rather than a concentration on binary notions of success and failure. Hirsch, for instance, like Kaplan, shows an interest in the impact of trauma films on spectators, particularly by the attempt to reproduce for the spectator an experience of once again seeing the unthinkable.[25] He argues for films that at least attempt to discover a form adequate for collective trauma, and perhaps we should acknowledge the *attempt* when analysing Eisenman's model for Germany's national Holocaust memorial, along with the significance of its selection by the *Nachgeborenen.*

Eisenman's blueprint for the memorial site was not, however, the only proposal to offer experiential encounters with the past. One of the most popular designs amongst the German public, media, and Jewish community, Renata Stih and Frieder Schnock's, *Bus Stop!* (Image: 3), would see red buses depart from the memorial site at regular intervals, taking visitors to the former concentration camps of Germany and Poland, and illuminated with the destination signs of Dachau, Ravensbruck, Buchenwald, Sobibor, Treblinka, and Auschwitz.[26]

This would not only create an itinerant memorial referencing the transportation of Jews, but also a protean social sculpture following, to some extent, the geographical reach of the Nazi extermination program. As trauma is contained not in an event as such, but in the way this event is experienced, sites such as Auschwitz become much more than physical settings of tragedies: they emerge as spaces to experience and re-experience events across time, full of visual and sensory triggers, capable of eliciting a whole palette of emotions.[27] So had this idea been commissioned, the new Berlin memorial would have axiomatic links to the places where genocide occurred. This version of *The Memorial to the Murdered Jews of Europe* would have engaged with the indelible experience of being at the source of trauma, in the places where trauma was conceived and vicarious trauma transmitted.[28]

***Image 3:*** Renata Stih and Frieder Schnock's *Bus Stop!* proposal. © Stih and
Schnock, Berlin/ARS, NYC/VG BildKunst Bonn/Berlin.
Image courtesy of Renata Stih and Frieder Schnock.

In Alison Landsberg's essay, 'Toward a Radical Politics of Empathy', she
conceives of Holocaust museums (and by extension concentration camp memorial
sites) as 'transferential spaces' where people enter into experiential relationships
with events they did not experience, thereby gaining access to 'sensually immersed
knowledges, knowledges which would be difficult to acquire by purely cognitive
means'.[29] This is supported by Harold Marcuse who writes that:

> The use of the memorial site exclusively for cognitive learning,
> without attention to emotional aspects of a visit, is not apt to
> promote the kind of learning that teachers want to take place at a
> memorial site (…) memorial sites should draw on their unique
> strength, namely the emotional appeal of a genuine historical site
> with authentic remains, and leave most of the intellectual
> learning for other, more suitable situations.[30]

Marcuse supports the idea that experiencing Holocaust memorials is not
contingent on cognition and that encounters with such mnemonic sites can, and
arguable should, include sensations of fear, empathy, sadness, and bewilderment.

Though devoid of artefacts, Eisenman's scheme can provide an emotional connection to the Holocaust the design's aforementioned strategies of intimidation. As a more direct, less ambiguous creation, Stih and Schnock's *Bus Stop!* also elevates the values of emotional encounters with Holocaust-related sites and memorials; it offers an intrinsic acquaintance for the vicarious witness, not because such experiences can mirror that of the victim, but rather because incomprehension essentially provides an understanding of the ungraspable Jewish experience. At memorial sites such as Sachsenhausen, the ruins of crematoria, and the heaps of personal effects displayed in the museum spaces, can cause empathetic identification with the victims. Empathy, especially as constructed out of mimesis, does not create emotional self-pitying identification with victims, but a way of both feeling for, while differing from, the subject of enquiry.[31] The popularity of a concept with mimesis intrinsic to its values suggests that reunified Germans were not drawn exclusively to abstract forms such as Eisenman's, but rather to experiential concepts regardless of genus, independent of designation or whatever category we might assign them. This concept of empathetic identification, essential to current modes of Holocaust pedagogy, can have a transformational impact on visitors.[32] In the example of Claude Lanzmann's documentary, *Shoah*, Dominick La Capra believes that empathetic identification with people and places enabled Lanzmann to feel that he was reliving–indeed suffering through–a past he had never in fact lived.[33] The aforementioned artefacts to which *Bus Stop's!* spectators would be transported to continue to provide a representation of reality, thus allowing us to suffer through, as Lanzmann does, a past that was not ours.[34]

When it comes to routine practices of memory, experience-based ideas, such as *Bus Stop!*, seek to circumvent the routinized or false practices of memory because they present a form of memory more tangible, tactile, and authentic in the sense that the visitor emotionally and physically participates in the memory.[35] As Karen Till elucidates, *Bus Stop!* encourages personal memory work through bodies moving through multiple space-times. The everyday spaces of the city, the moving buses, and the people moving through those spaces in the buses, the conversations in the buses–these movements, these becomings, *make up* the memorial.[36] In this sense, *Bus Stop!* offers a process not an answer, reflecting the Counter-monument tenet of creating mnemonic concepts as a more memorable way of remembering, through the participation required on the part of the viewer and the time the viewer must dedicate in order to complete the process of remembrance. As Stih and Schnock's official submission explains: 'Details, nuances, unexpected images and encounters turn the approach to memory sites into a formative experience. You take your time and you give it to the dead. For going to a former concentration camp is no simple day trip: it requires preparation in order to be able to stand the shock of comprehension'.[37] So like Eisenman's model, *Bus Stop!* would be participatory, innovative, and would, in contrasting ways, engage with Germany's vicarious trauma, in this case by imitating, albeit in a benign way, the deportations, the enforced movement of people and the restrictions that accumulated until all freedom was eroded to nothing.[38]

To cite a further example from the Berlin competition, I posit that trauma can be expressed in pioneering ways that attempt to negotiate the problem of incomplete memory whilst still relating to the poignancy of the past, of the absence of a destroyed section of society. Daniel Libeskind's, *Stone-Breath*, which reached the semi-final of the competition, evokes a spectacular vision of irreparability, irredeemable voids, and a wounded landscape, with its great broken wall, and its architectonic interpenetration of Berlin history that would have contextualised the memorial site.[39] Libeskind's design, which resembled the scarred walls of his plan for *The Jewish Museum,* also in Berlin, would have created a representation of trauma, not in a psychoanalytical sense, but rather in a material sense.[40] As Libeskind explains:

> I have read a number of texts, which illuminate the problem of trauma from the psychoanalytical perspective, but I believe that when one actually enters the space of that trauma, the space of the city, the trauma cannot be interpreted simply. That is the difference between talking about the problem and being in it. In a literary context, one can interpret trauma, one can cope with it in different linguistic settings. But no interpretation can eliminate the materiality, opacity, and thickness of the experience of walking, looking, touching, feeling where one is.[41]

Libeskind's design appears to fall between Eisenman's concept and Stih and Schnock's due to Libeskind's wish to create a site specific, tactile experience, whilst believing he could achieve that at a new site rather than one linked to the original places of murder. Libeskind's much-admired proposal would have delivered trauma in an architectural language right to the centre of Berlin. Though potentially esoteric, the broken wall, voids and wounded backdrop, would represent a country with permanent scars that wishes to move on whilst being fixated with its past. Like Walter Benjamin's interpretation of Paul Klee's *Angelus Novus*, the angel of history directs our gaze and thinking toward that which seems irredeemably lost, yet something that continues to haunt and torment our existence, something that can be read here as a metaphor for Germany's post-war situation.

The popularity of these three aesthetically divergent proposals suggests that Germans identified with the intended effects of trauma-related art. Whether the vicarious experience of trauma compares to an actual experience of trauma is questionable, but one must observe that in many regards the viewer can go through a similar experience and thereby a mediated or artificial encounter of trauma or terror.[42] Should one, for instance, relate the acoustic effects of Eisenman's design–the echo of Jackboots–then one may have a closer relationship with someone else's distressing past, whereas with *Bus Stop!* the viewer would have a more direct, tangible, and site specific appreciation of Jewish suffering. Moreover, such concepts can have a transformative impact by inviting spectators to be there emotionally but also to keep a cognitive distance and awareness denied to the victim by the traumatic process.[43]

Trauma amounts to a special form of memory; the traumatic experience has affect only, not meaning. It produces emotions–terror, fear, shock, and above all disruption of the normal feeling of comfort. With only the sensation sector of the brain active during trauma, the meaning-making faculty–rational thought and cognitive processing, namely, the cerebral cortex–remains shut down because the affect cannot possibly register cognitively in the brain. Not given meaning, the experience continually haunts the subject in dreams, flashbacks and hallucinations.[44] Germany's pursuit of a national Holocaust memorial led to the selection of a design–Eisenman's–that mirrored these effects and saw the most popular design amongst the German media and public–Stih and Schnock's *Bus Stop!*–also relate to a replication of emotions where the experiential supercedes the traditional focus on the visual entity of an artwork; where the primary function of the artwork is for one to be affected viscerally, emotionally, not by the visual entity alone, but by an insight into the origins of trauma that remain appropriately inaccessible, thereby replicating the original outcome of trauma, though not the conditions from which it emanates. I would therefore argue that these proposals received notable encomium because they are not part of the broad cultural storehouse of pre-established forms, but instead allow the spectator to be present emotionally whilst also keeping a cognitive distance that does not sanitise the traumatic traces. 1990's Germans–the *Nachgebegoren*–seemed to favour ideas that placed the vicarious witness in the position of the original victims' trauma, providing a sense of terror, fear, and shock, with designs that simultaneously gesture both to the existence of deep, inarticulable vicarious trauma and their own incapacity or unconscious unwillingness to deliver it.

Clark discusses a new format for social trauma via internet-based memorial sites, specifically Palestinian web memorials that record the deaths of children killed in the Israeli/Palestinian conflict. As Clark argues, 'Vernacular and official memorials provide outlets for a traumatized community to share their loss and vent their grief'. Witness testimony relates to social trauma as it 'permits a working through of trauma by the witness and personalizes the victims for the larger community'. The accessibility of web-memorials provides the community with increased opportunities to understand the trauma of their society, and in turn, work through their own experiences via the information and opportunities to contribute available through such sites. These provocative memorials serve as much more than places of commemoration, as they often ascribe guilt with the purpose of influencing public opinion. Strategies include an emphasis on the disproportionate number of deaths of Palestinian children and references to the nationality of the agent behind the weapon that caused each death. A commonality between this expression of social trauma and that of Eisenman's design for Berlin lies in the refusal to employ horrific details. Whilst *The Memorial to the Murdered Jews of Europe* relates to events seventy years before, it does relate to Germany's need to deal with its Nazi ancestry, and like the Palestinian web-memorials, consciously avoids graphic imagery whilst still managing to stimulate the viewer. The Palestinian memorials are, of course, much more political when compared to the Berlin memorial, with its non-apparent notions of guilt. Temporal factors must cause these differences, along with the axiomatic point that the overt politics of the web-memorials is perhaps inevitable for an on-going conflict.

Though the subject-matter of the Collins Mencarelli chapter is disparate to Clark's, the relevance of social trauma could not be more profound in a case such as Kyron Horman's disappearance, which led to a plethora of media coverage and the speedy creation of an on-line memorial, thus resulting in a global audience. At a more local level, such virtual and vernacular memorials perform a further task than creating awareness of the child's disappearance and the subsequent hope that he will be found. Such memorials, like those discussed by Clark, can also serve as places for communities to express their own trauma, due to the 'penultimate fear of all parents; that an innocent child is missing from a place that should be safe'. This newest memorial genre, the virtual, online memorial, demonstrates the potential for a community to preserve memory and cope with grief online. As Collins and Mencarelli argue, the online memorial gives us a space not restricted by physical limits: 'Its ease of access allows the expansion on the creativity and the possibility of scared spaces'. Whilst positive, this development also reveals contentious behaviour through the responses to the Kyron Horman Facebook memorial, through some of the site's viewers desecrating the virtual memorial with inappropriate and offensive comments. Though much of this behaviour is vandalism attributed to 'trolls' who might claim that their acts make 'political statements designed to expose the public's obsession with trauma', Collins and Mencarelli point out that such desecration interferes with healing and hope. Though *The Memorial to the Murdered Jews of Europe* has rarely been subjected to anti-Semitic graffiti (a company associated with the manufacturer of Zyklon B controversially supplied the anti-graffiti solution that coats all of the blocks) one often sees inappropriate behaviour there. The memorial's non-symbolic, no-prescriptive approach has resulted in children and adults playing amongst the blocks, thereby altering the memorial's meaning, as to many observers the site might appear like a site of leisure rather than one of remembrance.

Though one might initially consider this reception as defiling the memorial, the response usually stems from ignorance of the memorial's nature (or even of its being a memorial) rather than a conscious disrespect for the murdered Jews. Unlike the Kyron Horman Facebook memorial page, this reception does not deliberately and insensitively interrupt the original purpose of the trauma site.

Nevertheless, it demonstrates that sites of trauma, whether places where trauma occurred, newly constructed memorial sites, or virtual memorials, all encourage social interaction that can also have negative or questionable outcomes. Whilst regulation of trauma-related sites matters in order to reduce profanity and to provide respectful places of memory and contemplation, these examples also raise questions concerning the balance between the social nature of memorial sites–that increased restrictions might result in reduced opportunities to work through social trauma–and the reluctance to make them places associated more with proscription than memory. Though the traumatic response to Kyron's disappearance is 'based on the realization that child-protection safeguards and recovery procedures still do not work', a further trauma has arguably emerged through the response to the memorials formed in his honour: social trauma, due to its inclusive nature, might inevitably include callous inputs despite the sensitivity and continued trauma of a public tragedy.

## Notes

[1] Not entirely democratic and transparent, the decision-making process involved the public and media playing a seemingly ancillary role to the jurors and politicians. Public opinion, for instance, strongly favoured Renata Stih and Frieder Schnock's *Bus Stop!* Yet their proposal failed to make the 1995 shortlist of finalists, whilst an unpopular design by Christine Jackob-Marks was unveiled as the winner only to face rejection owing to upsetting Jewish sensibilities. It would, be very unusual, if not unprecedented, for a memorial to be commissioned by way of a public vote, so despite the aforementioned contradictions the commissioners and politicians stuck, to a large extent, with the paradigm for the creation of public artworks. The establishment of the memorial, however, followed an unusual process in that three official sponsors oversaw the project–the Memorial Association, the Cite-State (Land) Berlin, and the Federal Public–so perhaps for the first time ever, a private citizen initiative officially sponsored a state- or federally-funded cultural project.

[2] Professor James Young, the spokesperson for the 1997 Findungskommission, confirmed these primary reasons for Eisenman's selection. Interview, March 2011.

[3] The memorial occupies an area of Berlin where once the gardens between Hitler's office and that of his architect Albert Speer flourished. More sinisterly though, the north west corner of the memorial site formerly housed Propaganda Minister Joseph Goebbels's bunker, where, on 1 May 1945, in order to avoid capture by the on-coming Red Army, he and his wife Magda committed suicide shortly after she had poisoned her six children with cyanide capsules as they slept Anthony Beevor, *Berlin: The Downfall 1945* (London: Penguin, 2007), 380.

[4] Andreas Huyssen, *Present Pasts: Urban Palimpsests and the Politics of Memory* (Standord, CT: Stanford University Press, 2003), 81.

[5] Most prominent was the 1998 debate between Ignatz Bubis, leader of Germany's Jewish community, and writer and political activist, Martin Wasler, along with the extraordinary impact of Daniel Goldhagen's 1996 book, *Hitler's Willing Executioners*. In his book, Goldhagen posits that 'ordinary Germans', with their eliminationist anti-Semitist tendencies, bore responsibility for the atrocities rather than Nazi policies. Geoff Eley, *The Goldhagen Effect: History, Memory, Nazism–Facing the German Past* (Ann Arbor, MI: The University of Michigan, 2000), 53.

[6] Susannah Radstone, 'Trauma Theory: Contexts, Politics, Ethics,' *Other People's Pain: Narratives of Trauma and the Question of Ethics*, eds. Martin Modlinger and Philipp Sonntag (Oxford: Peter Lang, 2011), 14.

[7] Project instigators Lea Rosh and Eberhard Jäckel did not feel qualified to judge on aesthetics yet played a significant role in the selection process.

[8] Wolfgang Thierse, Speaker of Parliament, declared that the memorial was 'not solely for Jews but to help Germany confront a chapter of its history. See Ruth A. Starkman, *Transformations of the New Germany: Studies in European History.* (New York: Palgrave MacMillan, 2006), 237. Project instigator Lea Rosh, however, saw the memorial as being 'erected by the perpetrators to their dead victims' (William J. V. Neill, *Urban Planning and Cultural Identity* (London: Routledge, 2004), 14.

[9] Kai Erikson, *A New Species of Trouble: The Human Experience of Modern Disasters* (New York: W.W. Norton & Co., 1995), 184.

[10] In my interview with Peter Eisenman, the architect also said he, 'wanted a physical experience in the present tense because it would be so different to what one would have elsewhere. We wanted the Germans to see the Holocaust as everyday life.' He also elaborated on the acoustics, and how the undulating ground adds to this effect, as with a flat surface much of the echo would be lost. Interview, March 2011.

[11] Cathy Caruth, *Trauma: Explorations in Memory* (Baltimore: John Hopkins University Press, 1995), 5.

[12] Ibid.

[13] Dori Laub in Ann. E. Kaplan, *Trauma and Cinema: Cross-Cultural Explorations* (Hong Kong: Hong Kong University Press, 2004), 160.

[14] Simon Ungers, whose design was a leading contender for the 1994 competition, did not believe the Holocaust could be represented by any means others than abstraction. Interview with Sophia Ungers, December 2012.

[15] Approximately 70% of the 547 submitted designs were abstract.

[16] Mark Godfrey, *Abstraction and the Holocaust* (New York: Yale University Press, 2007), 4.

[17] Marianne Hirsch, *The Generation of Postmemory* (New York: Columbia University Press, 2007), 4.

[18] Kaplan, *Trauma and Cinema*, 18.

[19] Jill Bennett, *Empathic Vision: Affect, Trauma, and Contemporary Art* (San Francisco: Stanford University Press. 2005), 28.

[20] Quoted from the Press Release, 'The National Holocaust Monument is a Long Time Overdue' (*Das Nationale Holocaust-Denkmal ist längst überfällig)* 5 May 1994.

[21] Quoted from the Minutes of the jury's first meeting on 15 March 1995.

[22] Marita Sturken, *Tourists of History: Memory, Kitsch and Consumerism from Oklahoma City to Ground Zero* (Durham, NC: Duke University Press, 2007), 8.

[23] Jill Bennett, *Empathic Vision: Affect, Trauma, and Contemporary Art* (San Francisco: Stanford University Press, 2005), 29.

[24] Mark Godfrey, *Abstraction and the Holocaust* (NY: Yale University Press, 2007), 253.

[25] Kaplan, *Trauma and Cinema*, 19.

[26] Karen Till, *The New Berlin: Memory, Politics, Place* (Minneapolis: University of Minnesota Press, 2005), 165.

[27] Maria Tumarkin, *Traumascapes: The Power and Fate of Places Transformed by Tragedy* (Melbourne: Melbourne University Publishing, 2005), 12.

[28] Despite its unconventional, arguably non-conformist approach, *Bus Stop!* was the most popular design with the German public, and was also ranked eleventh out of the 528 proposals by the first jury. Gunter Schlusche, *Der Denkmalstreit - das Denkmal? Die Debatte um das 'Denkmal für die ermordeten Juden Europas' Eine Dokumentation [The Monument's Disputes: The Debate around 'The Monument for the Murdered Jews of Europe'–A Documentation]* (Berlin: Philo, 1999), 86. Amnon Barzel, former chair of the Council of Jews in Germany, also supported the concept and said that regardless of the memorial competition's outcome, *Bus Stop!* should be built in Berlin. Till, *The New Berlin*, 180.

[29] Alison Landsberg, *Prosthetic Memory: The Transformation of American Remembrance in the Age of Mass Culture* (NY: Columbia University Press, 2004), 23.

[30] Harold Marcuse, *Legacies of Dachau: The Uses and Abuses of a Concentration Camp, 1933-2001* (London: Cambridge University Press, 2008), 391.

[31] Landsberg, *Prosthetic Memory*, 22.

[32] David Bathrick, David Prager, Brad David and Michael D. Richardson, *Visualizing the Holocaust: Documents, Aesthetics, Memory* (Rochester: Camden House, 2012), 76.

[33] Dominick La Capra, *History & Memory after Auschwitz* (New York: Cornell University Press, 1998), 5.

[34] Despite the apparent merits of empathetic identification (primarily, emotional and visceral appeal), as La Capra posits, one cannot show empathy without intrusively arrogating to oneself the victim's experience or undergoing

(consciously or not) surrogate victimage, a point worth minding when evaluating the values of empathy. Ibid., 182.

[35] Kirsten Harjes, 'Stumbling Stones: Holocaust Memorials, National Identity, and Democratic Inclusion in Berlin,' *German Politics and Society* 23.1 (2005): 5.

[36] Till, *The New Berlin*, 182.

[37] See Stih-Schnock.de, Viewed on 5 December 2015, http://www.stih-schnock.de/bus-stop.html

[38] Despite receiving favourable reviews, *Bus Stop!* was ultimately rejected by the jury because several members of the jury felt it did not comply with the parameters of the competition's advertisement and questioned the feasibility of the concept in principle. Document outlining the jury's assessment of *Bus Stop!*, March 1995. Schlusche, *Der Denkmalstreit - das Denkmal?*.

[39] Shelley Hornstein and Florence Jacobwitz, *Image & Remembrance: Representation and the Holocaust* (Bloomington, IN: Indiana University Press, 2003), 45.

[40] According to jury member James Young, *Stone-Breath* ultimately faced rejection because of its potential confusion with a remnant of the Berlin Wall and also because similarity in appearance to Libeskind's already celebrated Jewish Museum, also in Berlin.

[41] Hornstein and Jacobwitz, *Image & Remembrance*, 45.

[42] Daniel Carter, *Hiroshima Mon Amour: The Art of Vicarious Trauma.* (Charllotsville, VA: University of Virginia Press, 2010), 2.

[43] Ann Kaplan makes a similar point regarding cinema where the viewer can enter the victim's experience through a work's narration.

[44] Bessel Van der Kolk, *Psychological Trauma* (Boston: American Physic Press, January, 1987), 167.

# Bibliography

**Primary Sources**

Interview with Peter Eisenman, conducted by Mark Callaghan on 17 March 2011.

Interview with Professor James Young, conducted by Mark Callaghan on 31 March 2011.

**Secondary Sources**

Bathrick, David, David Prager, Brad David and Michael D. Richardson. *Visualizing the Holocaust: Documents, Aesthetics, Memory.* Rochester: Camden House, 2012.

Beevor, Anthony. *Berlin: The Downfall 1945*. London: Penguin, 2007.

Bennett, Jill. *Empathic Vision: Affect, Trauma, and Contemporary Art*. San Francisco: Stanford University Press. 2005.

Carter, Daniel. *Hiroshima Mon Amour: The Art of Vicarious Trauma*. Charlottsville, VA: University of Virginia Press, 2010.

Caruth, Cathy. *Trauma: Explorations in Memory*. Baltimore: John Hopkins University Press, 1995.

Eley, Geoff. *The Goldhagen Effect. History, Memory, Nazism – Facing the German Past*. nc: The University of Michigan, 2000.

Erikson, Kai. *A New Species of Trouble: The Human Experience of Modern Disasters*. London, New York: W.W. Norton & Co., 1995.

Godfrey, Mark. *Abstraction and the Holocaust*. New York: Yale University Press. 2007.

Harjes, Kirsten. 'Stumbling Stones: Holocaust Memorials, National Identity, and Democratic Inclusion in Berlin.' *German Politics and Society* 23.1 (2005): 138-151.

Hirsch, Marianne. *The Generation of Postmemory*. New York: Columbia University Press. 2007.

Hornstein, Shelley and Florence Jacobwitz. *Image & Remembrance: Representation and the Holocaust*. Bloomington, IN: Indiana University Press, 2003.

Huyssen, Andreas. *Present Pasts: Urban Palimpsests and the Politics of Memory*. Stanford, CA: Stanford University Press, 2003.

Kaplan, Ann. E. *Trauma and Cinema: Cross-Cultural Explorations*. Hong Kong: Hong Kong University Press, 2004.

La Capra, Dominick. *History & Memory after Auschwitz*. New York: Cornell University Press, 1998.

Landsberg, Alison. *Prosthetic Memory: The Transformation of American Remembrance in the Age of Mass Culture*. New York: Columbia University Press, 2004.

Marcuse, Harold. *Legacies of Dachau: The Uses and Abuses of a Concentration Camp, 1933-2001.* London: Cambridge University Press. 2008.

Neill, William J. V. *Urban Planning and Cultural Identity*. London: Routledge, 2004.

Radstone, Susannah. 'Trauma Theory: Contexts, Politics, Ethics.' *Other People's Pain: Narratives of Trauma and the Question of Ethics*, edited by Martin Modlinger and Philipp Sonntag, 9-29. London: Peter Lang, 2011.

Schlusche, Gunter. *Der Denkmalstreit - das Denkmal? Die Debatte um das 'Denkmal für die ermordeten Juden Europas' Eine Dokumentation [The Monument's Disputes: The Debate around 'The Monument for the Murdered Jews of Europe' - A Documentation].* Berlin: Philo, 1999.

Starkman, Ruth. A. *Transformations of the New Germany: Studies in European History.* New York: Palgrave MacMillian, 2006.

Sturken, Marita. *Tourists of History: Memory, Kitsch and Consumerism from Oklahoma City to Ground Zero*. Durham, North Carolina: Duke University Press. 2007.

Till, Karen. *The New Berlin*: *Memory, Politics, Place*. Minneapolis: University of Minnesota Press. 2005.

Tumarkin, Maria. *Traumascapes: The Power and Fate of Places Transformed by Tragedy*. Melbourne: Melbourne University Publishing, 2005.

Van der Kolk, Bessel. *Psychological Trauma.* Boston: American Physic Press, January, 1987.

**Mark Callaghan**'s research and teaching centre mainly on contemporary memory culture. His Ph.D thesis at Birkbeck College, University of London, concerns the Berlin Holocaust Memorial Competition, perusing issues of national idenity, Jewish sensibilities, trauma theory, and artistic representations of genocide. Mark also graduated from the University of Manchester and Oxford University.

# Gaining Agency in Response to Trauma: The Role of Physical and Virtual Memorials

*Catherine Ann Collins and AnnaMaria Mencarelli*

**Abstract**
Trauma, whether individual or collective, often triggers the impulse to commemorate. Increasingly, scholarship has attended to both physical and virtual vernacular memorials as environments for memory preservation. In creating a place set apart from our daily routines, we gain space for the grief process. Vernacular memorials reflect what Foucault terms heterotopias of place and time. Our interest lies in the vernacular space, coproduced by family, friends and strangers who feel the need to have a place for mourning, for negotiating the means of their traumatic loss. One significant variant on the vernacular memorial concerns the use of the conventionalized form and rituals of roadside shrines to commemorate a child missing rather than dead. On 4 June 2010, Kyron Horman went missing from his school, and remains missing more than three years later. Through a case study of Kyron's physical and virtual memorials, we argue that the traumatic ambiguity of a missing child has led to a discourse of substitution wherein the act of commemoration (coproduction) begins to replace the traumatic ambiguity of the missing child. Whether reflecting highly personalized or more generalized cultural trauma, these physical and virtual spaces for memorialization reflect an emerging pattern of rhetorical responses to the trauma of missing children. The photographs serve as a coping mechanism that allows Facebook members to reproduce Kyron's past according to their preferred narrative; in this act they begin to gain agency and work through the trauma of his disappearance and society's failure to protect its children.

**Key Words:** Missing children, trauma, photographs, memorialization, grieving, heterotopian space.

*****

## 1. Introduction: A Missing Child as Public Trauma

When a child goes missing, it spreads a story that transcends socioeconomic, racial and geographical divides and settles itself in the heart of all parents as the penultimate fear; an innocent child is missing from a place that should be safe. The National Center for Missing and Exploited Children (NCMEC) estimates 800,000 children reported missing in 2010[1]: 7-year-old Kyron Horman was one of those 800,000. On 4 June 2010, Kyron disappeared from his elementary school and remains missing. In the first year after his disappearance rescue volunteers had contributed 20,000 search hours, and police followed 4,318 leads and conducted 3,500 interviews, at a cost of 1.44 million dollars.[2] Following the disappearance,

Kyron's photograph appeared in international newscasts, print media, on 57 billboards, hundreds of fliers, and on the side of trucks traveling the I-5 corridor along the West Coast of the United States. The public created more than 50 Facebook pages, the largest of which has 102,000 users across the globe. These memorials honour Kyron and advocate for his return.

Whether the loss is temporary or permanent, missing children create personal trauma and, in particular cases, disruptive cultural trauma. A child's abduction becomes a public tragedy when the loss threatens to reveal the deficiencies in societal structures. The Lindbergh kidnapping on 1 March 1932 constitutes the earliest highly publicized child abduction.[3] Unlike the Lindbergh baby, the son of a national hero, six-year-old Etan Patz was only well known to his family and neighbours in the SoHo community. Missing since 25 May 1979, his abduction prompted a nation-wide overhaul in the criminal justice system and advocacy for missing children. We believe that the traumatic response to Kyron's disappearance results from the realization that after thirty years of procedural requirements, child-protection safeguards and recovery procedures still do not work. Kyron's case disrupts the belief that a child is safe in school, and that missing children response systems make it unlikely those child abductions will long remain unsolved. Missing children create trauma for family and friends, as well as the community that has failed to protect them. Safeguard systems such as Amber Alert and the National Center for Missing and Endangered Children place responsibility for recovering the child on the individuals in the community: posters and amber alerts plead, 'if you see' this person, 'report' so that the child may be recovered. Three and a half years later, with on-going and extensive publicity of his missing status, Kyron's disappearance continues to elicit strong national and international concern and support.

## 2. Commemoration as a Response to Trauma

Trauma often triggers the impulse to commemorate in both private and public spaces. In the public sphere these memorial sites are both official and vernacular. In creating a *place* set apart from our daily routines, we gain *space* for the grief process. An official *place* serves as a sacred *space* that breaks normal routine (a requirement for mourning). Significant scholarship assesses public memorial sites, but increasingly attention has focused on both physical and virtual vernacular memorials that construct an environment for memory preservation in places set apart to allow space for grieving.[4] Our interest lies in the vernacular space, coproduced by family, friends and strangers who feel the need for, 'a meeting place for communication, remembrance, and reflection, separate from the "everyday",'[5] for negotiating the meaning of their traumatic loss. The physical site of a vernacular memorial is often chosen because of its proximity to the site of death or a near death experience. Rituals associated with pilgrimage to vernacular sites vary, but visitors often bring tokens of remembrance. Unlike a cemetery such a site requires no regular maintenance, so offerings weather and give clear indication of the passage of time. Some of these sites are visited, cleaned, and added to on a regular basis, others are *public* for only a few weeks.

One significant variant on the vernacular memorial concerns the use of the conventionalized form and rituals of roadside shrines to commemorate a child missing rather than dead. The act of commemoration (coproduction)[6] begins to replace the traumatic ambiguity of the missing child; commemoration becomes a means, albeit imperfect, for working through both the individual trauma of loss and the cultural trauma that the public experiences. The tension between keeping hope alive and mourning the missing child is complicated by the appropriation of the form embodied by vernacular memorials for the dead. A relatively new site for grieving in the United States, roadside shrines have become commonplace over the last twenty years. Now, traffic fatalities and murders are soon marked by flowers, cards, and religious as well as secular tokens of remembrance.

Vernacular memorials constitute, in Foucault's sense, heterotopian spaces with normal relations disrupted – places that change a site of trauma to a space for working through trauma. Heterotopian spaces function 'in relation to the remaining space' to create 'different real space as perfect, as meticulous, as well-arranged as ours is disorganized, badly arranged, and muddled'.[7] With physical vernacular memorial sites

> [t]he order brought by creating, maintaining, or visually acknowledging the site by looking and seeing it differently – not as the place of violent death but as space for remembering and honouring – offers relief from the chaos of traumatic memory and grief.[8]

When Kyron Horman went missing, a physical memorial was soon established at the site of his disappearance. Similar to the physical memorial created, the Bring Kyron Home Facebook page was the first online memorial developed shortly after his disappearance. Temporally, memorials provide a break in time that will extend the final moment of the missing/deceased's memory.

### 3. Progression of Commemoration: Physical and Virtual Heterotopian Space and Time

Whether commemorating the dead or missing, one of the prominent forms of memorialization consists in the inclusion of photographs of the victim. We will argue that these photographs reinforce the heterotopian character of the site and process of memorialization and further reinforce the complications incurred by borrowing the form of a traditional death memorial.

For Kyron Horman, commemoration has taken physical form in a *Wall of Hope* and virtual form in Facebook pages of remembrance. Whether reflecting highly personalized or more generalized cultural trauma, these spaces for memorialization reflect an emerging pattern of rhetorical response. The vernacular *Wall of Hope*, resembling shrines marking traffic fatalities, was initiated by Amber Schaechner two weeks after Kyron's disappearance, and initially consisted of 4 red balloons tied to the fence surrounding his school and a hand written sign entitled *Wall of Hope*.[9]

As a rhetorical artefact, the Wall epitomizes the coproduction of messages expressing hope for Kyron's return, empathy for his family, and anxiousness about his disappearance. Along with typical vernacular offerings – toys, balloons, and religious artefacts, personal letters addressed to Kyron and his family fill the fence. One reads, 'Kyron, We hope U come home soon. We pray that your safe', and another simply says 'Keep hope alive'. Others address the family such as one that urges his father, 'Don't give up, my friend. . . . Stay healthy for when Kyron comes home'. Some address Kyron: 'Kyron, love you so much buddy & hang in there, because we ARE coming for you sweetie'. Kyron's parents have also added their letters:

> My Ky, I love you! My heart aches every day and is empty until you come home. . . . I promise I will find you. I will never stop! Love Momma.

Some of the most poignant come from children, including one that reveals the child's doubt about Kyron's fate, 'I hope your parents find you soon and I hope you are safe and are alive'.

The Wall also displays Missing posters and seasonal classroom projects that frequently include Kyron's school picture (Image 1). Sylvia Grider explains, 'These artefact assemblages are sacred by virtue of the actions and intentions of the people who create and tend to them'.[10] Most vernacular memorials commemorate a life lost, but with a child missing and with the focus on a rhetoric of hope, even the newly adopted rituals and forms of the vernacular memorial do not fit. Over time, hope for recovery of a missing child becomes fragile, yet the need to memorialize, to work through the trauma of the disappearance has not abated. Anne Stone captures the difficulty associated with someone whose status is missing:

> When someone goes missing, knowledge is suspended and deferred. An aura of harm may thickly surround an interrupted narrative but cannot coalesce into certainty. . . .When someone goes missing, the real is at a remove, though a plenitude of possible representations remains. In the absence of the real, when a representation of the real is made public, that representation is malleable, shaped by the hands of strangers, and the gaps and

interstices of a stranger's knowing creates an impersonal identity, a gathering of cultural meanings over an obscured, private core.[11]

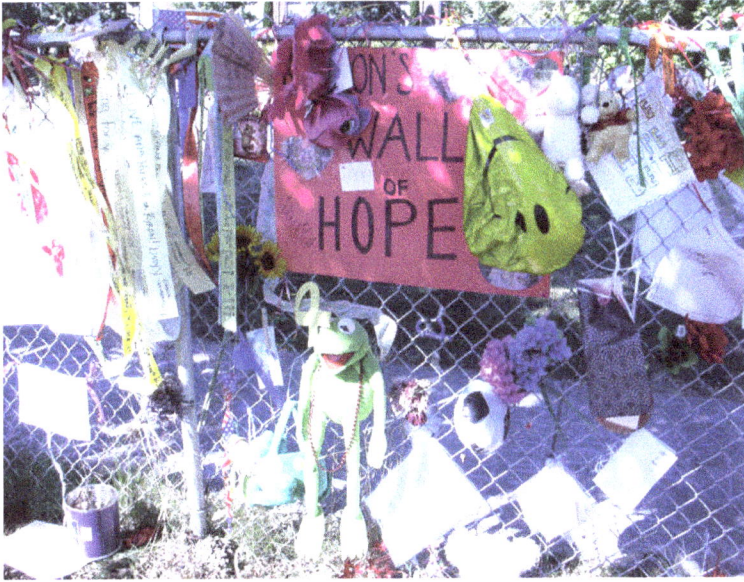

**Image 1:** *Wall of Hope* at Skyline Elementary, August 28, 2010.
© 2013. Image courtesy of Catherine Ann Collins

Instability in the site for commemorating complicates memorialization of Kyron. Grider contends these memorials function 'to draw attention to the previously ordinary place where some violent event occurred. The most distinguishing characteristic of spontaneous shrines are their proximity to the precipitating event'.[12] The original location of the memorial – on school property – marks the last place Kyron was seen – the place of departure. Maria Tumarkin has coined the term traumascapes 'to describe places across the world marked by traumatic legacies of violence, suffering and loss' in which 'the past is never quite over'.[13] Personal and cultural trauma is re-experienced in these places. Because Kyron went missing from school, locating a memorial on school grounds reinscribes the traumatic loss of a child from a place parents and the public trust to be safe. Unfortunately, this appropriate site for memorializing proved at the same time problematic. Concerned that children returning to school would have Kyron's continued disappearance 'staring them in the face',[14] and fearful that strangers visiting the Wall might pose a safety threat, the Wall was reassembled down the road. Locating the memorial close to the site of loss continued to matter to loved ones. Image 2 documents the Wall at its second location where new offerings continued to be added and marked the passage of time since the boy's disappearance. A final relocation occurred on 27 August 2011 when the Wall was re-erected on land surrounding the X-treme Edge Gym in Beaverton, miles away from the site of his disappearance.

Sites of memory, even in public places like the side of a busy road, become sacred spaces that seemingly should remain fixed. The first move was awkward, but the memorial remained physically close to the site of loss. The second move is disquieting, and while its coproduction makes it sacred, the frequent relocation inevitably changes the relationship between place and pilgrimage to the site.

***Image 2:*** Wall of Hope at Tualatin Valley Fire and Rescue, May 28, 2011.
© 2013. Image courtesy of Catherine Ann Collins

Establishing a physical place near the site of death seeks to create symbolic space for coping with trauma. Vernacular memorials are no longer bound to physical locations; they have emerged on the Internet. Facebook has become a site for commemorating personal tragedies as well as public traumas such as 9/11,[15] the Virginia Tech shooting,[16] or the death of celebrities. However distinctly these groups commemorate, all demonstrate the potential for a global community to preserve memory and cope with grief online.

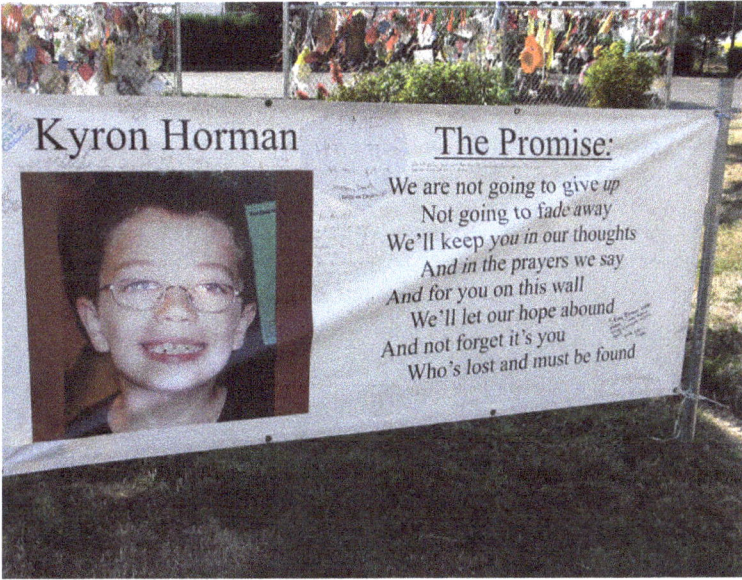

***Image 3:*** *Wall of Hope* in Beaverton, August 28, 2011.
© 2013. Image courtesy of Catherine Ann Collins

Commemoration as a response to trauma is also central to the Kyron Horman virtual memorials on Facebook which contain artefacts much like those left at the physical *Wall of Hope*, including virtual gifts for Kyron in the form of images found online – a picture that might cheer him up, or a photograph of presents meant for Kyron (such as physical teddy bears or frog figurines). These virtual tokens may be meant as presents that would bring joy to the child, but their existence solely as images prevents them from being utilized like the physical toys left at the *Wall of Hope*. Virtual tokens reinforce the heterotopian nature of offerings. Bringing offerings to a physical memorial represents the ritual of bringing gifts to the sick. Virtual offerings are a step further removed. Facebook memorials attempt to mirror the Wall. By including photographs of the Wall at all three locations, users can access the physical memorial virtually. Rather than making a physical pilgrimage, through Facebook members can send real offerings/messages to the memorial. The virtual pilgrimage ends by changing the physical memorial. When subsequent pictures showcase their offering, they re-affirm the user's coproduction.

One might assume that these online memorial or *RIP* pages are unlikely to solicit the same sacredness experienced at the physical grave or physical vernacular memorial site. We contend, however, that the members' coproduction will ultimately enact the commemorative function, a part of mourning and recovery from trauma.[17] As physical limits and informal rituals delineate the sacred space of a memorial, virtual memorials also limit the ways in which viewers may participate in commemoration in order to preserve sacredness at the site. The 'Psychic Help on the Kyron Horman Case' Facebook page limits the services the members may provide: 'you may not advertise your services here or jeopardize the case'.[18] The site encourages members to focus on the memory of Kyron or advocate for his safe return; reaping profits from his disappearance is regarded as profanity. Other Facebook pages restrict membership in the group by monitoring requests to join; some groups bar specific individuals, such as Terri Horman, Dee Dee Spicer, or supporters of either individual. Supporters of these banned individuals are warned that their comments will be removed. Monitoring the participation of Facebook members creates specific barriers to impiety and further delineates the site as sacred space.

Sociality at physical and virtual memorials, however, depends on careful monitoring. Not all visitors to commemorative sites prove respectful, and some have desecrated sites dedicated to Kyron Horman. At the *Wall of Hope*, for example, we found one disturbing message treated as an act of defilement; at a subsequent visit we discovered it had been painted over. The message written from the voice of the missing child reflected public suspicion that Kyron's stepmother was involved in his disappearance:

> I love you daddy. You will see me in another Time and Place
> where "I" Kyron (Special K) is No longer in Pain. Where "she"
> can no longer hurt me Dad.

Desecration of online memorials like the vandalism seen at the physical memorial have a similarly disturbing effect. Online vandals, also called trolls,[19] create fake identities and accounts in order to post offensive images and messages. Many trolls claim that their acts are political statements designed to expose the public's obsession with trauma.[20] Trolls target those online users that they label as 'grief tourists', individuals who have no ties to the victim, but visit memorial pages out of a need for attention that they masque as grief.[21] Kenan Malik's essay on the disappearance of four-year old Madeline McCann poses the question that some trolls on online memorials similarly ask: 'But why has this personal tragedy become a national, indeed international obsession?'[22] He contends that the issue has less to do with any particular child and more to do with 'a desire for vicarious identification with someone else's pain. . .a way of remoulding identity and forging social bonds'.[23] These faked emotional responses trolls argue justify their desecration of online memorial sites. Whitney Phillips contends that trolls 'emphasize the visceral, resulting in an aesthetic which both mirrors and monsters the objects of their ridicule' when they 'force their victims to confront. . .[their]

fear of helplessness, fear of losing a loved one, fear of human parts'.[24] By compromising the sacred space of online memorials, though, these trolls unknowingly inflict further damage on those who genuinely use the space as a site for mourning and commemoration. From its onset, trolling 'has proven to be a public relations nightmare for the Facebook brand'.[25]

The administrators of three Facebook groups dedicated to Kyron Horman were interviewed for the frequency of trolling on their site. The results vary but each administrator faced the necessity of monitoring and removing actions taken by trolls. Created a few weeks after Kyron's disappearance, *Ribbons for Hope – Kyron Horman*, a page that encourages visitors to post flyers and send messages to the physical *Wall of Hope*, has received at most 10 suspicious comments. The administrator of the page told us:

> The limited trolling is understandable given the purpose of the
> site is limited to dispersing flyers and sending in messages of
> hope to Kyron; there is less reason for people to troll. Readers of
> the page want Kyron to be found, and thus the page supports
> hope and spreads the word to keep Kyron's face out there.[26]

Unfortunately, a limited amount of trolling is not characteristic of all the Kyron Facebook groups; administrators for these sites report that they need to be constantly on the lookout for unsavoury and disrespectful comments. Only with careful and vigilant combing through posts can they prevent unwanted comments and actions from these disrespectful visitors. Unfortunately, vandalism has not developed recently in online memorials, and the development of trolling commemorative pages follows the pattern of desecration of physical memorials. Just as the physical desecration was covered by painting over the offensive text, so too do the online memorials and their administrators attempt to cover or hide the offensive postings. Still, the trolls present a current and troubling issue in the development of online memorials. In order to cope with collective trauma, memorialization demands sacred space; desecration interferes with healing and hope. Whether physical or virtual, desecration demands a response, but defining desecration ties up with our communal sense of order and identity and can be highly contested. Goodman and Gorden's seminal essay on desecrating the flag[27] reminds us that some consider a flag burning an intolerable act of desecration, others an act of symbolic speech. Since both the physical and virtual forms of memorial are coproduced, and those contributing to the memorials have different conceptions of privileged speech, issues of desecration inhere, even in the places and spaces for remembrance, and may lead to conflict.

Like the *Wall of Hope*, virtual memorials create the space for coproducers to preserve Kyron's memory, negotiate how mourners will deal with the trauma of his disappearance and ambiguity of his current whereabouts, and privilege how the community will appropriately act on Kyron's behalf. We observed in both mediums heterotopian qualities and the capacity for individuals to work through trauma.

Foucault argues that heterotopias may also reflect disruptions in time, what he terms heterochronias: '[t]he heterotopia begins to function fully when men are in a kind of absolute break with their traditional time'.[28] Visiting the memorial, taking time to commemorate, constitutes a break in time, but the heterochronia extends to the visitor's conception of Kyron as well. Interestingly, Kyron's father told reporters that he buys clothes and age-appropriate toys for the larger, older Kyron. For most of the public, Kyron is frozen as the same 7-year-old he was at his disappearance. The Wall preserves unchanged the child at the age of his symbolic disappearance/death, thereby disrupting time. Temporal disruption similarly manifests itself in the Facebook pages. Users do not refer to him as the now 11-year-old, but as their 'sweet baby blue'.[29] Photographs and messages offer an identity tightly bound to the mythic innocent child. As Julia Kennedy notes in tributes to missing British child Madeline McCann: 'the idealized construction of Madeline manifest in the recurrent use of the words "angel", "innocent", "beautiful", and "cute" exemplifies personal identification through symbolic signifiers of perfect childhood'.[30] Emphasizing youth and innocence magnifies the fear produced by the child's status as missing. Messages and offerings at The Wall are not age-appropriate but static as if he will always love Cars-themed items and red-eyed tree frogs. We have found only one visible change in Kyron's identity, namely the circulation of an age-progressed photograph, rather infrequently employed. Although authorities had hoped this image would help to identify the now older Kyron, few Facebook pages use it, with some voicing scepticism[31] about the accuracy of the image. The perceived need for authenticity and the desire to preserve the myth of innocent childhood precludes his aging on the Facebook memorials.

Though distinct, the different Facebook pages all reflect ambiguity and hope that if no physical evidence proves Kyron is dead, he may still be alive. This struggle between hope and closure is voiced throughout the Facebook groups in posts epitomizing the ambiguity of Kyron's situation. Numerous messages left for him on the Facebook pages vocalize the belief that Kyron will read the messages one day. As one user puts it 'there's really only one kind of closure I want'.[32] The question in missing children cases is when to close a case. Generally the case closes upon return of the child or corpse, but when years have passed with little progress made, it throws the public into a dissonance wherein they sustain the trauma of the child's disappearance in order to keep Kyron or other missing children alive in their hopes.

## 4. Asserting Agency through Personal Expression on Facebook

Having discussed the general nature of physical and virtual memorial sites for Kyron, we turn our attention to photographs of Kyron that serve as the primary form of expression that coproducers of the memorial sites employ. We agree with Sullender's claim: 'when it comes to grief, especially vicarious grieving, we are visual creatures'.[33] Original and altered images of Kyron contribute to the space for memory work and trauma response. In his classic study of grieving, Erich Lindemann claims preoccupation with the image of the deceased characterizes the grieving process.[34] Photographs have long been regarded as testaments to lives lost, whether the portrait of a dead child or the image of life moments. The photograph reminds those left behind of the life that was, and triggers remembrance and acceptance of loss. 'Memory freeze-frames; its basic unit is the single image. . .the photograph provides a quick way of apprehending something and a compact form for memorializing it'.[35] The photograph displayed at funerals, attached to roadside memorials, and published in newspaper obituaries celebrates the life of those who have died. Images of Kyron dominate the Facebook pages we have analysed. The most viewed page, 'Missing Kyron Horman', contains 148 unique photographs of Kyron (excluding altered images).

Posed in front of his science fair exhibit, the most prominent photograph was taken just before Kyron's disappearance. Multiple versions focus on his face alone, or Kyron from the waist up, or as an extreme close-up on a large banner titled 'The Promise' (Image 3). The image enlarged to poster size is displayed with a hand written letter from Momma. The photograph figures prominently on the Missing posters (Image 4), and on electronic billboards along I-5, making it the most recognized image of the missing boy. All Facebook pages display this image in their Timeline, Albums, Cover Image and/or Profile Picture.

If trauma means a loss of agency, then personal expression through online memorials can begin to reinstate agency. In commemorating, the individual coproducer no longer remains in a passive state, but intervenes in the grieving process to come to terms with the reality of their loss.[36] This is LaCapra's distinction between acting out the trauma – being 'haunted or possessed by the past and performatively caught up in the compulsive repetition of traumatic scenes' – and working through the trauma.[37] In multiple ways Facebook users employ Kyron's image to try to cope with his disappearance. They alter his photographs by cropping, adding clip art, icons, borders, animation, text or background (Image 5) to control his narrative.

In altering the image and adding textual amendments, Facebook users fashion a story of Kyron's response to his current situation and forecast a better future. For them, the final photograph of Kyron at the science fair is not the end of his story. Desiree's words to the news station manifest this collective effort: 'I stare at that picture everyday and I just want to take him out – just take him out of that picture'.[38] The final image of Kyron at the Science fair proves his existence. He was there, wearing the cargo shorts and CSI tee shirt, but the image does not imply his presence here any longer. In retelling Kyron's story through photographs, contributors to the Facebook pages keep Kyron alive in their minds and in the public's attention to his disappearance. Telling his story contributes to the broader narrative of missing children and thereby begins to address the fear that safeguards do not work. We noted at the beginning of this essay that missing children safeguards like Amber Alert depend on individuals in the community being observant and reporting sightings of missing children. When Facebook co-producers bring attention to Kyron through eye-catching images and photomontages of Kyron's life, they actively engage in calling the public's attention to his case. By modifying Kyron's image, the users alter the storyline, placing him in frames, cropping images so that Kyron is accusing his kidnapper, or adding text to suggest his own opinions. Images, especially those altered, function as a rhetorical statement – their alteration reflects the intention of the construer. We are no longer seeing mere opinions of Kyron's whereabouts or facts about the case; users are now creating for themselves and other Facebook users a storyline with Kyron still present, if only in photographic form. The photographs, then, serve as a backdrop for a carefully constructed message. Sometimes the message is one of hope as in Image 6 depicting Kyron in the present, walking toward the viewer through a doorway. The message focuses on the desired future of the little boy, a narrative in which he will return safely.

In some cases, Kyron's reconstructed images offer opinions on his whereabouts. At other times they serve as a message of accusation, as is the case in Image 7. Photographs of Kyron juxtapose him with his stepmother, Terri Moulton-Horman, thought by many involved in Kyron's disappearance. In Image 7 the photograph and text create a narrative in which characters are associated with good (Kyron), bad (Dee Dee Spicer, friend of the stepmother) and evil (Kyron's stepmother). When Kyron's story is told in this manner, resolution demands pressure leveled against Kyron's stepmother and her friend.

Other manipulated images position a photograph of Kyron in active frames; the viewer can follow the direction of Kyron's pointing to the profile image displaying a picture of Terri Horman behind bars or an image that appears to be a mug shot of his stepmother.[39] The positioning is becoming more common on Facebook pages because the cover image directly indicates the referent of the profile image as the object of discussion.

Image 8 illustrates how layering and composition create an identity for Kyron. The image showing Kyron waving cropped from one of his many soccer poses is then placed over a background shot of Skyline Elementary School, the final place he was seen.

*Image 4:* Cropped Science Fair Image on a Missing Child Poster.
© 2013 Kaine Horman. Image courtesy of Kaine Horman

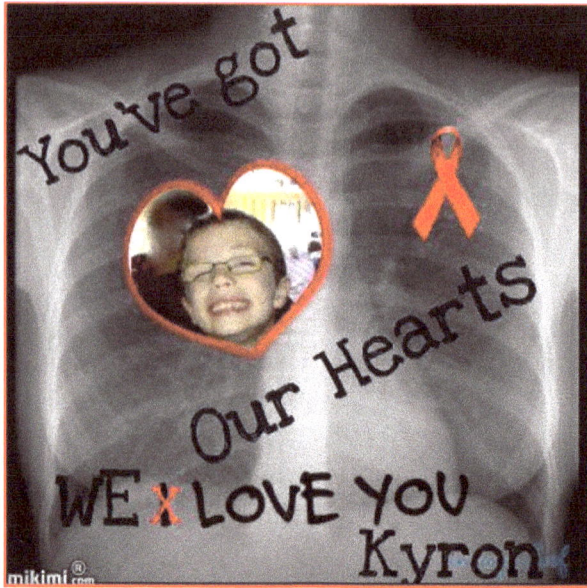

***Image 5:*** Photograph of Kyron cropped and inserted into this photo frame.
© 2013 Kaine Horman. Image courtesy of Kaine Horman

***Image 6:*** Altered Image of Kyron in the Future[40]
© 2013 Kaine Horman. Image courtesy of Kaine Horman

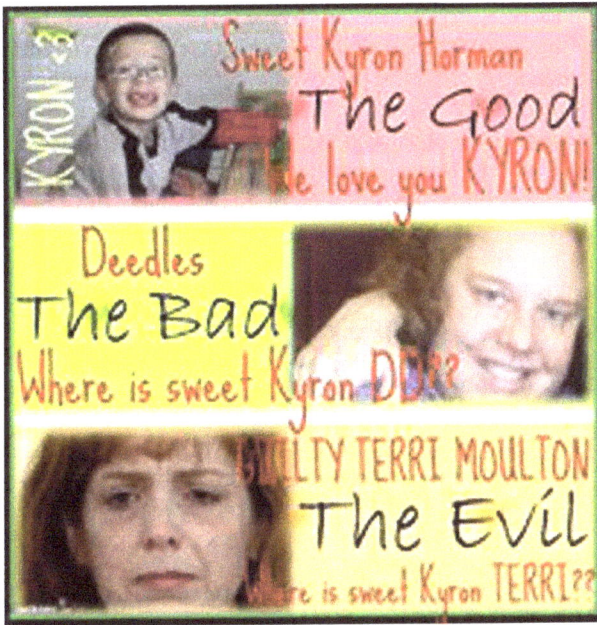

***Image 7:*** Creating a Narrative of Good vs. Evil[41]
© 2013 Kaine Horman. Photograph courtesy of Kaine Horman

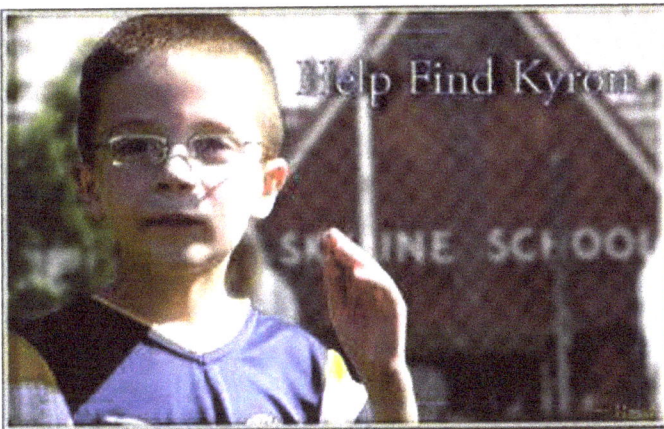

***Image 8:*** Re-visualizing Kyron's Final Moments[42]
© 2013 Kaine Horman. Image courtesy of Kaine Horman

Although accounts of Kyron's last moment say that he waved to his stepmother inside the building before he supposedly went to class, the manipulated image, complete with somber expression, places him outside of the school. One can give multiple interpretations of this image, but regardless of the narrative the viewer adopts, the manipulation illustrates an attempt to revisualize Kyron's final moments (outside of the school instead of inside). The selected photograph of Kyron with an expression of unwilling parting leads some viewers to interpret the image as confirmation of their belief that Kyron was taken by force.

Images not altered can still function to retell Kyron's story. A picture of Kyron with his classmates is accompanied by a direct message to the boy: 'good morning Kyron, this is what you should be doing now.'[43] Other messages continue to put his image in the present tense by asserting that he still enjoys doing the activity depicted in the photograph.

We have seen a similar move reporting the continued celebration of Kyron's birthday. 2013 marked the third consecutive year of Kyron's disappearance, but it is also the third year Kyron's birthday was celebrated by his family and the public. The message for these parties is to 'let Kyron know we did not forget him'.[44] The parties reflect an exigence for commemorating Kyron's memory, discussing the dangers of abduction, and celebrating his birthday with the hope that he will join the party one day. These messages use consistently present or future tense: 'when he gets home', 'are his favorite treats', and 'would enjoy hearing'. The messages do not treat Kyron as no longer able to attend parties or celebrate birthdays, but rather as *detained* or *unable* to celebrate at this time. The use of present tense changes the character of the commemoration – unlike celebrations for the deceased where birthdays are remembered as what the individual will not celebrate themselves, Kyron's birthdays are celebrated as though he were about to join the festivities (See Image 9).

The tense shift is transferred to the photographs, so that they are not artifacts of *what has been*, but *what is* or *what will be*. In like manner, users will crop Kyron's image, many times in action poses, and place them into scenes so that he is no longer in the scene of his disappearance, but in some sort of event or action of the present. This suggests, as supported by the captions accompanying these images, that Kyron is not dead or even irreparably lost; he is *living* through the photographs and stories of others touched by his disappearance.

The presence of manipulated images on the Facebook pages complicates our understanding of Kyron's virtual commemoration in three ways: this form of commemorative coproduction changes Kyron's identity for the producer and the potential viewer of the memorial site, it alters the status of the image as a form of commemoration, and it should prompt changes in the way in which we view commemorative spaces in the future.

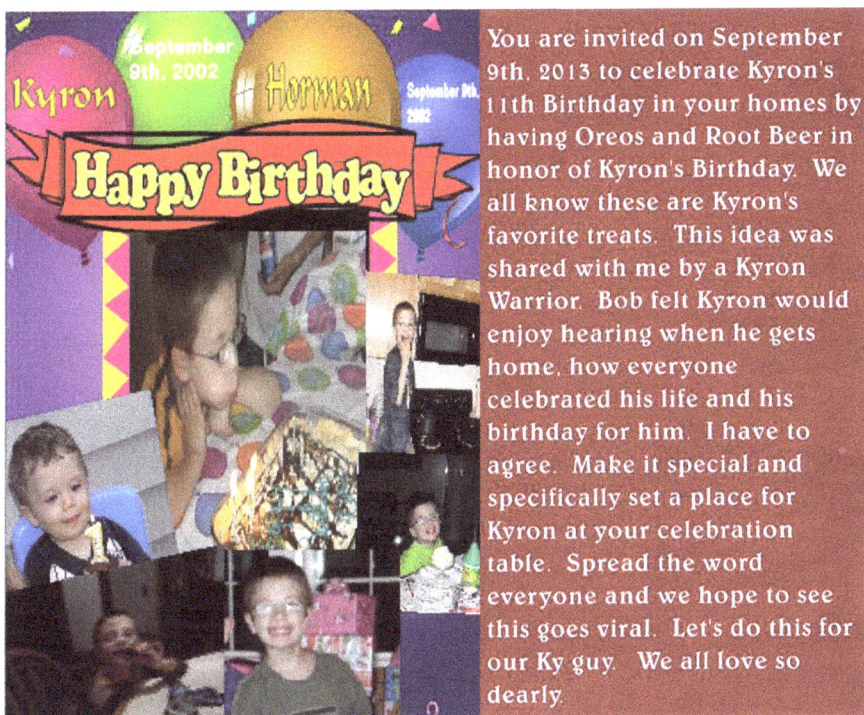

***Image 9:*** Birthday Celebration 2013, 11 Years Old[45]
© 2013 Kaine Horman. Image courtesy of Kaine Horman

Many of the earliest alterations of Kyron's photographs connect to his identity. The *Anti Terri Horman Facebook* page[46] sports a Red-Eyed Green Tree frog with boxing gloves. This mascot was created because of Kyron's interest in the amphibians and because his science fair project dealt with the life of the red-eyed tree frog. Kyron's identity closely tied to these signs has developed further as the images display more of his personality. In this sense, the image and its alterations, represent the identity of the missing. Kyron exists as a referent, and the referent of the photograph is closely tied to the identity of this missing child. Since the first monumental missing child's case, the photograph has functioned as the most critical tool in the search for the abducted. Even as technology advances, photographs remain central to search and rescue efforts, especially because age-progressed images give insight into the possible appearance of the long-term missing. Whether a photograph appears on milk cartons, on the news, on the side of trucks or online, the images signify the child's identity. The altered photographs and signs do not represent Kyron, but represents who or what the audience wants Kyron to be.

Although, the celebration of birthdays and holidays marks the passage of time, his age remains that of his disappearance. Little contention over Kyron's static age exists. Users embrace this identity despite the recent construction of an age-progressed photograph. The photograph's break in time also creates a break in time for Kyron's identity.

Facebook users' proclivity to alter images of Kyron suggests that we can no longer, in this age of photo enhancement and manipulation, view the photograph strictly as a referent of the past. Roland Barthes articulated the punctum of the photograph as the 'truth' of its prior existence, or 'that-has-been'.[47] He leaves it open to the viewer of the photograph to ponder the future of the referent.[48] Is it possible that now, we, as story-telling animals,[49] can make a shadow of an individual's experience, a form of a living and continuing story? Certainly, the Facebook users construct visual stories of Kyron's immediate presence. So the magnitude of the believability of the photograph or its authenticity is not at issue here. Of central importance, the audience can use and alter photographs to construct a living identity. We use the term living not in the sense of life or death, but rather of growth, change, adjustment and adaptation to its environment, that is to say, as the story of the user. Kyron's identity is living in the same sense our forebears called the constitution living because it has the capacity to adapt to changing circumstances. The photograph is a heterochronia, but not in the way we first believed. We postulated that the photograph constitutes a break in time because it offers a space in which the past can exist in the present. It did not occur to us that in this space the past could not only exist, but also thrive and transfer into the future. We find now a new perspective on the photograph's ability to break time. The past can become the present or future for the pilgrims to these heterotopias (physical and virtual commemorative sites).

What in the event of a missing child does allow for this break in conventions of photography? Is it the medium itself? Does advanced technology allow more accessibility and encourage our manipulation of the medium? The issue, we think, lies less in manipulating the appearance of authenticity and more in reflecting the human need to cope with trauma.

The virtual nature of online memorials reinforces these sites as heterotopias in which space and place, temporality, and role relationships are disrupted: 'virtual memorials blur the boundaries between the living and the dead, enabling relationships to continue after death'.[50] The Internet gives others the ability to '"create" and "grow" their child in images and text'.[51] Virtual memorials allow members to communally grieve, regardless of location or time zone. As technology advances and these online platforms develop more user-friendly ways to create spaces, we expect the use of these spaces to continue and develop. This does not mean they will replace the physical memorials – as evidenced by the continued visitation of and commemoration at the physical *Wall of Hope*. We can no longer ignore the differences in the development of commemoration, especially with regard to memorials advocating for the missing. The online space illustrates that in times of collective trauma, the access to a public space for constructive coping will be needed. The possibilities for innovative commemorative forms, as well as desecration, will continue to tax co-producers of commemorative sites to protect these critical spaces as sacred sites for trauma recovery. Virtual memorials are already experiencing pushback from trolls who challenge the sacrality of these sites for grieving. Does the ease of access to online memorials make them less sacred? Are the trolls correct in assuming that the online memorials are mainstreaming trauma? The ways in which our online communities respond to the pushback will change the future of commemoration studies. It seems clear, however, that the image will remain central to the use of these online spaces to respond to the trauma of the dead and missing and that they will be co-constructed by others grieving or trying to keep hope alive. In the three years that we have studied the Facebook sites, we have seen a move to more intimate alterations of the photographs. The images appear constructed endearingly, taking time, effort and tools to construct the visual spaces. Whereas in the past the images frequently displayed poor cropping or overuse of animation and alteration, now the images reflect more complex methods of alteration. Additionally, the images are being used in different ways on the pages. Photographs are not just postings; they are also cover images, profile shots, or thumbnails of events dedicated to Kyron. The expansion of the image's repertoire results in part from Facebook's move toward a visually concentrated space as opposed to text-concentrated. The newest Facebook device, the timeline, encourages users to tell their story with pictures. Clearly the online sites are visual phenomena communicating our way of perceiving life and tragedies. The online memorials give us a space not restricted by physical limits: its ease of access allows the expansion on the creativity and the possibility of sacred spaces.

The photographs serve as a coping mechanism that allows Facebook members to reproduce Kyron's past according to their preferred narrative; in this act they begin to gain agency and work through the trauma of Kyron's disappearance and society's failure to protect its children. Images of Kyron offer space for reflection as they simultaneous distort by freezing his representation and thereby discourage closure of the traumatic incident. Just as the space for memorializing, the relocations of the site, and the disruptions of time make the Wall heterotopian place/space, so too does the photograph, as an object, disrupt normal relations of space and time.

## 5. Conclusion

We have argued that memorials for missing children follow the form of vernacular memorials; they are physical places for memorializing, and heterotopian spaces for coping with the trauma of loss. Family, friends, and strangers engage in pilgrimage as they come to physical memorial sites and attempt to work through their grief. Research, however concludes that for missing loved ones, the ambiguity of their status sustains the trauma because 'unresolved or incomplete mourning results in stasis and entrapment in the traumatic process'.[52] Virtual memorial sites similarly offer places for commemoration. Both forms of memorials result from co-production as visitors establish, add to, and comment on the sites and the person commemorated. As different as physical and virtual sites may seem, in the case of Kyron Horman they all display photographs as representations of the lost child who is mourned.

In a very different sense, photographs can go beyond a quick form of memorializing and alternatively create shock value; Susan Sontag argues that the 'photographs are a means of making "real" (or "more real") matters that the privileged and the merely safe might prefer to ignore'.[53] The science fair photograph has similar shock value, in reminding the viewer that Kyron went missing from school. The photograph elicits a deep-seated fear that presumably safe places in fact are not. The photographs help jar the viewer into a heterotopian space for mourning Kyron and for facing the trauma from society's failure to protect children and return those missing. Even though the forms of memorialization provide a way of coping with loss, the perpetuation of hope reinforces the trauma of Kyron as a missing child. We argue that the traumatic ambiguity of a missing child has led to a discourse of substitution wherein the act of commemoration (coproduction) minimizes the trauma. Within the paradox, commemoration becomes an albeit imperfect means for beginning to work through both the individual trauma of loss for those who knew Kyron personally and the cultural trauma of loss the public experiences when structural mechanisms for the protection of children fail. Finally, we agree with other scholars of online grieving, that the living relationship between pilgrim to the memorial and the deceased or missing alters the relationships possible: 'what we can learn is that a renegotiation of that relationship between the deceased and bereaved has the chance to become both a normal and necessary part of the grieving process; an opportunity for the bereaved to grow from the experience'.[54]

## 6. Reflections on Public and Private Trauma

All three essays in this unit focus on memorials as a response to trauma. They range from Mark Callaghan's case study of the physical commemoration in *The Memorial to the Murdered Jews of Europe* to our focus on both a physical site – *The Wall of Hope* and on virtual memorials on Facebook, and finally to Jeanne Clark's case study of four web memorials (although one of the web memorials also intended to create a physical museum of commemoration). All of these memorial sites focus on the memory of trauma and are designed to prevent the repetition of the originating trauma – the murder of six million Jews, the death of thousands of children in the on-going Israeli-Palestinian conflict, and the disappearance of 10-year old Kyron Horman. In each of these memorial sites, information matters less than recreating the experience of trauma; in highlighting the emotional impact of the memorial, each seeks to minimize the passive intellectual response to traumatic events. Callaghan writes that the Berlin memorial 'was designed to reflect a state of anxiety and confusion, as an insight into the experience of others.' Photographs of children in the other sites studied in this unit become in Clark's words, 'markers of innocence' that offer a shared substance between those caught up in the trauma and national as well as international visitors to the memorials.

Issues of identity emerge in all three essays and offer a second form of compatibility between these three explorations of memorials to private and public trauma. In Callaghan's case study the memorial is official. Strategically located in prime real estate in central Berlin, it both memorializes those lost in the Holocaust and confronts uncertainty about German national identity and guilt over this period of the nation's history. Clark similarly argues that the memorials she studies are caught up in defining Palestinian and Israeli identity. Bridging the divide between official and vernacular memorials, Clark's sites construct the 'identity of both the mourned victim and the mourning community.' Kyron Horman's physical and virtual memorials are solely vernacular; they engage pilgrims to these sites by encouraging their role as co-producers who construct Kyron's identity as well as their own through the form and content of their tributes to the missing child.

One major difference in the three case studies lies in the non-representational *Memorial to the Murdered Jews of Europe* and the representational memorials depicted by Collins and Mencarelli, and Clark and relying heavily on photographic images. The photographs reinforce a belief in the innocence of children. Images of children at play, in school, surrounded by friends and family, or sleeping peacefully reinforce the horror of their death or disappearance. Clark references this as the political function of memorials. In the case of Kyron Horman, American society has failed to protect children at school or recover them promptly if abducted, and individual citizens have failed to find a missing child. Where the Berlin memorial 'defies narrative construction,' the Palestinian and American memorials embrace verbal and visual narratives as a way of working through trauma.

Despite their differences in intent and form, the memorials we have collectively studied reflect Khalili's contention that 'commemoration is dialogic and shaped by the constant interaction with its audience' which 'allows for ambiguity and polyvalence'.[55] The experience-focus of the Berlin memorial, as Callaghan notes, does not always produce reverence, and hiding among the stelae, like the presence of trolls on web memorials, makes one wonder what form commemoration would have to take to reach some audiences. Yet each of the commemorative sites we have collectively critiqued has demanded we break time as it draws us into a recognition and reflection on traumatic events that should not be forgotten.

# Notes

[1] National Center for Missing and Exploited Children, '2010 Annual Report,' viewed 25 June 2012, http://www.missingkids.com/missingkids/servelet/ResrouceServelet?LanguageCountry=en_US&PageId=3679.

[2] 'FBI Steps up Role in Search for Kyron,' video posted 24 February 2011, viewed 27 July 2012, http://www.katu.com/news/local/116871428.html?tab=video&c=y.

[3] 'The Kidnapping,' OPB, viewed 26 June 2012, http://www.pbs.org/wgbh/amex/lindbergh/sfeature/crime.html.

[4] See Brian Caroll and Katie Landry, 'Logging on and Letting Out: Using Online Social Networks to Grieve and to Mourn,' *Bulletin of Science, Technology & Society* 30 (2010): 341-349; Brian De Vries and Judy Rutherford, 'Memorializing Loved Ones on the World Wide Web,' *OMEGA* 49 (2004): 5-26; and Carla J. Sofka, 'Social Supporter "Internetworks" Caskets for Sale and More: Thanatology and the Information Superhighway,' *Death Studies* 21 (1997): 553-574.

[5] Holly Everett, *Roadside Crosses in Contemporary Memorial Culture* (Denton, TX: University of North Texas Press, 2002), 3.

[6] Kirsten A. Foot and Steven M. Schneider, 'Online Action in Campaign 2000: An Exploratory Analysis of the U.S. Political Web Sphere,' *Journal of Broadcasting and Electronic Media* 46.2 (2002): 228.

[7] Michel Foucault, 'Different Spaces,' *Aesthetics, Methods, and Epistemology*, trans. Robert Hurley, ed. James D. Faubion, vol. 2 (New York: New Press, 1998), 184. See also Elizabethada A. Wright, 'Rhetorical Spaces in Memorial Places: The Cemetery as a Rhetorical Memory Place/Space,' *Rhetoric Society Quarterly* 35.4 (2005): 51-81.

[8] Catherine Ann Collins and Alexandra Opie, 'When Places Have Agency: Roadside Shrines as Traumascapes,' *Continuum: Journal of Media & Cultural Studies* 24 (2010): 109-110.

[9] Michelle Cole, 'Parents, Other from Community Return Questionnaires Sunday in the Effort to Find Kyron Horman,' *OregonLive*.com, last modified 20 June 2010, viewed 15 June 2012. http://www.oregonlive.com/news/index.ssf/2010/06/parents_others_from_community.html.

[10] Sylvia Grider, 'Spontaneous Shrines and Public Memorialization,' *Death and Religion in a Changing World*, ed. Kathleen Garces-Foley (Armonk, NY: M.E. Sharpe, 2006), 248.

[11] Anne Stone, 'Bearing Partial Witness: Representations of Missing Women,' *Review of Education, Pedagogy, and Cultural Studies* 31.2-3 (2009): 221-236.

[12] Grider, 'Spontaneous Shrines,' 248.

[13] Maria Tumarkin, *Traumascapes: The Power and Fate of Places Transformed by Tragedy* (Melbourne: Melbourne University Press, 2005), 12.

[14] Teresa Blackman, 'Moving Kyron's Wall of Hope for Security,' KGW.com video, last modified 17 August 2010, viewed 15 June 2012, http://www.kgw.com/video/featured-videos/Kaine-Horman-visits-Wall-of-Hope-100787279.html.

[15] Aaron Hess, 'In Digital Remembrance: Vernacular Memory and Rhetorical Construction of Web Memorials,' *Media Culture Society* 29 (2007): 812-830.

[16] Johanna Sumialia, 'Networked Diasporas: Circulating Imaginaries of Violence,' *Jurnalism și communicare* 3 (2009): 75-80.

[17] For a review of the scholarship on online grieving and the states of mourning see, Kimberly Falconer, et al., 'Grieving in the Internet Age,' *New Zealand Journal of Psychology* 40.3 (2011): 79-88.

[18] *Psychic Help on the Kyron Horman Case*, (Facebook), last modified September 2013, viewed 14 October 2013, https://www.facebook.com/pages/Psychic-Help-on-the-Kyron-Horman-Case/103688263073130.

[19] See, for example, Alice Marwick and Nicole B. Ellison, '"There Isn't Wifi in Heaven!" Negotiating Visibility on Facebook Memorial Pages,' *Journal of Broadcasting and Electronic Media* 56.3 (2012): 378-400.

[20] Whitney Phillips, 'LOLing at Tragedy: Facebook Trolls, Memorial Pages and Resistance to Grief Online,' *First Monday* 16.12 (2011): np.

[21] Ibid.

[22] Kenan Malick, 'Mourning Sickness in a Culture of Fear,' *Bergens Tidend* (24 May 2007), viewed 22 October 2013, http://www.kenanmalik.com/essays/bergins_madeline_print.html.

[23] Ibid.

[24] Phillips, 'LOLing at Tragedy.'

[25] Ibid.

[26] AnnaMaria Mencarelli, email message from Ribbons of Hope Administrator, 4 September 2013.

[27] Richard J. Goodman and William I. Gorden, 'The Rhetoric of Desecration,' *Quarterly Journal of Speech* 57.1 (1971): 23-31.

[28] Foucault, 'Different Spaces,' 182

[29] 'Kyron Horman World Soldiers', *Facebook*, viewed June 2012, https://www.facebook.com/pages/Kyron-Hormans-World-Soldiers/161645780592018?fref=ts.

[30] Julia Kennedy, 'Don't You Forget about Me: An Exploration of the "Maddie Phenomenon" on *YouTube*,' *Journalism Studies* 11.2 (2010): 232.

[31] Ibid.

[32] Ibid.

[33] R. Scott Sullender, 'Vicarious Grieving and the Media,' *Pastoral Psychol* 59 (2010): 192.

[34] Erich Lindemann, 'Symptomology and Management of Acute Grief,' *American Journal of Psychiatry* 101 (1944): 141-148.

[35] Susan Sontag, *Regarding the Pain of Others* (New York: Picador Farrar, Straus and Giroux, 2003), 22.

[36] Kevin Wang and Peter Gloviczki, 'Sense of Community in the Virtual World: An Ethnographic Exploration of Online Memorial Groups' (paper presented at the Ethnography Division of National Communication Association Annual Convention, San Diego, California, 21-24 November 2008).

[37] Dominick LaCapra, *Writing History, Writing Trauma* (Baltimore, MD: The Johns Hopkins University Press, 2001), 21.

[38] 'The Search for Kyron Horman - Part2,' video, viewed 2 June 2012, http://www.kgw.com/video?id=123072893&sec=773704.

[39] Ibid.

[40] *Kyron Horman World Soldiers*

[41] *Roseburg Supports Kyron Horman,* (Facebook), viewed June 2012, https://www.facebook.com/RoseburgLovesKyronHorman

[42] Ibid.

[43] *Praying for Kyron Horman Today?* (Facebook), viewed September 2013, https://www.facebook.com/pages/Praying-for-Kyron-Horman-Today/238849536186600?ref=br_tf.

[44] Ibid.

[45] Ibid.

[46] *Anti Terri Horman Page*, viewed 15 June 2012, https://www.facebook.com/pages/Anti-Terri-Horman-Page/191989190837433

[47] Roland Barthes, *Camera Lucida: Reflections on Photography*, trans. Richard Howard (New York: Hill and Wang, Farrar, Straus and Giroux, 1981), 77.

[48] Ibid, 88.

[49] Walter R. Fisher, *Human Communication as Narration: Toward a Philosophy of Reason, Value, and Action* (Columbia, SC: University of South Carolina Press, 1987), 63. Fisher argues that in addition to being rational, humans are storytellers who constitute their lives in the stories they choose to tell.

[50] Lisa M. Mitchell, et al., 'Death and Grief On-line: Virtual Memorialization and Changing Concepts of Childhood Death and Parental Bereavement on the Internet,' *Health Sociology Review* 21.4 (2012): 413-431.

[51] Ibid.

[52] Robert J. Lifton, 'The Concept of the Survivor,' *Survivors, Victims, and Perpetrators: Essays on the Nazi Holocaust*, ed. Joel E. Dimsdale (New York: Hemisphere, 1980), 124.

[53] Sontag, *Regarding the Pain*, 7.
[54] Natalie Pennington, 'You Don't De-Friend the Dead: An Analysis of Grief Communication by College Students through Facebook Profiles,' *Death Studies* 37 (2013): 619.
[55] Laleh Khalili, *Heroes and Martyrs of Palestine: The Politics of National Commemoration* (Cambridge: Cambridge University Press, 2007), 91.

## Bibliography

*Anti Terri Horman Page*. (Facebook). Viewed 5 September 2013. https://www.facebook.com/pages/Anti-Terri-Horman-Page/191989190837433

Barthes, Roland. *Camera Lucida: Reflections on Photography*. Translated by Richard Howard. New York: Hill and Wang, Farrar, Straus and Giroux, 1981.

Blackman, Teresa. 'Moving Kyron's Wall of Hope for Security.' *KGW.com* video. Last modified 17 August 2010. Viewed 15 June 2012. http://www.kgw.com/video/featured-videos/Kaine-Horman-visits-Wall-of-Hope-100787279.html

Caroll, Brian, and Katie Landry. 'Logging on and Letting Out: Using Online Social Networks to Grieve and to Mourn.' *Bulletin of Science, Technology & Society* 30 (2010): 341-349.

Cole, Michelle. 'Parents, Other from Community Return Questionnaires Sunday in the Effort to Find Kyron Horman.' *OregonLive*.com. Last modified 20 June 2010. Viewed 15 June 2012. http://www.oregonlive.com/news/index.ssf/2010/06/parents_others_from_community.html

Collins, Catherine Ann and Alexandra Opie. 'When Places Have Agency: Roadside Shrines as Traumascapes.' *Continuum: Journal of Media & Cultural Studies* 24 (2010): 107-118.

'Desiree Young v. Teri Moulton Horman.' Last modified July 2010. Viewed 27 July 2012. https://www.facebook.com/#!/DesireeYoungVTerriMoultonHormanOnlineDiscussion.

De Vries, Brian, and Judy Rutherford. 'Memorializing Loved Ones on the World Wide Web.' *OMEGA* 49 (2004): 5-26.

Everett, Holly. *Roadside Crosses in Contemporary Memorial Culture*. Denton, TX: University of North Texas Press, 2002.

Falconer, Kimberly, Mieke Sachsenweger, Kerry Gibson and Helen Norman. 'Grieving in the Internet Age.' *New Zealand Journal of Psychology* 40.3 (2011): 79-88.

'FBI Steps up Role in Search for Kyron.' *KATU.com* video. Posted 24 February 2011. Viewed on 5 August 2015.
http://www.katu.com/news/local/116871428.html?tab=video&c=y.

Fisher, Walter R. *Human Communication as Narration: Toward a Philosophy of Reason, Value, and Action*. Columbia, SC: University of South Carolina Press, 1987.

Foot, Kirsten A. and Steven M. Schneider. 'Online Action in Campaign 2000: An Exploratory Analysis of the U.S. Political Web Sphere.' *Journal of Broadcasting and Electronic Media* 46.2 (2002): 222-244.

Foucault, Michel. 'Different Spaces.' *Aesthetics, Methods, and Epistemology*. Translated by Robert Hurley, edited by James D. Faubion, 175-185. Vol 2. New York: New Press, 1998.

Goodman, Richard J. and William I. Gorden. 'The Rhetoric of Desecration.' *Quarterly Journal of Speech* 57.1 (1971): 23-31.

Grider, Sylvia. 'Spontaneous Shrines and Public Memorialization.' *Death and Religion in a Changing World*, edited by Kathleen Garces-Foley, 246-264. Armonk, NY: M.E. Sharpe, 2006.

Hess, Aaron. 'In Digital Remembrance: Vernacular Memory and the Rhetorical Construction of Web Memorials.' *Media Culture Society* 29 (2007): 812-830.

Kennedy, Julia. 'Don't You Forget about Me: An Exploration of the "Maddie Phenomenon" on *YouTube*.' *Journalism Studies* 11.2 (2010): 225-242.

Khalili, Laleh. *Heroes and Martyrs of Palestine: The Politics of National Commemoration*. Cambridge: Cambridge University Press, 2007.

'The Kidnapping.' OPB. Viewed 26 June 2012.
http://www.pbs.org/wgbh/amex/lindbergh/sfeature/crime.html.

*Kyron Horman World Soldiers*. Last modified June 2012. Viewed 13 June 2012. https://www.facebook.com/#!/pages/Kyron-Hormans-World-Soldiers/161645780592018.

LaCapra, Dominic. *Writing History, Writing Trauma*. The Johns Hopkins University Press, Baltimore, 2001.

Lifton, Robert J. 'The Concept of the Survivor.' *Survivors, Victims, and Perpetrators: Essays on the Nazi Holocaust*, edited by Joel E. Dimsdale, 113-126. New York: Hemisphere, 1980.

Lindemann, Erich. 'Symptomology and Management of Acute Grief.' *American Journal of Psychiatry* 101 (1944): 141-148.

Malick, Kenan. 'Mourning Sickness in a Culture of Fear.' *Bergens Tidend* (24 May 2007). Viewed 22 October 2015.
http://www.kenanmalik.com/essays/bergins_madeline_print.html.

Marwick, Alice and Nicole B. Ellison. '"There Isn't Wifi in Heaven!" Negotiating Visibility on Facebook Memorial Pages.' *Journal of Broadcasting and Electronic Media* 56.3 (2012): 378-400.

Mitchell, Lisa M., Peter H. Stephenson, Susan Cadell, and Ellen MacDonald. 'Death and Grief On-Line: Virtual Memorialization and Changing Concepts of Childhood Death and Parental Bereavement on the Internet.' *Health Sociology Review* 21.4 (2012): 413-431.

National Center for Missing and Exploited Children. '2010 Annual Report.' Viewed 25 June 2015.
http://www.missingkids.com/missingkids/servlet/ResourceServlet?LanguageCountry=en_US&PageId=3679.

Pennington, Natalie. 'You Don't De-Friend the Dead: An Analysis of Grief Communication by College Students through Facebook Profiles.' *Death Studies* 37 (2013): 617-635.

*Praying for Kyron Today*? Viewed September 2013.
https://www.facebook.com/pages/Praying-for-Kyron-Horman-Today/238849536186600?ref=br_tf.

*Psychic Help on the Kyron Horman Case.* Last modified September 2013. Viewed 14 October 2013. https://www.facebook.com/pages/Psychic-Help-on-the-Kyron-Horman-Case/103688263073130.

*Roseburg Supports Kyron Horman.* Viewed June 2012. https://www.facebook.com/RoseburgLovesKyronHorman.

Sanderson, Jimmy, and Pauline Hope Cheong. 'Tweeting Prayers and Communicating Grief over Michael Jackson Online.' *Bulletin of Science Technology & Society* 30 (2010): 328-339.

'The Search for Kyron Horman - Part2.' video. Viewed 2 June 2012. http://www.kgw.com/video?id=123072893&sec=773704.

Sherman, Daniel J. 'Art, Commerce, and the Production of Memory in France After World War I.' *Commemorations: The Politics of National Identity*, edited by John R. Gillis, 186-211. Princeton, NJ: Princeton University Press, 1994.

Sofka, Carla J. 'Social Support "Internetworks" Caskets for Sale, and More: Thanatology and the Information Superhighway.' *Death Studies* 21 (1997): 553-574.

Sontag, Susan. *Regarding the Pain of Others.* New York: Picador Farrar, Straus and Giroux, 2003.

Stone, Anne. 'Bearing Partial Witness: Representations of Missing Women.' *Review of Education, Pedagogy, and Cultural Studies* 31.2-3 (2009): 221-236.

Sullender, R. Scott. 'Vicarious Grieving and the Media.' *Pastoral Psychol* 59 (2010): 191-200.

Sumialia, Johanna. 'Network Diasporas: Circulating Imaginaries of Violence.' *Jurnalism si Communicare* 3 (2009): 75-80.

Tumarkin, Maria. *Traumascapes: The Power and Fate of Places Transformed by Tragedy.* Melbourne: Melbourne University Press, 2005.

Wang Kevin and Peter Gloviczki. 'Sense of Community in the Virtual World: An Ethnographic Exploration of Online Memorial Groups.' Paper presented at the Ethnography Division of National Communication Association Annual Convention, San Diego, California. 21-24 November 2008.

Wright, Elizabethada A. 'Rhetorical Spaces in Memorial Places: The Cemetery as a Rhetorical Memory Place/Space.' *Rhetoric Society Quarterly* 35 (Fall 2005): 51-81.

**Catherine Ann Collins** is a Professor of Rhetoric at Willamette University. She writes and teaches in the areas of visual rhetoric, the rhetoric of war, memory and memorials. Her most recent works on trauma theory explores 9/11 and war memorials, roadside shrines, and memorials to a missing child.

**AnnaMaria Mencarelli** is currently pursuing a masters degree in healthcare communications through Boston University with plans to apply to medical school in 2015.

# Part 2

# Representing Trauma

# Images of Suffering: Trauma and Homer's Troy in Euripides' *Hecuba*

## Lisa B. Hughes

**Abstract**
Euripides' *Hecuba*, an Athenian tragedy of the fifth century BCE, begins as the eponymous queen of the recently fallen Troy awakens from a nightmare, that a doe was torn from beneath her knees, by a mangled wolf, and that Achilles' ghost rose from above his tomb demanding a fresh prize. Awaking, she fears for the lives of her two children, Polydorus and Polyxena, and realizing these images need to be interpreted she says: 'O Helenus, I need you now, interpreter of dreams! Help me, Cassandra, help me read my dreams!' This same insistent need, to interpret returns of a wound, is the work of trauma theorists, such as Caruth and LaCapra. In this chapter, I'll show how *Hecuba*, especially as it recalls Homer's graphic depiction of the death of Hector, explores the representation of trauma, especially by thematizing looking at suffering. The play is read and considered along with notions such as the return of the repressed, working through, and catharsis.

**Key Words:** Greek tragedy, Homer, Euripides, catharsis, theatre, repetition compulsion, acting out, working through.

*****

## 1. Wounds in Homer and Euripides

In Homer's *Iliad*, Hecuba, the queen of Troy, sees her son Hector die in a duel with Achilles. A person could not imagine a more horrifying end for her son, and she watches it all from the walls of Troy, helpless. As Achilles approaches Hector, first Priam, his father, begs Hector to return to Troy, and save his own life, then Hecuba opens her robe and pleads with him by the breasts that nourished him not to face Achilles alone. Both parents are unsuccessful in their pleas, and all of the twenty-second book theatrically recounts in heart-breaking and gruesome detail the horror the parents witness from the wall.[1] When Hector falls, his death is generally regarded as a proleptic representation of the fall of Troy. The significance of the *Iliad* to the development of Greek identity in the historical period cannot be overstated, and later writers allude to this very duel most.[2]

Centuries after Homer, in 425 B. C. Athens was in its sixth year of a devastating war that they would eventually lose in a way so crippling that even their flowering democracy was overturned. In the midst of the fighting, Euripides wrote a play called *Hecuba*, named for the queen of the recently fallen Troy, and familiar to his audience from Homer's *Iliad*. The play is set immediately after the fall of Troy in Thrace, a liminal space between Greece and Troy, where the Greek male victors, Agamemnon, Odysseus and others, are stranded for lack of wind, along with the female Trojan captives, especially Hecuba, her daughter Polyxena, and the chorus. Here Hecuba continues to relive the death of Hector and the fall of Troy through the deaths of her two children, Polydorus, here sent to Thrace to their family friend Polymestor with the gold of Troy, as a safety measure, and Polyxena, later killed on the tomb of Achilles, in order finally to secure favourable winds.

Against the backdrop of the Peloponnesian War, the suffering of the Trojan women clearly serves as a metaphor for the contemporary situation. *Hecuba*, especially as it recalls Homer's graphic depiction of the death of Hector, and the theatrical nature of its presentation, thus explores images of suffering associated with the trauma of the war. The play is often criticized for a lack of unity, as it offers no Aristotelian cause and effect between what Hecuba suffers upon the death of Polyxena and the grim revenge she takes on Polymestor for killing her son, Polydorus. And though this apparent schism has often been cited as evidence of the lack of cohesion and integrity of the piece, by reading the play in its Homeric context and in light of Freud's repetition compulsion, it explains, and even necessitates, the duality of the plot.[3] The play exemplifies the return of the repressed, working through, and transference, as discussed by Freud and LaCapra.[4] Of especial interest are the ghost of Polydorus and his appearance in the prologue and in the dream of his mother Hecuba; the death of Polyxena, and the way that it reproduces elements of Hector's death in the *Iliad*; and the revenge that Hecuba takes on Polymestor, unobstructed by her enemies, the Greeks. In its original context the play *Hecuba* itself becomes a site of trauma, and shows the interplay of physical wounds, psychic wounds, and wounds to the body politic. The audience of Athenian citizens witness suffering in the same way as the characters on the stage.

## 2. The Recurring Dream

The prologue spoken by the ghost of Polydorus, the youngest son of Hecuba and Priam, the brother of, and a surrogate for, Hector has the double effect of connecting this text closely with *Iliad* 22, while suggesting also that the play will comment on returns of wounds. In the discourse on trauma, ghosts are symptoms of an unresolved past that keeps intruding on an uncertain present.[5] This ghost provides the background to the play, invoking *Iliad* 22 conspicuously. He provides the simple explication that he was killed by a family friend, Polymestor, here in Thrace where he had been sent to protect the family gold, and that his unburied corpse needs a grave. He makes clear that the current situation directly results from the duel between Hector and Achilles: 'But as long as Troy's great ramparts stood proud/and unbreached, so long as our towers held intact/ and Hector, my brother, prospered in the fighting, I flourished . . .'[6]

In addition, the ghost of this youngest son tells of a much larger and more terrible ghost, one whose presence haunts the play with memories of the duel in *Iliad* 22. The ghost of Polydorus warns of Achilles' unappeased ghost appearing before the Greek army, and demanding the slaughter of Hector's sister Polyxena on his grave. In the prologue then, Achilles is apparently still engaged in the moment of the duel with Hector, and two of Hector's siblings as possible surrogates for him repeat that moment compulsively.[7]

The play proper begins as Hecuba awakens from a nightmare.[8] She has dreamt that a doe was torn from beneath her knees, by a mangled wolf, and that Achilles' ghost rose from above his tomb demanding a fresh prize. Awaking, she fears for the lives of her two children, Polydorus and Polyxena, and realizing the need to interpret these images, she says: 'Disaster I dreamed. Terror on terror. O Helenus, I need you now, interpreter of dreams! Help me, Cassandra, help me read my dreams!' (*Hec.* 87-89). Through the intrusive images of both the ghost and the dream we are invited to consider the assertion that repeated images of suffering and death form our collective and cultural unconscious, and to question meaning found in reading them.[9]

Long before Athenians had made the theatre a central venue for working through communal suffering, Homer presented Hector's death in a highly theatrical way, with his mother Hecuba sitting on the wall looking, as an audience. Her dream here at the beginning of the play, and in fact the whole play itself, results from the impact of this Homeric image on Hecuba, and even on the Greek populace, so steeped in Homer. The play does not simply allude or respond to the duel between Achilles and Hector, and Hector's death, but further develops the image of Hecuba as portrayed as a *spectator* to the same. As such, it does not merely encourage a reading of this play as a text about looking at pain, but it demands such a reading.

That Hecuba, Achilles, and the others are to be thought of as traumatized follows from LaCapra's description: 'This is very clear in the case of people who undergo a trauma. They have a tendency to relive the past, to exist in the present as if they were still fully in the past, with no distance from it. They tend to relive occurrences, or at least find that those occurrences intrude on their present existence, for example, in flashbacks; or in nightmares. . .'[10]

This Athenian vase, from *ca.* 515 BCE emphasizes that the element of Hecuba's looking mattered as much as as the actual death and mutilation of her son's corpse. The tragedy of Hector alone is not the subject, but the experience of his parents witnessing his suffering. The black figure on the far left is Priam, and the white figure next to him his wife Hecuba. Including the parents within the frame, the painter of the vase imagines us looking at and involved in the suffering of Hecuba, looking at and involved in the suffering of Hector—of us, looking at her looking. The play does that too.

When Hecuba awakens, she feels disturbed by a dream of Polydorus, and fearful about what the day will bring. In this immediate context the chorus of female Trojan captives confirm her dream that her daughter, Polyxena is to be sacrificed on the tomb of Achilles, as a bride and a war prize. Hecuba's response – 'Oh grief, what can I say? What are the words for loss?'[11] – signals this play's concern with how to represent trauma.[12] To read the play as a response to *Iliad* 22 entails answering the question 'Why is Hecuba dreaming of Achilles?" and especially "Why is she dreaming he wills the death of her child?'[13] Clearly Hecuba continues to experience that Homeric event, asleep and waking, and in this play she'll relive the death of Hector and the fall of Troy through the deaths of two more children, her daughter Polyxena and her son Polydorus. Hecuba's dream links this play to *Iliad* 22, and immediately we find Hecuba, and ourselves, located in a loop of reliving the injury sustained there when Hecuba watches Achilles chase her son around the walls of Troy as if in a dream:

> If ever he made a dash right on for the gates of Dardanos to get quickly under the strong-built bastions, endeavouring that they from above with missiles thrown might somehow defend him, each time Achilleus would get in front and force him to turn back into the plain, and himself kept his flying course to the city. As in a dream a man is not able to follow one who runs from him, nor can the runner escape, nor the other pursue him, so he could not run him down in his speed, nor the other get clear.[14]

***Image 1:*** Water jar (hydria) with the chariot of Achilles Dragging the corpse of Hektor. © 2013. Museum of Fine Arts Boston

Significantly, Homer never specifies if the dream adopts the perspective of the chaser, the fleer, or the Greek and Trojan spectators. I suggest he embraces all these perspectives. The rest of the action in Euripides' play occurs in the immediate context of a dream, which recalls this original wound.

The *Iliad* repeats Hector's death compulsively. Immediately after Achilles stabs him to death, the other Greeks approach his corpse and all stab it themselves, as if to kill him again, or keep on killing him. Since Achilles does not derive the satisfaction he expected he ties Hector's corpse to his chariot, further mutilating him, compulsively repeating the act of killing him as if in repeating the act he will eventually get satisfaction from it. As Hecuba views this from the wall, as seen on the vase above, we are told that in grief she pulls out her hair, and wails. Thus both Hecuba and Achilles compulsively repeat that moment.

The chorus tells Hecuba about the appearance of Achilles' ghost and his demand. Achilles' dissatisfaction continues as does his compulsion to keep killing Hector, and now he demands Polyxena, a surrogate Hector, to be slaughtered on his tomb. This demand comes from an Achilles long since dead, who still appears to his own troops, haunting their imagination. Not only in dreams, Freud claims, does the traumatic event recur but also in hallucinations, such as this. Achilles continues to haunt not only the dreams of Hecuba, but also the Greek army, an audience of the past duel between Hector and Achilles. They too experience a return of the repressed, continuing to kill Hector, much as Achilles did in life. The multiplicity of those continuing to be haunted by Achilles speaks to the profound and lasting effect of *Iliad* 22.

Hecuba tells Polyxena the news of the decree, and Odysseus arrives immediately to confirm it. When Polyxena understands the fate that awaits her, her behaviour and her words associate herself with her brother Hector, especially as he appeared in *Iliad* 22, and in a close reading of these two passages together one can see Hecuba's loss of Polyxena as part of a repetition compulsion; she keeps living the moment of Hector's duel with Achilles. A number of details link them, first in Polyxena's speech through which she embraces her fate, and later in the messenger's report of her death.

Most importantly, Polyxena defines herself and her worth by her relationship to Hector, implying that her kinship to him governs her behaviour. As she leaves the stage and her mother, Polyxena reminds us of her fraternal bond and locates herself within the world of *Iliad* 22 when she asks what message she should take to Hector and Priam. This important collocation of names links the scenes, for Hector and Priam appear together for the first time in *Iliad* 22, in the heart-breaking scene, shared intimately also with Hecuba, then again in Polydorus' prologue to this play. Looking closely at this image of suffering from the *Iliad* allows us to understand the repetition here.

Before the chase and the simile of the dream, the aged and pitiful Priam begs his son Hector not to fight alone outside of the wall. Priam knows that Hector's fall

will cause the fall of Troy, and he describes what the future will hold in such an
event. Priam imagines the future in sad detail:

> . . . Oh take pity on me, the unfortunate still alive, still sentient
> but ill-starred, whom the father, Kronos' son, on the threshold of
> old age will blast with hard fate, after I have looked upon evils
> and seen my sons destroyed and my daughters dragged away
> captive.[15]

In short, he imagines the setting for this very play.[16] Lamenting his bereavement of
many fine sons, Priam expresses particular concern over the uncertain fates of two
of his children, one of whom the *Iliad*'s audience already knows to be dead, the
other of whom is Polydorus. Then vividly and fearfully contrasting the shame and
the ugliness of a murdered old body with the beauty of a mortally wounded youth,
he appeals to Hector to have pity:

> . . . For a young man all is decorous when he is cut down in
> battle and torn with the sharp bronze and lies there dead, and
> though dead still all that shows about him is beautiful; but when
> an old man is dead and down, and the dogs mutilate the grey
> head and the grey beard and the parts that are secret, this for all
> sad mortality, is the sight most pitiful.[17]

Hecuba makes a similar prayer to her son, as uncovering her bosom she asks for
his pity lest he deny her the opportunity to mourn and bury him. In their pleas, both
parents offer visual imagery that suggests the frailty of the uncovered human body.

After both parents issue their tearful appeals, Hector debates with himself and
resolves that it is better to oppose Achilles and face death nobly than to live in
shame. In the course of this debate, he imagines a few different scenarios, which he
rejects. First he considers offering Helen, the original cause of the conflict, in
exchange for his life. Next he rejects the idea of approaching as a suppliant for fear
of being killed naked, like a woman, and finally he expresses willingness to receive
the spear in his chest, and Achilles attacks, claiming that with his death Hector will
pay for his slaughtered companions. When at length Achilles overcomes him, his
soul leaves his body, renouncing courage and youth; at the sight of this beautiful
body the Greek army strike out and violate it. Every detail of this scene is repeated
or in some way answered in the first part of *Hecuba*, which centres on Polyxena's
death.

In her general grieving and in her direct appeal to her daughter, Hecuba covers
many similar important points of the parental appeals to Hector. Like Priam in the
*Iliad*, Hecuba moans the great loss of children she has suffered, and she expresses
trepidation and uncertainty as to the fates of two of her children, one of whom is

Polydorus. In the *Iliad* her husband had consoled himself in the fact that if Lycaon and Polydorus were still alive, he could ransom them for gold; likewise Hecuba here tries to barter for the life of her daughter. As the chief concern of Homer's Hecuba was that she be able to mourn her son's body, so similarly this Hecuba expresses the desire to administer last rites to her daughter. Likewise her bare breasts, which evoked such a powerful image in Hecuba's attempt to win Hector's devotion, also matter to Polyxena in expressing devotion to her mother. In her farewell, immediately after she anticipates going down to Hector, Polyxena bids farewell to the breasts that nourished her.

The quality of the girl's thought, too, resembles her brother's in many respects. As Hector debates the options that lay open to him, he reduces the question to a choice of meeting death bravely or living in shame. He imagines a scenario in which some inferior person could say of him that he ruined his people, and he decides he could not live with that shame. Polyxena too imagines the future, being forced to bake bread and scrub floors; and her bed, before worthy of kings, is now violated by a slave. Odious as these prospects are, it is not their performance with which she finds herself unable to live, but with the name of slavery. And like her brother, she decides that to die nobly is much better than to live in shame.

Not only do the siblings simply reject a shameful life, but they both also fantasize in apprehension that they might suffer a death worthy of someone far inferior. When Hector toys with the possibility of bargaining with Achilles, and pleading for his life, he quickly dismisses the idea, lest he be killed naked, like a woman. Euripides remembers this expression of fear and he uses it to link Polyxena's death with this scene from the *Iliad*, for she meets her death exactly as a naked woman. But on her recalibrated scale of honour, she too can imagine a death beneath even that. When her mother informs her of the Greeks' decree, Polyxena vividly narrates the death that awaits her, comparing her own slaughter to that of a squawking, frightened lamb. The thought of dying in shame like an animal clearly contributes to Polyxena's resolve for shortly hereafter she voices her plan to meet death bravely and silently. All of this suggests that in Polyxena's death, we, and Hecuba, are reliving the death of Hector.

### 3. What the Messenger Saw

Odysseus leads Polyxena offstage to meet her death at the hands of Neoptolemus, Achilles' son and surrogate. We hear the details of it through the herald Talthybius, finding ourselves in something of a discursive loop that explores the meaning of trauma. The returns of Hector's wound continue as we watch a play about a woman listening to a messenger giving a report about a wound he witnessed. Another distancing frame is added, just as in the vase painting above, when Talthybius occupies Hecuba's position, and watches the scene directly. Hearing of Polyxena's death, Hecuba insists to Talthybius: 'Tell me. Let me hear it all, everything, no matter how it hurts.' Dramatizing the burden of bearing witness,

Talthybius the messenger responds: 'There is a cost in *telling* too, a double price of tears, for I was crying when your daughter died, and I will cry again while telling you, lady. But listen.'[18]

A great deal is gained by reading this speech as a kind of epic production, as a response to Homer, and I would say to *Iliad* 22 in particular.[19] The scene that Talthybius describes strikingly resembles the setting of the Homeric dual between Achilles and Hector, notable especially for the theatrical aspect, with a highly conspicuous audience: 'The whole army of the Greeks,/drawn up in ranks, was present at the execution.'[20] As Greeks and Trojans had watched the duel between Hector and Achilles, so all the Greeks are present here, watching. Verbs of seeing and hearing are thematized in this play, emphasizing their powerful capabilities. The very space where this is produced, the theatre, derives from a verb denoting seeing, as the theatre is the place where we see.[21]

As Talthybius describes it, Polyxena and Neoptolemos, the sister of Hector and the son of Achilles, recreate the Homeric dual. This is anticipated by Polyxena's appeal to Hector and Priam as she had left the stage, and then by repeated references to Neoptolemos, not by name but as the 'son of Achilles.'[22] After Polyxena is led, theatrically, before the audience of Greek soldiers, Neoptolemus utters a prayer to his father that reminds us that the ghost of Achilles has been haunting both Hecuba and the Greeks since the opening of the play, and that Achilles is the director of this performance.

Hector's death is attributable to numerous things, including that he must share in responsibility for the rape of Helen; that, as the preeminent Trojan warrior, his death will bring the most honour to Achilles; and that, according to Achilles' demands, Hector's death will pay for the Achaeans he slaughtered, especially that of his beloved friend Patroklos. The play, too, is ambiguous about the reasons for Polyxena's death. Will it procure favourable winds, or will her death as the preeminent Trojan princess bring Achilles the most honour? It thereby serves also as a recruitment tool to induce other Greek warriors toward such battle prowess. Hecuba speculates further that Achilles views this as payment for his friends slaughtered in battle, the same motive he expressed for Hector's death, evidence that Hecuba, at least, sees this as a repetition.

Deciding against running, Hector declares that he will stand willingly, and face what wounds may come. Offering his breast to Achilles, clad and armed in gold, he receives a mortal wound in his neck. Similarly, Polyxena speaks, asking to be freed, so that she can face her death willingly, and with dignity: 'Of my own free will I die, / Let no man touch me ... Let me die free.'[23] She then makes the startling and powerful gesture of ripping her peplos, and baring her breasts. Talthybius describes her beauty as bare and lovely, like a statue of a goddess. Then recalling the golden arms of Achilles which felled Hector, his son Neoptolemus stabs Polyxena with a golden sword.[24] And because of their gestures, and their youth, and their beauty, both become represented as beautiful corpses that elicit a strong response from the Greek army.

The image of the statue sharply contrasts the very physical and graphic description that follows upon Neoptolemus' stabbing her: '... the blood/ gushed out, and she fell, dying to the ground/ but even as she dropped, managed to fall somehow/ with grace, modestly hiding what should be hidden/ from men's eyes.'[25] Some things, apparently, should be hidden from men's eyes, and also kept out of the speech.[26] Still, even as Talthybius tries to put this gesture in the most positive light possible, a palpable evil lies below the surface of his speech, that even he is compelled to elide, as if to say both at the same time: 'Your daughter was just slaughtered in a violent and sexualized way', and 'It was all fine, nothing bad happened.'

This tension, between the horror of the corpse and the need to imagine it as beautiful, replicates Priam's distinction between the grotesqueness of an old man's corpse and the (imagined) beauty of a youthful one (see above). LaCapra warns against this impulse to 'transvalue the traumatic event into an occasion for the sublime'.[27] We shall return to this tension in concluding WHAT?, as the messenger's response may somewhat indicate what our response, as the audience, might, or should be.[28] The wounding of Polyxena wounds those who witness it, those who speak about it, and those who hear it. In this, the play renders a theatrical version of the vase painting, insofar as it focuses on the pain of watching as much as on the pain of being injured.

## 4. From Suffering to Daring: Acting out and Working Through

The final visual horror for Hecuba comes when Talthybius leaves, and the chorus arrive carrying the corpse of Polydorus. We are to imagine it initially covered, as Hecuba at first assumes it is Polyxena, then fears it may be Cassandra. In a dramatic moment, they uncover the corpse, and she looks upon her naked, dead son. Her first words could be spoken by the Hecuba of the vase painting, 'Oh me! *I am looking at* my dead son!'[29] Further, we should imagine the corpse as mutilated as the chorus says he was washed ashore from the sea. This is consistent with what Polydorus says of himself in the prologue: 'Here, pounded by the surf, my corpse still lies,/ carried up and down on the heaving swell of the sea, unburied and unmourned.'[30] This is precisely the kind of mutilation Hector receives in the *Iliad* and on the vase painting, as Achilles drags his corpse around the city walls, his mother watching. And in Hecuba it is yet another iteration of her experience of beholding the death of her son.

According to Freud, the victim of trauma will continue to relive the trauma, until finally she masters it. For LaCapra too, 'the return of the repressed,' 'acting out,' and 'working through' entail critical aspects of reading trauma, and what begins as suffering often finds creative outlet. In the immediate grip of the wound, Hecuba asked 'what are the words for loss', but halfway through the play, after losing Polyxena and Polydorus, she seems to find creative outlet. In the end, after much 'acting out,' Hecuba finally can be said to 'work through' her loss, though at a great cost to herself and her humanity.[31]

Throughout the first half of the play Hecuba uses the language of suffering, expressing herself repeatedly with the Greek word '*tlaw*'. In the Greek language, already recognizing the relationship between suffering and acting out that Freud will notice, the word for suffering has the same root as that for 'daring' '*tolmaw*'. A sufferer, if she suffers enough, will ultimately dare something. The fusion of daring and long suffering inherent in the word *tlaw* and its various forms provides a linguistic link between the Hecuba of the first and the second halves of the play. When she looks on the naked corpse of her son, the chorus refer to her as 'wretched', 'talaina' a related term, and one that she had just used of herself. Whereas at first she is victimized by Polymestor and the Greeks, she shortly will make the former her victim, and thus will come to embody both aspects of suffering and daring inherent in the word '*tlemon*'.

The final iteration of her repetition compulsion comes in the revenge she exacts on Polymestor in the second half of the play. This time, she attempts mastery of the situation, rather than yet another enactment of loss. Her turnaround crucially comes soon after the messenger, Talthybius, narrates the death of Polyxena in a highly theatrical way. Hecuba serves as visual audience while hearing about Talthybius' experience and immediately the trajectory of the play changes from suffering to acting.

LaCapra has discussed 'acting out' and 'working through' in ways that can usefully guide our reading of the second half of the play. He begins with 'acting out', the tendency in the traumatized to repeat traumatic scenes, as I'm suggesting Hecuba does with the death of Hector. In the next step, 'working through', the victim gains some distance, and 'acquires the possibility of becoming an ethical agent'. It will be important for our understanding of Hecuba that possibilities of 'working through' still do not imply transcendence or any notion of a cure.[32]

To succeed, Hecuba must enlist the help of her enemy and captor, but initially Agamemnon stands aloof, refusing to look at her. Whether from an understanding that she herself suffers from having seen the gruesome death of Hector and the corpse of Polydorus, or from understanding the impact that seeing the suffering and death of Polyxena has had on Talthybius the messenger, as Hecuba tries to enlist the aid of Agamemnon, she does so by asking him to look at her, at the pitiful image of suffering she projects is. This perpetuates the image of looking begun in *Iliad*, and illustrated on the vase, and it also begins the reversal inherent in working through as now she desires to be the object of the gaze, not the subject: 'Pity me./ Be like a painter. Stand back, see me/in perspective, see me whole, observe/ my wretchedness. . .'[33] She offers herself as the Hector figure on the vase, if only Agamemnon will become Hecuba, and watch with emotional involvement.

Not only does she ask him to look at her, but, specifically as a painter would, as an aesthetic object, capable of evoking emotion in the same way, for instance, that a theatrical audience might watch a play, or the same way the Greek army had just seen Polyxena bear her breast like a statue. She invokes the power of art to create meaning. Instead of looking, however, Agamemnon listens to her appeal, guaranteeing his lack of interference, but not his active aid. In refusing to look at her, Agamemnon attempts to separate himself from her suffering, refusing to adopt the role of Hecuba from the vase. In this, he distinguishes himself from Talthybius, whose speech revealed his involvement in the spectacle he witnessed. Both men, in their different responses, demonstrate the complexity of victimhood that LaCapra points to, and the problem of making sympathizers and witnesses trauma victims themselves. We should note the distinction carefully, as ultimately we will find ourselves in their position, using either as a possible model for our response. Speaking of a historian's challenge, but in ways that can apply to witnesses in general, he recommends, 'trying to work out some very delicate relationship between empathy and distance.'[34]

Maintaining his distance, Agamemnon nevertheless admits that he pities Hecuba, and he agrees passively to allow her to take revenge, to orchestrate a little theatrical spectacle of her own. He refuses, however, to become an actor in it. She calls Polymestor and his sons to her tents, a potential foregrounding of theatricality in that the word for tent, '*skene*', is the same word for stage. Hecuba stages her revenge just as the staged duel between Achilles, and the sacrifice of Polyxena. When Polymestor arrives at her tent she will blind him and kill his own small children. Both actions suggest attempts at reversals of what she herself has suffered. And like Polyxena's death, the 'duel' between Hecuba and Polymestor can read as yet another return of the duel between Hector and Achilles, wherein Hecuba again acts out, this time from the position of Achilles, the victimizer. By LaCapra's standards, she may be moving along the continuum towards 'working through', having gained some agency, but the depravity of her involvement suggests that any cure or transcendence eludes her. The text, however, in its obvious construction of a repetition of which Hecuba is *unaware*, engages in *working through*, thus allowing *us* to work through the trauma that gives rise to the play and to Hecuba's action. As Whitehead says of contemporary trauma fiction, '...the haunting power of a traumatic past ... can be readily identified by the attentive reader but remains beyond the reach or grasp of the characters themselves.'[35]

The past traumatic event was the slaughter of Hector in *Iliad* 22, described in a hunting image, with Achilles as a hunting dog, and Hector as a fawn.[36] When Polymestor has been blinded and his sons murdered, he emerges from the tent, bestially, on all fours and raging. He imagines himself still as the predator, but by the end of his speech he has clearly become the prey. Initially he says: 'Where? Where shall I run? Where shall I stop? Where? Like a raging beast I go, running on all fours to track my quarry down!' (*Hec.* 1056ff). Now, Hecuba relives the image from the perspective this time as the aggressor, not the victim. The dream image of Achilles chasing Hector around the walls of Troy in the *Iliad* finally reverses as Hecuba, acting on behalf of Hector (and his stand-ins, Polyxena and Polydorus) becomes the predator, rather than the prey, and the oft repeated chase scene from *Iliad* 22 has reversed. Hecuba's metaphorical status as the hunting hound both identifies her role and her action with Achilles of *Iliad* 22, and anticipates the literal metamorphosis into a hound and prophesized for her in this play: '*changed to a dog, a bitch with blazing eyes*' (*Hec.* 1265).

Killing Polymestor's children seems like a clear reversal of Hecuba's losing Hector, and then his stand-ins, or of working through it, but blinding him less so. But if Hecuba has been living with that image in her mind since she first watched his death in *Iliad* 22, she has now put the image of Polymestor's own dead children into his psyche, and then guaranteed that he will have this image not in his eyes, but much worse, in his mind. It has been suggested that in Greek tragedy an unseen event can nevertheless manifest itself 'as an interior reality in the protagonist's psyche' and that this event can lead to trauma for the audience too.[37] Hecuba watched Hector's death, and saw his corpse as she saw the corpse of Polydorus. But she is equally moved by the internal image she has of Polyxena's death as described by the messenger Talthybius. Polymestor experiences the death of his children in the same way. He becomes doomed to relive his wound indefinitely now, just as Hecuba frozen on the vase, unable to look away, always and only seeing the death of Hector. Likewise we have become involved with the suffering by watching it.

## 5. Looking at Suffering: Mimesis and Catharsis

In this chapter I have considered how this play might have worked upon its original audience, as well as how it might work on a contemporary audience, providing a lens through which to view the representation of traumatic experience. The answer to this question, both for antiquity and now involves understanding mimesis and catharsis from Aristotle's *Poetics*. Mimesis means imitation, or representation, and though Aristotle refers to drama here, the term applies to art in general. Humans have a natural urge to 'represent' reality in such a way that seeing this representation can lead to a 'catharsis'.[38] Aristotle never defines what he means by catharsis, and interpretation ranges from a therapeutic notion of a purge, to a purification, to an intellectual clarification.[39] Catharsis brought about through pity and terror here materializes only if seen close enough to recognize so as to pity, but distant enough to feel safe so as not to succumb to terror. When tempering the understanding of Aristotle by reading him along with LaCapra, one can consider the possibility of cathartic degrees, rather than insisting on all or nothing.[40]

To understand how Euripides' *Hecuba* might have assisted in working through for the Athenians in 425 BCE we should remember Phrynichus' 493 BCE tragedy, *The Sack of Miletus*. The play depicted the real life crushing Greek defeat at the hands of the Persians, and the historian Herodotus tells us Athenians fined the poet for causing too much pain. Too close, the event affected everyone, and as Talthybius said, 'some things should not be seen'. The aesthetic distance in *The Sack of Miletus* was not great enough, and certainly now they could not watch a play about the Peloponnesian War either. Using mythic elements to talk about painful current topics works better, and the figure of Hecuba symbolized long suffering when this play was performed.

The poet in the fifth century then had to repress traumatic events causing too much pain to experience, or to create some aesthetic distance to watch without looking away. Transferring them to an earlier, mythological time can enable the audience to work through them. To talk not about the defeat of the Athenians, but about the defeat of Troy – not to talk about the cruelty of the Athenians but that of the mythical Greek heroes. Still, while Euripides transfers the suffering to the enemy, the Trojans, he shows the Greeks watching the suffering of the Trojans, and how much pain it causes nevertheless. Talthybius traumatized to see the death of Polyxena, Agamemnon resisting looking at Hecuba, and Achilles, as he had killed Hector in the *Iliad*, continue to haunt the collective imagination of the whole army watching, as his returning ghost demonstrates.

Although the Greeks ultimately win the Trojan War, they still carry hidden wounds. Throughout the Trojan saga, though she suffers the most, Hecuba still remains the one *somatically* intact person. Hector is penetrated by the sword of Achilles, Polyxena by the surrogate sword of his son, Neoptolemos who also penetrates the body of Priam, over an altar. Even Achilles himself will ultimately receive a mortal wound from Paris' arrow. Hector's wife Andromache has become the war booty of Achilles' son, Neoptolemos, who will penetrate her sexually. All the other Trojan women in the play experience a similar fate, most notably, Cassandra with Agamemnon. Earlier Cassandra had been raped by Ajax. Hecuba was given as a slave to Odysseus, who out of respect for his own wife and for the age and status of Hecuba does not plan to make her a concubine. Hecuba alone remains somatically intact, while at the same time she is shown to receive the most wounds through her eyes, so as to be the most psychically fragmented. In this she may function as a model for the victorious Greeks, as physical intactness costs emotional pain, to the individual and to the body politic.

What solution can heal such a wound? We must not confuse the question of what Aristotle meant by catharsis, with the question of *what tragedy can do*. The intellectual, therapeutic, aesthetic, civic, or religious pleasure felt by a particular audience at a particular time does not depend on what Aristotle meant by the term. Despite some disagreement on the specifics of catharsis, there is general agreement that something important happens when a body of people gathers to watch a representation of a painful action. Shakespeare has famously used Hecuba in *Hamlet* as the subject to illustrate a play's power to move. Hamlet watches a play and asks how it affects an audience: 'What's Hecuba to him, or he to her,/ That he should weep for her.'[41] For however brief a time, the play is a reality to its audience.

The audience, like Hecuba, remains physically intact, though assailed with painful images and narrations, and possibly psychically wounded. The play then shows that achieving the correct distance from the source of pain is key to working through it, as LaCapra also said. Speaking of the catharsis of tragedy, the critic, I. A. Richards says: 'Pity, the impulse to approach, and Terror, the impulse to retreat, are brought in Tragedy to a reconciliation which they find nowhere else, and with them who knows what other allied group of equally discordant impulses. Their union in an ordered single response is the catharsis by which Tragedy is recognized, whether Aristotle meant anything of this kind or not.'[42]

Hecuba, Talthybius, and Agamemnon all offer a range of involvement available to the observer. For the Athenian audience, the painful unmediated realism of *The Sack of Miletus* proves too realistic, like the unblinking gaze of Hecuba, too close and too raw to offer a catharsis. The detachment of Agamemnon lies at perhaps the other end of the spectrum. As he says, he feels pity, one of the components, but no fear, and he refuses to become a participant. Talthybius the messenger, on the other hand, offers a middle ground, and a model for our engagement as the audience. He has a double status, as both participant and observer in the action, as should an ideal audience. For, in order for the drama to work for them, 'they too must relinquish some of their distance, they must become participants.'[43] And if the audience must watch, and become involved, as Hecuba does, they are also granted distance. The messenger cried when he saw Polyxena's death and he cried to recount it, but he does so with coherent and compelling language, not, like Hecuba, at a loss for words. In discussing the theatricality of Euripides' *Bacchae*, Barrett makes claims for the audience's relationship to the messenger that apply here as well: 'That is, not only are the spectators in one sense required, like Pentheus to become "actors"; they also command a comprehensive, masterful view' and they, like the messenger engage in 'a collective tranquil contemplation of what is staged.'[44] The Athenian audience sees filtered pain, aestheticized pain, and can therefore more potentially achieve catharsis.

In the figure of Hecuba we see inseparably both the trauma of a city and of an individual, and a sense that these wounds will repeat forever. The play ends with a trial, though, with Agamemnon the judge between Polymestor and Hecuba. Ultimately Agamemnon sides with Hecuba, in her crimes against Polymestor, but he does so through judicious reason, not passion, the 'collective tranquil contemplation' of the arguments. This evidences, I would suggest, that the play attempts to work through, rather than compulsively repeat. Murder trials in Athens replaced the *lex talionis*, or law of retribution, which perpetuated cycles of passionate vengeance killing of the type seen in Homer. A court of law, like a theatre, is a place where competing narratives are staged with the hope and belief of reaching a workable sense of truth and justice both for jurors and for a theatrical audience. Despite frequent acknowledgements of their own frustrating limitations of epistemology and of expression, both are ultimately pragmatic institutions.

This working through works to the good that LaCapra identifies as one of the ultimate goods that can come from trauma, even if it can never heal. Now, in the present of the play and of the audience, it becomes more important than ever to understand trauma narratives because through them we engage in meaningful civic behaviours, such as the search for justice. For LaCapra, in working through, we can 'change the causes of this cause insofar as they are social, economic, and political and thereby attempt to prevent its recurrence as well as enable forms of renewal.'[45] This is an important outcome, in the time of the Peloponnesian War.

I do not mean to suggest a happy ending in this dark play, to risk the very charge of 'transvaluing the traumatic event into an occasion for the sublime.' I agree that a truly traumatic event cannot be healed in any comprehensive way. Nevertheless it does, however, afford at least a first step toward working through.[46] *Hecuba*, the play, repeats discursively and thus helps us work through the repetition of the original trauma, just as this chapter, and in fact this whole book represent such traumas as another way of working through and mastering our various pasts, always already sites of trauma.

## Notes

[1] Michael Lynn-George, *Epos: Word, Narrative, and the Iliad* (Atlantic Highlands, NJ: Humanities Press International, 1988), 50-54, discusses theatrical aspects of Homer and the relationship between epic and drama, as does Richard Garner, *From Homer to Tragedy* (London: Routledge, 1990).

[2] Garner, *From Homer to Tragedy*, 9.

[3] The problem of its disjointedness is summarized by D. J. Conacher, *Euripidean Drama: Myth, Theme and Structure* (Toronto: University of Toronto Press, 1967), 146-65.

[4] Sigmund Freud, *Beyond the Pleasure Principle*, trans. James Strachey (New York and London: W.W. Norton, 1961); Dominick LaCapra's *Representing the Holocaust: History, Theory, Trauma* (Ithaca: Cornell University Press, 1996), *History in Transit: Experience, Identity, Critical Theory* (Ithaca: Cornell University Press, 2004) and '"Acting out" and "Working through" Trauma, *Yad Vashem* (1998).

[5] Anne Whitehead, *Trauma Fiction* (Edinborough: Edinborough University Press, 2004), 13-14.

[6] *Hec.*16-20. Unless otherwise stated, all translations of *Hecuba* are from *Euripides III*, eds Grene and Lattimore, (Chicago: University of Chicago Press, 1958), and of the *Iliad* are from Homer's *Iliad*, trans. Lattimore, (Chicago: University of Chicago Press, 1951).

[7] Euripides could easily have made the ghost of Achilles a dramatized character, and surely Achilles' ghost would have been more awe-inspiring than that of Polydorus. That he mentions him without dramatizing him calls attention at once to his absence and his presence as a haunting revenant. To understand the significance of the pervasiveness of the absent ghost of Achilles to this play, consider the importance of the unseen implied interlocutor of Mouth in Antropova's chapter in this volume.

[8] Cathy Caruth, *Unclaimed Experience: Trauma, Narrative, and History*, (Baltimore and London: The Johns Hopkins University Press, 1996), 63-64, following Freud and Lacan offers 'awakening' as a significant figure of literary trauma. '. . . the trauma of the nightmare does not simply consist in the experience *within* the dream, but in *the experience of waking from it*. It is the experience of *waking into consciousness* that, peculiarly, is identified with the reliving of the trauma.'

[9] For more on dreams in Greek tragedy, and in *Hecuba* specifically see G. Devereux, *Dreams in Greek Tragedy*, (Oxford: Oxford University Press, 1976).

[10] LaCapra, '"Acting out" and "Working through" Trauma,' 2.

[11] *Hec.* 154-5.

[12] Caruth, *Unclaimed Experience,* 5. She says of a traumatic text: 'these texts, each in its turn, asks what it means to transmit and to theorize around a crisis that is marked, not by a simple knowledge, but by the ways it simultaneously defies and demands our witness.'

[13] Devereux, *Dreams in Greek Tragedy*, 270. He agrees, saying of Hecuba's dream, 'Few literary dreams have so high a degree of dramatic functionality' though we disagree on the actual function.

[14] *Il.* 22.194-201.

[15] *Il.* 22.62-70.

[16] Justina Mossman, *Wild Justice*, (Oxford: Oxford University Press, 1995), 23. (1995:23) also sees *Iliad* 6 and 22 as important subtexts of the play in terms of its being a fulfillment of the dread prophecies of Hector, Priam, and Hecuba.

[17] *Il.* 22.71-76.

[18] *Hec.* 516-520.

[19] James Barrett, *Staged Narrative: Poetics and the Messenger in Greek Tragedy*, (Berkeley and Los Angeles: University of California Press, 2002), xvi-xvii. Against the generally accepted practice, and with great success, Barrett reads the messenger speeches as part of the rhetoric of the play showing that 'typically the

tragic texts endow the messenger with a narrative voice that closely resembles that of epic, and that this explains his success on two grounds. First, the approximation to Homer in itself carries a powerful authority that resounds uniquely in the Greek literary tradition. . . Second, in appropriating the narrative voice of Homer, the messenger employs a number of narrative strategies that work to claim a privileged status.'

[20] *Hec.* 521-3.

[21] For the pervasive verbs of seeing and their significance in this play see Froma Zeitlin, 'Euripides' *Hekabe* and the Somatics of Dionysiac Drama', *Ramus* 20 (1991): 53-94.

[22] *Hec.* 24, 523, 528.

[23] *Hec.* 546-550.

[24] C. Segal, 'Golden Armor and Servile Robes: Heroism and Metamorphosis in *Hecuba* of Euripides', *AJP* 111 (1990): 304-17. He discusses the importance of the images of gold in Hecuba in relation to the golden arms of Achilles. To his discussion I should add that his mention in the parodos, and his description as being clad in golden armor (109-11) obviously makes us think of his visual appearance in the *Iliad* in his duel with Hector.

[25] *Hec.* 567-71.

[26] If we read this with 'Speaking of the unspeakable' it helps us understand this part of the messenger speech. Both Mouth and Talthybius experience something they cannot process, but their coping strategies differ. Mouth simply become inarticulate, whereas Talthybius suppresses the worst.

[27] LaCapra, *Writing History, Writing Trauma*, 190. Schaub (this volume) notes a similar phenomenon in *Losing North*, and she writes, 'Discourse means ways of talking the world into being, or organizing a chaotic mass of sensations into a coherent structure. When feelings become too chaotic, hence menacing, one may circumscribe them or block them out. The text does just this. Where it notices contradictions, it smooths them out; where realities prove too threatening, it forgets them; where realities prove too threatening, it forgets them altogether.'

[28] Barrett, *Staged Narrative*, 102-131.

[29] I use my own translation here of the line '*oimoi, blepw de paid' emon tethnekota*' as in this case it is more literal and more to the point.

[30] *Hec.* 27-29.

[31] Later, Hecuba will defend this action by saying that at times like this, actions have precedent over words. In this she points to a similar concern as that expressed in the work of Antropova and Schaub in this collection. All three central characters point to an ultimate failure of language but Hecuba alone finds this alternative way out rejecting language altogether in favor of action.

[32] LaCapra, '"Acting out" and "Working through" Trauma', 6.

[33] *Hec.* 807-809.

[34] LaCapra, '"Acting out" and "Working through" Trauma', 7-8.

[35] Whitehead, *Trauma Fiction*, 85.

[36] *Il.* 22.188-92.

[37] Panayioa Chrysochou, 'The Si(eye)ght of Trauma: Oedipal Wounds, Tragic Visions, and Averted Gazes from the Time of Sophocles to the Twenty-First Century,' *Journal of Literature and Trauma Studies* 1.1 (2012): 15.

[38] Mimesis itself is a fraught term as there is not agreement about the extent to which reality can be accurately represented. Caruth, *Unclaimed Experience*, says that one betrays or compromises an event's unrepresentability by trying to represent it. In this volume, both Antropova and Schaub readings challenge the idea of representability.

[39] For a discussion of this range, and further bibliography, see Donald Keesey, 'On Some Recent Interpretations of Catharsis,' *The Classical World* 72:4 (1979) 193-205.

[40] LaCapra, *History in Transit*, 141-2, resists the reductive and false dichotomy of either total transcendence and mastery or valorization of trauma with endless acting out and aporias.

[41] Shakespeare, *Hamlet*, (II. ii. 553-54).

[42] I. A. Richards, *Principles of Literary Criticism* (London: Keegan, Paul, Prench, 1925), 245-6.

[43] Charles Segal, *Dionysian Poetics and Euripides' Bacchae* (Princeton: Princeton University Press, 1982), 225.

[44] Barrett, *Staged Narrative*, 129.

[45] LaCapra, *History in Transit*, 119.

[46] In this respect, one thinks of Jules Dassin's *Never on a Sunday* (1960), and Melina Mercouri's character Illya's refusal to read *Medea* correctly. When told that Medea really did kill her children to punish Jason, she insists, 'Yes. She gets him back, and everybody go away and everybody is happy and they go to the seashore. And that's all!' I share Schaub's caution when she suggests that *Losing North* may consist in 'a first step towards rehabilitation'.

## Bibliography

Allen, James T. *A Concordance to Euripides*. Berkeley: Univ. of California Press, 1954.

Barrett, James. *Staged Narrative: Poetics and the Messenger in Greek Tragedy*. Berkeley: Univ. of California Press, 2002.

Berger, James. 'Trauma and Literary Theory.' *Contemporary Literature* 38.3 (1997): 569-582.

Caruth, Cathy. *Unclaimed Experience: Trauma, Narrative, and History*. Baltimore and London: The Johns Hopkins University Press, 1996.

Chrysochou, Panayiota. 'The Si(eye)ght of Trauma: Oedipal Wounds, Tragic Visions, and Averted Gazes from the Time of Sophocles to the Twenty-first Century.' *Journal of Literature and Trauma Studies* 1.1 (2012): 15-26.

Scheff, Thomas, J. *Catharsis in Healing, Ritual, and Drama*. Berkeley: Univ. of California Press, 1979.

Conacher, Desmond J. *Euripidean Drama: Myth, Theme and Structure*. Toronto: Univ. of Toronto Press, 1967.

Devereux, George. *Dreams in Greek Tragedy*. Berkeley: University of California Press, 1976.

Edwards, Mark. *Homer: Poet of the Iliad*. Baltimore: Johns Hopkins University Press, 1987.

Freud, Sigmund. *Beyond the Pleasure Principle*, trans. James Strachey, New York and London: W.W. Norton, 1961.

Garner, Richard K. *From Homer to Tragedy: The Art of Allusion in Greek Poetry*. London and New York: Routledge, 1990.

Grene, David and Lattimore, Richmond. Eds. *Euripides III*, Chicago: U. of Chicago Press, 1958.

Keesey, Donald. 'On Some Recent Interpretations of Catharsis.' *The Classical World* 72.4 (1979): 193-205.

King, Katherine C. 'The Politics of Imitation: Euripides' *Hekabe* and the Homeric Achilles,' *Arethusa* 18 (1985): 47-66.

LaCapra, Dominick. *History in Transit: Experience, Identity, Critical Theory*. Ithaca and London: Cornell University Press, 2004.

————.*Writing History, Writing Trauma*. Baltimore and London: Johns Hopkins University Press, 2001.

Lattimore, Richmond, trans. *The Iliad of Homer*. Chicago: U. of Chicago Press, 1951.

Lynne-George, Michael. *Epos: Word, Narrative, and the Iliad*. Atlantic Highlands, NJ: Humanities Press International, 1988.

Mossman, Judith. *Wild Justice*. Oxford: Oxford University Press, 1995.

Richards, Ivor A. *Principles of Literary Criticism*. London: Kegan Paul, Trench, Trubner, 1925.

Rothberg, Michael. *Traumatic Realism*. Minneapolis: University of Minnesota Press, 2000.

Segal, Charles. *Euripides and the Poetics of Sorrow*, Durham, 1995.

————. 'Golden Armor and Servile Robes: Heroism and Metamorphosis in *Hecuba* of Euripides', *AJP* 111 (1990): 304-17.

————. *Dionysian Poetics in Euripides' Bacchae*. Princeton: Princeton University Press, 1982.

Whitehead, Anne. *Trauma Fiction*. Edinburgh: Edinburgh University Press, 2004.

Zeitlin, Froma I. 'Euripides' *Hekabe* and the Somatics of Dionysiac Drama', *Ramus* 20 (1991): 53-94.

**Lisa B. Hughes** is a classicist and Chair of the Program in Comparative Literature at The Colorado College. Her teaching and research interests include ancient drama in cultural context and the classical tradition in American culture.

# 'Split in two chronologically': Loss and Dis/Orientation of the Emotional and Geographical Exile in Nancy Huston's *Losing North*

## Danielle Schaub

**Abstract**

With its reflections on the self caught between countries and languages, Nancy Huston's essay *Losing North* leads itself to a psychoanalytical and textual exploration of loss and dis-orientation resulting from the experience of exile borne in part of a need to distance the self from childhood traumatic experiences, namely her mother's walking out on the family, never to return. Based on the author's experience of expatriation, the essay records, with humour, nostalgia and rationalisation alternately, a variety of emotions and dis/advantages to her condition that bring to mind the theories of Klein, Winnicott, Bion and Kristeva. With their focus on self-hate and guilt, lack of holding and continuity, false and true self, severed links and bond, disorientation, these theories help explain the likely sources of the text's ruptures. Close reading and deconstructive approach, in turn, confirm the psychoanalytical theories as they highlight what Jacqueline Rose would consider writing that reveals unconscious phenomena. Indeed in its attempt to deconstruct the metaphor of losing north, the text loses ground increasingly while its voice remains continually floating, language drifting away from the speaker's centre of self. Although the text clearly struggles to engage in a Derridian practice of word play to get beyond unitary meaning, the textual voice follows a unidirectional, indeed unidimensional thread, avoiding affective planes, erasing the feminine, thereby perpetuating its own entrapment. *Losing North* thus illustrates a particular exploitation of Derridian word play, fabricating associations while probing, and grappling with, meanings of disorientation to avoid letting trauma seep into it and particularly the emotions related to the maternal.

**Key Words:** Exile, childhood loss, dis-orientation, psychoanalytical theories, literary and psychoanalytic explorations, deconstruction, erasure of the feminine and the emotional.

*****

## 1. Introduction

With its reflections on the self caught between countries and languages, Nancy Huston's essay *Losing North* leads itself to an exploration of loss and dis-orientation borne in part of the choice to live in exile.[1] In Huston's case, the choice presumably also results from an unconscious desire to distance herself from childhood traumatic experiences, namely her mother's walking out on the family, never to return.[2] Based on the author's experience of expatriation, the essay records, with humour, nostalgia and rationalisation alternately, a variety of emotions and dis/advantages most exiles would recognise about their new lives, particularly if their dislocation involves both language and culture estranging them from themselves. Among these, confusion, embarrassment, unrest, distress and turmoil, solitude, disruption, enlightenment, enrichment whirl as in a toccata and fugue, emphasising the virtuosity of the composer-cum-writer in conveying her reflections based on her life experiences. The essay focuses on the problematics of cultural exile, by offering a selection of reflections on land, language, home and adoptive culture, family, racism, adjustment and roots, the true and false self, the silenced self, home and abroad, the split, distance, the expatriate and the 'impatriate' realities, and fear of estrangement. Huston has entitled the sections of her essay 'Take-Off', 'Orientation', 'Disorientation', 'The Mask...', '... And the Pen', 'False Bilingualism', 'Nature and Nurture and Nature', 'The Misery of the Foreigner', 'The Arrogant Mosaic', 'Relatively Relative', 'The Three Daughters-in-Law', 'Memory Gaps', and 'Other Selves.'

With the epigraph from Gerard Manley Hopkins—'My own heart let me have more pity on; let / Me live to my sad self hereafter kind, / Charitable; not live this tormented mind tormenting yet'[3]—Huston allows readers to sense the wound at the heart of the experience. And if that did not suffice, the quotation from Romain Gary that makes up the entire initial section, 'Take-Off', ascribes the choice of a new country and language to self-hatred. The text explores the split that causes the exile to wear a mask and to immerse in life as if on stage, clarifying the realities faced and their multiple impact. The progression marks the passage from territory or geography to the psyche, informing psychological repercussions stemming from expatriation and its original traumatic cause for self-hatred, in this case the disappearance of the mother. In examining the traumatic experiences of childhood loss, engendering lack of holding and continuity, self-hate and guilt, severed links/bond, disorientation, false and true self aggravated by self-chosen exile, the theories of Freud, Klein, Winnicott, Balint, Bion and Kristeva ground the text and explain the likely sources of its ruptures. Close reading and deconstructive approach, on the other hand, highlight the patterns that the text exploits to avoid letting trauma seep into it and particularly the emotions related to the maternal.

## 2. Relevant Psycho-Analytical Theories

Freud's *Beyond the Pleasure Principle* contributes insightful clarification of the processes at hand in Huston's *Losing North*.[4] For one, it explains the textual voice's drive to shield itself from pain and to look for ways of experiencing pleasure. For another, by reflecting on the 'compulsion to repeat' countering the pleasure principle, it justifies the textual insistence on examining unpleasant or distressful realities as an attempt to regain control. Finally, Freud's reminder about the speculative character of his work serves as a reminder that the present discussion does not presume to offer more than speculations on the textual content.[5] Freud's considerations in 'Mourning and Melancholia' may also apply to the Huston's essay in that the text's erasure of the maternal and distancing from the homeland may point to unconscious withdrawal from consciousness of the object-loss.[6] Freud contends that linked with aggression and hatred, an ambivalent attachment to the lost object results in melancholia, a process that denies loss and introjects it into the self, so that loss of the ego occurs.[7] However, the text does not disclose straightforward depression, rather questionings around belonging, betrayal of the homeland and the self, a form of intellectual defence mechanism that puts the childhood wound at bay, somehow putting a balm on it so that it cannot draw cathectic energy.

In this respect, Melanie Klein's work on envy and gratitude, on love and hatred, and particularly her formulations regarding the paranoid-schizoid and depressive positions, throw light on phenomena the textual voice of Huston's *Losing North* raises.[8] The text does not give evidence that the voice is blocked at the level of the paranoid-schizoid position. Neither does it clarify whether the mother's absence started at the time she left the family, causing an interruption in the feeling of security, or whether it simply concretely prolonged her absence-in-presence before her departure. In the first case, up to when she left, the mother must have reflected the anxieties the child projected onto her, digesting and returning them with love so that the child could feel less in danger of contamination by the bad external and internal forces. But by leaving and not securing continuity in maternal care, the mother could not help contain the child's aggression and hatred. In absence, the mother figure underwent destruction owing to frustration and hatred, triggering guilt. As the destruction of the loved object yields another destructive impulse that annihilates the source of protection and haven that gave the child meaning, the child must have experienced the depressive position and depressive guilt in the form of sorrow and nostalgia (triggered in the text as it works through the realities of exile and expatriation). In response to her anxieties, the child must have used her ego defences to deny dependence on the mother, whose absence only contributed feelings of loss; in an attempt to alleviate the wound the child-come-young adult simply chose to put a distance between herself and the absent mother, illusorily ridding herself of her dependence. On the other hand, if the mother could not provide security on account of psychic absence, the expatriation of the child-come-adult would not just amount to running away from the mother object but perhaps to connecting to the mother object as her essence equates with exile and absence.[9] Whether the mother corresponds to one model or the other, the text, however, shows that 'all the disparate roles . . . embraced and then rejected' encompass attempts to 'conjure up the love of the person who is usually the very symbol of proximity and presence'.[10]

An extension of the textual problematic relation to the mother, Winnicott's theory of the true and false self suits the previous quotation in that the roles adopted correspond to ways to secure recognition from the mother.[11] The text also refers to the need to play a part akin to Winnicott's false self. Winnicott argues that the false self stems from compliance to the environment that the individual cannot control rather than from spontaneity and serves a key role in social functioning, driving to conformity; on the other hand rooted in the psyche, the true self relates to the unconditional desires and needs of an individual, which emerges with good-enough mothering. When overwhelmingly constraining, compliance may stifle the true self so much that the false self dominates, causing the self to perform as if on stage or depleting the true self of its vitality and energy in such a manner as to cause psychic death.[12] Winnicott's 'The Theory of the Parent-Infant Relationship' also applies.[13] His notion of continuity offered by the good enough mother capable of holding the infant's experience by surviving his/her destructiveness does not materialise in Huston's text for the simple reason that the mother's alienation signals interruption of ties provoking lack of continuity. Intimately related to this lack, Winnicott's theory of the mind and psyche-soma (1949) offers insights into the focus of the text on the mental to the detriment of the emotional and corporeal.[14] With its split between the North and the South, the text evidences that the rupture resulting from the imperfect, mother-less environment impinges on the healthy development of the psyche-soma.

Given the estrangement and the cessation of interaction at hand, Bion's 'Attacks on linking' (1959) inevitably proves relevant to Huston's *Losing North*, not because her essay deals with schizophrenics, but because it points to rupture, division, disorientation essentially resulting from attacks to sever bonds with the absent mother, akin to the fragmentation schizophrenics bring to their thinking and linguistic expressions.[15] By walking out on the family, the mother referred to in *Losing North* does not cater for the emotional and physical needs of her children so that the bond with the native land snaps as does the illusion of safety in maternal care. For the sake of protection, or rather not to suffer from the absence and not to feel loss, the self takes a distance, cuts ties, seeks independence. Deprived of roots, the self experiences a sense of inner exile, causing double mourning, that of the self in inner exile and that of the self in outer exile in a country and language alien to the native ones. Here an incursion in another language might explain the destructive mechanism at hand: in Spanish, the word for mourning—*duelo*—also denotes *duel* so that the word throws light on another aspect of territorial exile particularly suited in this context, namely that of severance at both ends. Owing to defence mechanisms to eschew absence, those leaving cut off ties with the family left behind, who in turn cease to take an interest in the new lives of the uprooted, engaging in a symbolic duel that attacks links. The destructive impulse then replaces the engagement in mourning to lighten the burden of disconnection.

An extension of Bion's theory, Kristeva's *Strangers to Ourselves* (1991), with its reflections on strangers in a society and country not their own as well as feelings of strangeness within the self, applies most particularly to Huston's essay, as the latter illustrates Kristeva's theory most appropriately.[16] Kristeva contends that 'a secret wound, often unknown to himself [sic], drives the foreigner to wandering', as if of his/her own accord, as if in utter indifference for the world left behind, for the severed ties with the home environment and family; the posed indifference in fact originates in defence mechanisms not to see the wound.[17] She attributes the need for exile to the estranged, misunderstanding or absent mother, and to the search for a land promising intoxicating independence far from the original roots, which either overburdened by love and/or control, or failed by emotional or physical absence. Leaving behind origins, the stranger must set foot and take place elsewhere, make choices, adjust, escape routine and rest, cringing at reminiscences of the old country, incapable of treasuring landmarks, for none exist because of the maternal loss.[18] On the surface, the stranger appears indifferent, heartless, untouchable, though deep down profoundly affected by aggression, exclusion and discrimination; feelings engendered by these, Kristeva adds, hide behind self-assurance, determination and fortitude, all masks concealing the non-existent self. As a result of the wound inflicted by the mother, the stranger suffers from self-hatred borne, as Freud would have it (1917), from the introjected wounding mother;[19] hatred and anger directed to the self find expiation, so to speak, by turning them to others as a statement of existence; however, excited by a passion or a goal, the stranger settles down in complete, consuming fusion.[20] *Losing North* reveals patterns matching Kristeva's findings: leaving the homeland to distance herself from the mother whose absence left her rootless, the speaker does not realise the reason for her exile, nor notices that she severs the maternal and emotional from her discourse and then after reacting to discrimination embraces the new culture with excessive zeal to the point that she writes in the adoptive language.

With regard to linguistic acquisition, Kristeva remarks that, by learning the language of the adoptive country, the stranger escapes the yoke of the mother tongue because it exists outside its prohibitions.[21] Learning the new language outside the realm and the passions of the maternal unlike infants, the stranger, Kristeva notes, finds in it a haven, for it offers a new self through the manipulation of words without restriction and the creation of verbal constructs free of fear but also fraught with artificiality and devoid of unconscious connection, enthusiasm or aversion. Severance 'from the maternal source of words' disempowers true self-expression, thereby hiding and silencing the self while engendering a sense of anguish and dejection because of the lost roots.[22] In this respect, the speaker in *Losing North* discusses at length in undeniable mastery her mixed feelings vis-à-vis the French language, different selves, loss of connection with the originary family, loss of memory. Her reflection on the pursuit of the perfect word in front of the computer informs the disconnection from the self she imagines would have developed if it were not for uprooting herself.[23]

However, what emerges from Huston's writing stays in line with Kristeva's reflections in *Black Sun: Depression and Melancholia*, in which she explores depression and its discourse in an attempt to restore its symbolic power, in an attempt to work it through and benefit from it.[24] Going back to her ideas in *Black Sun*, in *La Haine et le pardon* (Hatred and forgiveness) (2005), Kristeva notes that an ordeal puts humans to the test allowing either for depression to set in or for a challenge of values and certitudes that allow to move beyond borders.[25] Without ordeals or rather by denying them, one makes do with an identity fiercely protected with limits and principles rather than liberating uncertainties.[26] Depressive speech underscores the loss and/or the absence underlying signification; somehow acknowledging it, art and literature secure a 'sublimatory hold over the lost Thing' that counteracts loss by naming it;[27] thus writing that springs out of depression alleviates it because the process of signification that writing yields affords mourning through distancing representation, turning away from the attachment to the lost object precisely through its translation into words. The process of identification by naming through which the self recovers the lost object leads to forgiveness and mourning so that separation becomes bearable, thereby restoring meaning as argued in *La Haine et le pardon*, in which Kristeva posits literature as an often superior rival to psychoanalysis for its bibliotherapeutic value. Literature and psychoanalysis reveal the multiple faces of hatred without which psychic life cannot exist but offer forgiveness—'par-don' (for-giveness, or by gift) as she says—not because they erase the existential unease but because through their gift (*par-don*) they enable a psychic and even physical rebirth.[28] Such rebirth emerges from literature and art precisely because through their interpretation they display madness in the light of reason, therefore giving meaning to the nonsensical, elucidating desire and hatred through transference and counter-transference, securing other selves, unforeseeable connections, new channels.

## 3. Stylistic and Compositional Reflection of Trauma[29]

In her discussion of Melanie Klein's theory of psychic negativity in the emergence of the subject, Jacqueline Rose suggests a reading of texts 'interested in the moments when writing slips its moorings, when it fails . . . its own tests of coherence, revealing . . . its "other" scene', thereby demonstrating 'the triumph of the unconscious'.[30] Examined in this manner, Nancy Huston's *Losing North* reveals a particular pattern of slippages. The text appears to lose ground increasingly as it perpetuates a search for an *originary source* in an attempt to deconstruct the metaphor of losing north. The textual voice remains continually floating, language drifting away from the speaker's centre of self. *Losing North* illustrates a particular exploitation of Derridian word play, fabricating associations while probing, and grappling with, meanings of disorientation. However, though language undergoes a process of explosion, the text remains bound within unitary phallocentric patterns. Deconstruction in *Losing North* pursues the traces of intellectual abstractions, leaving the threads of emotional, physical and sensual responses largely unexplored, thereby erasing connection to the ground.[31] Although the text clearly struggles to engage in a Derridian practice of word play to get beyond unitary meaning, the textual voice follows a unidirectional, indeed unidimensional thread, avoiding affective planes, erasing the feminine, thereby perpetuating its own entrapment.[32]

Deconstructive patterns demand diverging exploration beyond the positive/negative binaries of meanings and associations available to any sign. But both institutionalized censorship and spatial/temporal limitations of writing necessarily constrain what can be said in a particular context. Nevertheless, with regard to free-associative writing, a different aspect comes into play. If Jauss, who formulated reader-response theory, had been around when Derrida challenged classical philosophy with his theory of deconstruction, he would likely have commented on particular ways that writing/reading teases out threads of meaning.[33] He would have noticed that limitations in the directions of unravelling are less attributable to the particular sign traced than to the dis/ability of the text to get beyond its confines. For on a psychological level the pattern and extent of deconstruction reveals unconscious barriers to authorial intent in deconstructive discourse.[34]

While acknowledging a particular bilingual/bicultural dilemma, the voice in the text of *Losing North* avoids exploiting associations available in English or extensions beyond the limits of modern French to bleed into different languages or older root forms. Play is bound by restricting French to the particular realms of human cognition, leaving the emotional, the sensual and the exotic out.[35] Although the text tries hard to work its way out of phallocentric paradigms, its own logocentric terms pull it back. Loss of the north appears as a threat because of its correspondence with the head, the cerebral, and the Western European masculinist brand of intellectual space that erases or marginalizes the body and the mother/land. The narrator maintains a non-emotional stability. The tunnel vision or muffled voice thus created prevents free-play of the floating signifier. Language is disallowed a flow that would textualise a borderless perspective, encourage the subversion of limited meanings, and reveal the absent-centre of difference and deferred possibility between terms which Derrida performs as 'différance'.[36]

From the very beginning, the text and its strands 'slip their moorings':

Take-Off

'I do not like myself. Yes'. The words of Sviatoslav Richter.

To begin with, self-hatred. For whatever reason.

All sorts of behaviour can be inspired by self-hatred. You can become an artist. Commit suicide. Adopt a new name, a new country, a new language.

All of the above (Romain Gary).[37]

The title of the section 'Take-Off'—the only words by the author of *Losing North* —intimates a variety of concepts. Beyond implying the starting point of an activity, particularly in the light of Nancy Huston's repeated allusions to Romain Gary and her understanding of his premises, the title suggests a place where to start from and therefore even gratitude not to be alone on the strange boat that ferries exiles of the heart. But its French version, 'Envoi', also alludes to a burdensome child sent off to distant relatives or an unknown destination like a neatly packed parcel.[38] The appropriation of Romain Gary's words in this context yields to Klein's notion of self-hatred originating from the sense of loss the child experiences in western contexts: separation from the mother sets in almost from birth since the baby is not tied to the mother's body.[39] At the same time, the appropriation of self-hatred calls to mind Freud's considerations of melancholia transforming object-loss into ego-loss.[40] The text later refers to the lost mother in such fashion that one may presume the loss caused the speaker to cut off her ties with the native, that is, maternal land, the appropriation of Gary's words may point to the speaker's turning hate of the absent into self-hatred in melancholia, which, as Kristeva explains, results in exile.[41]

These feelings foreground further textual emotional erasures, instabilities and abstractions. In particular, self-hatred affects the perception of human grounding, the very subject of the next section:

> Orientation
>
> To be disorientated is to lose the east.
>
> In French, 'losing north' means forgetting what you were going to say. *Losing track of what's going on. Losing your marbles.* It is something you should avoid at all costs. Something that's always spoken of negatively, to say that one hasn't done it. 'My, he certainly doesn't lose the north, does he?' is the way the expression is used. Never 'Ah, too bad—he's lost the north'.[42]

While the title 'Orientation' suggests the human capacity to locate oneself in time and space or even the direction chosen for an activity or an enterprise, the text does not embark on a quest for grounding or enlightenment. For under 'orientation', comes its negation 'to be disorientated', marking loss of bearing, not self-grounding. In this case, the tracing goes back to losing the east. However, the tracing stops short of examining other implications of losing one's east, such as losing ties with one's very birth, or losing the exotic where the sensual finds a realm for infinite experimentation in speech, movement, behaviour, appearance.

Such curtailed tracing seems to correspond to Bion's consideration of attacks in which the mind attacks the mind's perceptiveness and cognitive faculties.[43]

This unitary reference leads to a leap to the north, yet another cardinal point, one that seems to obsess and perhaps also possess the textual voice. Interestingly, here again the voice speaks the strands of a disembodied situation. A gerund is defined as loss of cognitive or perceptual faculties, forgetting what *you* meant to say, not what *I* meant to say, yet another form of attack on linking. Both the gerund and the personal pronoun stress the speaker's lack of involvement while the content refers to the intellect—cold, unemotional, unsensual.[44] Intention, not impulse nor desire, drives the mind formulating the definition, echoing the sourceless italicised definitions that follow, the one focusing on intellectual fuzziness while recalling the original lack of direction implied by the turn of phrase, the other stressing loss of control. And the voice proceeds to pontificate: 'It's something you should avoid at all costs', rehearsing what the reader senses as an order, an echo of right and wrong paradigms, which calls to mind Winnicott's reflections on compliance and the false self.[45] True the original meaning behind the ban lies in the intention of the idiom's interpreter to relate to its use in the negative, but the double negation of the following sentence implies the need to defy and beat the possibility. Yet, contrary to the final statement of the paragraph, the idiom in French works in the affirmative too: 'J'ai perdu le nord' (I've lost the north), I might say to beg forgiveness for some incoherent behaviour. In addition, the example of how one uses the idiom expresses admiration for the male who shows resourcefulness or smartness.

Where does the feminine stand in this context? The only personalised examples of usage refer to a male. The use of the indefinite pronoun 'one' (translated from the French *on*) also implies the power of the male gender.[46] So the female gets lost behind the generic pronoun. In addition, the French version describes losing north as 'une chose qui ne se fait pas', which relegates the female to the forbidden by virtue of the gender attached to *a thing* (une chose), signifying the loss of the female that becomes an emasculated self, held in check.[47] But as the voice is concerned with the loss of 'the thing', it also evokes castration and the loss of the *originary stage* when separation of the self and the maternal had not set in. In other words, to lose one's head means to lose the masculine and the ability to separate one's thoughts from any emotion or desire. According to Klein, speech production starts when the child needs to name the absent mother; language originates in the lost sense of complete unity with the source of sensation within ourselves, that is, when an obstacle to the mother/baby relationship comes up and forces the baby to become conscious of a split identity and name the absent mother in an attempt to modify the anxiety of loss.[48] Thus although the text seems to challenge the Kleinian construct by engaging in tracing, it remains trapped within the methodology of self-effacement, perhaps out of self-hatred.

With its focus on the north, the text remains perpetually disoriented—not in a poststructuralist sense of having lost an 'originary source' (arche) or 'destination' (telos), which Derrida argues inevitably occurs with relinquishment of the metaphysical 'one' at the centre.[49] Instead, the text remains locked in a longing for a north, and its disorientation results from having lost not only the east but also the other cardinal points. In his Jungian *Dictionary for Dreamers*, Chetwynd equates the four cardinal points with 'the four faculties of the mind: intellect, emotion, intuition and sensation'.[50] The south with its reference to 'earthly warmth', love, and 'passion' represents the maternal, the site of emotional responses, the body.[51] The east stands for the exotic and the west for the intuitive, the 'unconscious modes of knowledge'.[52] All these cardinal points are closely connected with the maternal whose absence caused childhood trauma, accounting for the favouring of the north and the head. Such partiality could well go back to attacks on linking à la Bion directed against the maternal object and all that it represents and/or illustrate the theory of Winnicott according to which deficient mothering may encourage an excessive development of mental functioning to the detriment of the psyche-soma.[53]

The text continually cries out its fear of losing the north, the head, the intellect. Yet even the north need not be a unitary concept. Are there not many norths? Take a Corsican, a Moscovite, a Montrealer, and an Inuit; each one of them perceives the north differently. In addition, the north also happens to be the homeland of the narrator (Canada) but within Canada her birthplace is located in the west (Calgary). So to the intuitive value attached to the west, the text also adds the maternal since the speaker was born there. The unidimensional reading of disorientation, which does not encompass exploration of regions beyond the boundaries of the permissible such as female longing, actually reveals that such opening cannot be effected because the textual voice has lost her bearing by losing the maternal. The narrator has to situate herself only in the north in order not to succumb to guilt and self-hatred. Her obsession with not losing north calls to mind Joan Rivière's Kleinian interpretation of psychic conflicts, namely 'the ego's need to dissociate itself from the unpleasure' through object-relations of a negative order.[54]

Once in the north, the narrator feels she must negotiate her identity on new terms to secure acceptance from her adoptive country. However she perceives her presence as invasive and conditioned within particularly limiting restraints that she unquestioningly poses as unilaterally French. As such, the voice imposes constant control over expression in order not to violate the highly stereotypical terms imagined as pre-requisite conditions for attainment of some idealised notion of national status in the new country. Consequently, the narrative remains restricted to an idealised target, imagined as Francophile, but actually pertaining only to the dominant discourse of a very particular sector—the French male intellectual elite. In an attempt at attaining at-one-ment status, that is, the fleeting and metaphysically idealised notion of *French national*, the narrative traps itself within a linguistic barrier whose borders seem to threaten self-destruction. This entrapment evokes Winnicottian notions of the false self complying with societal demands.[55] The elision of all the cardinal points, bar the north, then signifies acquiescence to cerebral modes of communication. The attempt to break out in a deconstructive pattern, while continually ploughing within a particularly limited field, shuts down even perception of other entry points to French identities—deconstructed, hybrid, and non-homogeneous forms of identity—available outside the narrow confines of becoming 'one of the boys.' Conformity to the intellectual codes of the French establishment stifles the creative abilities of the true self, somehow illustrating Winnicott's theory of the true and false selves.[56]

The text's construction of French expectations also recalls Kristeva's allegations in *Strangers to Ourselves* that, in order to elicit acceptance, the foreigner must stick to the rules of the adoptive country.[57] However, the narrative voice could negotiate space for herself by breaking boundaries and experimenting with the emotional, the intuitive and the exotic, by exploding linguistic singularity itself through moving beyond a monolingual frame. The French text, however, avoids bringing such modes into play, betraying its entrapment within the very discursive modes it attempts to escape.[58] The narrative continually re-erects linguistic and ideological walls confining the narrator to a status of alienated other, while the text recirculates an ever-escaping horizon of Francophile identity whose metaphysical status remains aloof and unobtainable. As such, language in the text remains flat, monotone, and abstract, totally avoiding acknowledgment of the emotional hemisphere. In this respect, the text offers an example of what Kristeva calls 'verbal constructs . . . centered in a void, dissociated from both body and passions', typical of a foreigner's new language bound to remain artificial 'like algebra or musical notations'.[59]

Barring a bipolar pattern of exclusivity that disallows recuperating patterns of *différance* available on multilingual levels, the text underscores the mutual untranslatability of the French and English languages or the lack of correspondences between them in its reflections on the English translation of 'perdre le nord' (losing north):

> *To be all abroad* is what my excellent French-English dictionary suggests by way of translation. An expression which, taken literally, means to be in a foreign country. But if, in turn, you take the English-French dictionary and look up the expression *To be all abroad*, what you find is *to be scattered every which way*, or *to the four winds, to talk twaddle, to be off one's rocker—* which is not at all the same thing![60]

The narrator consults a particular dictionary as if this were a singular and all-expressive source, bi-passing the English potential for unravelling. Though conscious of the flexibility and/or contradictions of translations, the textual economy remains stagnant and cannot find a means of exchange to accrue other forms of profit. The avoidance of a readily available multilingual deconstruction as possibility raises a question, namely, whether the text is trapped or whether the discursive mode itself traps the narrator, preventing her from touching upon the emotional, the sensual, and the intuitive, causing her to attack these as possible links to the hated mother, as Bion might have noted.[61] The first person pronoun at last enters this passage with the words *my dictionary*, but as the reference book remains unnamed, even this use of a personalising pronoun ends up essentialising because it presents a unitary source, the one and only dictionary.

French in *Losing North* appears to strangle the narrative voice into a dispassionate whisper, and the narrative, entrapped within its own constructions, does not foreground its limitations. The *Robert and Collins Dictionary*, for instance, offers more than *to lose one's way* to translate the geographical concept; it also proposes liberating translations, like *not missing a trick* or *keeping his wits about him* [sic].[62] The narrative in *Nord perdu*, however, appears to be fighting so hard for acceptance into the male French intellectual circle that it cannot imagine celebrating whatever remarkable *originary force* empowers it, what unique wealth of untranslatable pain fires it to try so hard and go so long. The voice that tries to break out of dualities by bringing in *my* dictionary rather than *the* dictionary, condemns itself to absolution to a single, unquestioned, and stable text as metaphysical referent. Again conformity crushes the creative connection to the self, in a manner reminiscent of Winnicott's false self constraining the true self.[63]

The textual voice does show awareness of differences by highlighting confusion over and over again. Nevertheless, it remains blind to its own evidence, overlooking the possible exploitation of the 'magma *between languages*, in which words lose their meanings, refuse to mean, start out meaning one thing and end up meaning quite another'.[64] The text does not record that any dictionary, such as any other text, remains the cultural-historic construct of its author/s, quite often trapped within gender issues that keep the female in check. The magma would point to the incapacity of language to enunciate female realities because the generic masculine imprisons the female voice. At the same time, the confusion resulting from the magma may also indirectly allude to Freud's theory of melancholia or to the projected hatred of the loved object onto the ego, where accusation and reproach shift from the one to the other in confusing fashion.[65] In this case words would signify feelings that lose their objective meaning because they have been misplaced.

This goes back to the idea of lost bearings. The narrator had to situate herself only in the north to forget the rift with the maternal and to negotiate an identity that would match her idea of the acceptable. On account of the unitary, dualistic and exclusive construct assumed to please, she does not exploit *l'entre-deux* nor takes the contradictions to good account by creating a new identity, fluid, multi-faceted. For the narrator establishes that she lives within the limits of conventions, principles, logic by saying 'What I should have said. Theoretically. What I was supposed to say, in the event that I had something to say',[66] rather than 'What I could have said' or 'wanted to say', if she had allowed her true self to resist compliance to the accepted norm.

Why should the voice not have something to say, let herself go, and exploit her creativity? She does see the holes in the dominant French constructs, proving perfectly capable of making acrobatics with language. The narrative indeed performs incredible linguistic feats, tracing associations, parallels, visions. But, for lack of a self-critical outlook, for a lack of a connection to the self, it remains short of transgressive patterns or subversive exploitation of the linguistic flexibility afforded by multiple languages and cultures. Disempowerment originates from the fight for access to an intellectual circle favouring a masculinist outlook. Metalanguage by excellence, the discursive celebrates the cerebral experience of language devoid of affective charge, not breaking out of phallocentric syntax evidenced in 'an unusual amount of attention to individual words, figures of speech, *manners* of speaking'.[67] Herein lies the ego's need for protection against its fears, for not accessing its darker realms that would connect her to the wound that led to exile. A form of attack on the maternal related to Bion's theory, the preference for the cerebral over the emotional generates associations that do not provide links with the memories of the hurt that like a volcano awaits explosion.[68] Connections remain limited to the cerebral, disempowering the flow of truly free reparative associations.

Discourse means ways of talking the world into being, or organising a chaotic mass of sensations into a coherent structure. When feelings become too chaotic, hence menacing, one may circumscribe them or block them out. The text does just this. Where it notices contradictions, it smoothes them out; where realities prove too threatening, it forgets them altogether.[69] It does not name what its narrator has lost, offers no blood and flesh description of the north, no sensual and emotional perception. The north remains a Cartesian construct, big and empty, devoid of people and physical characteristics. Disembodied, the text insists on the loss as disempowering. Yet leaving may mean embracing, reflecting, expanding horizons. The narrator erases her native city in favour of her adoptive Paris and, by switching languages and cultures, agrees to 'be involved in *theatre, imitation, make-believe*', a life of imaginary constructs, those favoured by Winnicott's false self.[70]

Contrary to Eva Hoffman, the speaker enters 'a life in a new language' of her own accord, willingly severing her ties with the past.[71] In 'La Structure, le signe et le jeu dans le discours des sciences humaines', Derrida insists on the disruption of the centre, by which he means that humans have no access to a reality unmediated by unstable cultural perceptions, the result of their being social and linguistic animals.[72] However, by aborting and erasing historical and bodily connections and therefore by attacking possible links in a Bionian sense, the narrative in *Losing North* denies the possibility of a wholistic textual existence beyond (and outside) academically textualising itself. The narrative even essentialises the narrator's own experience of motherhood, reducing its importance by mentioning her own children through an impersonal generalisation between brackets, and indeed suggesting her own presence in absence.[73] Though not enacting total erasure, such decentring signals a minor form of Bion's attacks on linking.

Owing to the text's reductionist tendency in front of life experiences, it universalises the reality of exiles, singing different self-exclusive identities: 'People in exile are rich—rich with the accumulated sum of their contradictory identities'.[74] The narrator's considerations about feeling French, or not, disclose an elusive sense of identity resulting from a conviction of not belonging:

> 'Do you feel French now? people often ask me. (To live abroad is to be perpetually subjected to silly questions.)
>
> What on earth might it be like to 'feel French'? How would I know, were it to happen to me one day?
>
> Foreigners can be given French nationality (the verb 'to naturalise' in French also designates what taxidermists do to dead animals); they can be given French diplomas and French honours, they can even be elected to the glorious French Academy and cherish dreams of French immortality... They will never be French for all that, because no one has the power to give them a French childhood.
>
> So the answer is: no.
>
> (Even *with* a French childhood, there are any number of people who have a hard time feeling French! Without one, it's impossible.)
>
> *Your childhood stays with you all your life, no matter where you go.*[75]

With such conviction, the notion of integration, intertwining, crossbreeding does not even come up.[76] The textual voice favours terms such as exile, expatriates (up against the lucky 'impatriates'), never considering immigrants who do connect past and present. For want of grounding, the narrator cannot fathom that one can feel a citizen of many places with cross-connections, not just an accumulation of identities at cross-purposes. A passport only makes a person a citizen on a legalistic level. Emotional connection with the land, its inhabitants, and its language, however, offers a kind of citizenship that surpasses such formalities.

Accumulation of realities and experiences in different languages does not necessitate seeing oneself as multiple exclusive identities with clear-cut boundaries like a toy whose secret compartments pop open one at a time, never in conjunction. People who inhabit more than one culture multiply these realities and experiences, thereby increasing the number of facets to the diamond of identity. The hybrid perspectives that varied cultures and/or languages afford change perceptions of identity to the extent that one can choose to realise van Herk's vision according to which 'the immigrant becomes magician of the self', modulating new, inclusive signs of identity.[77]

Though the narrative shows awareness that the absolute does not rule, that humans are composites made up of their different ages, it erases the past and brings in only such quotations antagonistic to a non-native French identity. As such, the text serves as a projection by which outsiders are blamed for the subject's sense of discontinuity, detachment of emotional, sensual, and intuitive responses. The presence of two cultures then becomes a schizophrenic construct, the narrator inhabiting physically and mentally either one realm or the other, with no crystallisation or cross-enrichment ever possible. Yet overlapping happens on the level of the unconscious when the metaphysical feelings of being 'really' French are equated with eating a bar of chocolate after breaking up with a partner.[78] Suddenly the gustatory offers the connection with the past, with the maternal, whose soothing enables rewarding self-images, regardless of the objective fact that chocolate stereotypes less the French than Belgian or Swiss identity.

Halfway through the book, the text insists that the French language offers a lesser emotional charge than the previous linguistic state, as evidence of the narrator's flight from the potential danger of anger, guilt and self-hatred linked to an affective life (Klein), to a past in a maternal tongue shaped by English.[79] Linguistic arguments, unemotional language, intellectual wordplay—these present a welcome escape into indifference. The lack of emotional impact that the French language affords recalls psychological discussions of language and the self: 'it [the French language] was not my mother', the narrator tells us.[80] Interestingly, the description of the piano and English or the harpsichord and French and their respective emotional impact translate in generalising terms her own perception of Kristeva's consideration of language, as if to reduce the affective charge[81]:

> I see *English and the piano* as motherly instruments: emotional, romantic, manipulative, sentimental and crude. In both, variations in dynamics are emphasized, exaggerated, imposed, flagrantly and unavoidably expressed. *French and the harpsichord*, on the other hand, are neutral, intellectual instruments. They require control, restraint and delicate mastery; their expressivity is infinitely more subtle, discreet, refined.

> Speaking French or playing the harpsichord, in other words, there are never any violent surprises or explosions.[82]

The same happens when the narrator admits her shunned emotions indirectly: 'What I was running away from when I turned my back on English and the piano seems quite clear'.[83] This loss of the mother as elision of the mother tongue results in emotional anaesthesia and atrophy of the sensual and intuitive senses.[84] In turn, it encourages an intellectualist cerebral spinning of words. Suzette A. Henke considers that life writing provides therapeutic liberation. But to reach mental healing, 'scriptotherapy' demands writing out the traumatic experience and re-enacting it through words.[85] *Losing North* does not reconstruct the story of the narrator's debilitation. The text rather consists of scraps, fragments, episodes around identity and language, pointers to the psychic fragmentation in a Bionian sense originating in the mother's walking out on the six-year-old narrator and her siblings. The book consists in a first step towards rehabilitation, pointing to the source of trauma.[86] Rehabilitation perhaps occurred in the writing of the mother leaving her children behind, in *Slow Emergencies*.[87] But the textual voice in *Losing North* is still experiencing the lost maternal north, as the title of the book indicates. Memories of the past are not dwelt on, merely touched upon, and, when encountered, compared to an electric signal, then to a sieve, full of holes allowing the pain of experiences to escape.[88] Memory itself proves problematic; the textual voice obsesses about Alzheimer's disease while avoiding and erasing whole episodes of the experiential past, in a Bionian fashion.[89]

Freud's writings on trauma indicate that those who have had traumatic experiences are not 'much occupied in their waking lives with memories of their accident. Perhaps they are more concerned with *not* thinking of it'.[90] Perhaps the text of *Losing North* circumvents trauma and sensual experience to avoid vulnerability through reduction to cliché or a sensationalist text. Shoshana Felman's discussion of Holocaust survivors addresses the estranging quality of testimony, echoed in Elie Wiesel: 'loneliness glimpsed in each of [his] sentences, in each of [his] silences'.[91] In a similar fashion, towards the end, in 'Other Selves I', the narrator concentrates on what she does not do, acts of omission caused by staying at home, presumably to write, a lonely act not unfamiliar to academics. Somehow the omitted acts concern her relations with beings emotionally related to her. An opening seems afforded by a non dualist realisation that different facets of one's being interact: the narrator notes that 'in one way or another—by way of telephone conversations, letters, photographs, or simply memories—all of these worlds were part of my day today'.[92] Vague images associated with trains bring about nostalgia for the past and the realisation that her career as a writer rests on her lost connection with the maternal. Moving terms describe her illumination:

I suddenly see with crystal clarity that my vocation as a novelist dates back to my childhood—when, to reassure myself and perhaps even to survive, I had to learn to convincingly conjure up the love of the person who is usually the very symbol of proximity and presence —but who, in my case, was far away and permanently inaccessible. And it's quite possible that all the permutations I've put myself through, all the disparate roles I've embraced, then rejected . . . have been my own way of asking . . . 'Like this, Mummy?'[93]

Echoing Kristeva's reflections in *Strangers to Ourselves*, the speaker's search for approval poignantly grasps what drives her, the nostalgia for the lost connection with her mother, forever re-enacted through her narrative. She then explains that opening up to the multiple identities invented, also in accordance with Kristeva's findings, amounts to 'go[ing] mad. In order to preserve our sanity, we make ourselves short-sighted and amnesic. We strive to keep our experience within certain fixed limits'.[94] Literature offers a leeway, for 'the novel celebrates our miraculous capacity to recognize others in ourselves, and ourselves in others'.[95] Somehow she reaches a conclusion similar to Kristeva's according to which we all are 'strangers to ourselves', an equally universalising phrase to reduce the pain of realisation.[96] In that context, at times the narrative voice most suitably addresses the reader, also enhancing the essentialising process. In relation to geographical exile, for instance, the voice remarks:

> *Here*, you set aside what you used to be. . . . you don't want to bore them [your interlocutors] by giving them a crash course on Western Canada . . . everything that shaped you, contributed to making you. . . .
>
> *There*, you set aside what you've become. Yes—the folks back home take little interest in the things you've been thinking, saying, reading, seeing and doing, day after day for decades.[97]

By addressing the reader, the textual voice presumes recognition, whether the reader shares the condition of geographical exile or simply of exile to the self. Basically it points to alienation as a human condition.

The last section, 'Other Selves II', elaborates once again on the multiple options of the expatriates who live imagining what they could have been if they had stayed behind.[98] There generalisations nonetheless give way; the text of *Losing North* finishes with a lively fantasy—all south, east and west—in touch with emotions:

. . . there's a *me* who continues to live back there. . . . She's a spunky dame . . . taller and heftier than [I]. . . . she dishes out life all around her, ruffling hair or whacking bottoms according to the needs of the moment, she doesn't mind a little vice and a little violence every now and then, it does her good, she hollers when she feels like it, cusses like a sailor, plays poker with a vengeance and drinks her beer straight from the bottle. . . she plays the clown, plays the whore, doesn't give a hoot what people think. . . [99]

Sensual, emotional and intuitive, all the images of what the narrator could have been if she had stayed behind interconnect in a fluid song celebrating life, not classified in square little boxes, not bound by syntactic norms. But the text returns to drab reality, the real voice swallowing the dream, echoing Kundera: 'this lightness of being is perfectly unbearable. Who can accept the idea of having only one life?'[100] After the foray into creative flexibility, resisting the stifling norms of syntax, subverting accepted roles, letting imagination loose, the ambivalence afforded by exile and its concomitant split realities, identities, linguistic perception recalls Kristeva's stranger, forever with a foot in the adoptive country and the other in the native land.

## 4. Conclusion

Allowing fragments only to appear not to unravel the threatening strands of identity, the narration in *Losing North* describes dislocation in universalising statements. By doing so, the script suppresses an understanding that linguistic shortcomings originate in a radical disruption.[101] Somehow, the gaps effected by the traumatic break with the maternal unsettle the narrative voice of *Losing North* in such a manner that it causes a rift in the projected sense of self, resulting in a repetitive insistence on exclusive identities rather than an enriching intertwining forming a sensual/intellectual continuum. Under the guise of universalisation, the textual voice raises the issues of combining languages and cultures, but insists on limiting presentations of realities through negation, hiding behind impersonal forms to avoid tackling the trauma head on.[102] Contrary to *The Goldberg Variations* where Huston says '*I* for thirty different people', in *Nord perdu*, the narrative shuns the 'I' substantially and drowns itself in the universal, indefinite pronoun 'on' (one)—dispassionately avoiding a textual mirror of inner angst.[103] In *Losing North*, the pronoun *on* (one) is translated as *you*. But with both versions, even when the text addresses its readers, the narrative voice hides behind the 'you' or 'we', in an effort at distancing the self. An overwhelming disruption with the separation from the maternal and the ensuing loneliness and kleinian self-guilt leads to the narrative voice's marginalising and even effacing records of any past unitary sense. The universalising tendency of the textual voice quite likely translates the desire to belong, to be like others, while the negations of reality correspond to the lack, the loss. Trauma filters in through linguistic turns of phrases and, particularly, through omissions[104] and negations in the text. A first attempt to explore the effects of trauma, albeit indirectly or unconsciously, as if they have not been assimilated into full cognition yet, the text glints here and there, embracing liberating views that empower the emotional. Language is used tentatively, not exposing truth as such. The text does not offer testimony; it points towards vaguely delineated '*action* that exceeds any substantialised significance' and '*impact* that dynamically explodes any conceptual reifications and any constative delimitations'.[105]

Yet several signs—the recovery of ancestry, the appeal of the natural, the realisation that freedom and restraint may be combined—indicate that the north and the south can be reunited by agreeing to 'acquiesce and embrace what has happened and to renounce continuing anger about it'.[106] Can a true voice emerge from *Nord perdu*?

> For years now, in both my writing and teaching, I've been speaking out against the Sartrian model of self-engendering the 'all-culture' stance that declares: *I am a rational, sovereign, free and autonomous adult, entirely the product of my own will.*[107]

The text adds: 'Although . . . I've often spoken out against this model, I must admit that it has also been my own'.[108] Contradictions abound, but having somehow engaged in analysis of the self in a manner that recalls the theories of Freud, Klein, Winnicott, Bion and Kristeva, the text has sought forgiveness as Kristeva describes in *La haine et le pardon*, that is, not by seeking to erase its unease but by securing meaning, opening up to new beginnings, engendering new openings enabled by transfer and interpretation; self-critical awareness might open eyes and pave ways for more flexible perceptions of multifaceted realities and acceptance of self within an unbearable lightness of being. Pursuing the lost by reshaping and recharging depressive discourse to seek meaning for it, Huston's writing deals with the loss, trying to sublimate it by looking at its effects, naming it by circling it closer and closer, eventually identifying it so as to come to terms with it in the future by working through grief. In so doing she helps her readers work through their own in bibliotherapeutic fashion, just as the entire essays collected in this book create meaning of traumas by revisiting them and discussing their variegated features.

## Notes

[1] Nancy Huston, *Losing North: Musings on Land, Tongue and Self* (Toronto: MacArthur & Co, 2002). Wherever the argumentation requires the use of the French text, reference will be made to *Nord perdu*. Nancy Huston, *Nord perdu suivi de Douze France* (Arles: Actes Sud/Leméac, 1999).

[2] Though the voice heard does not belong to a fictional character but to the author of the essay, critical comments on behavioural or psychological responses do not consist in firm allegations but only point to possible psychoanalytical interpretations of the textual transmission. The author may meditate on her own experiences, but the text only presents the reflections of a persona rather than a case study of a flesh-and-blood individual in therapy. In literary studies, as Berman notes, '[t]he unique contribution of psychoanalysis may not be discovering objectively the true unconscious content of works of art, but rather enriching the exploration of the potential transitional space evolving between artist, work of art and readers or viewers, enhancing our sensitivity to multiple meanings and complex emotional influences of art.' Emanuel Berman, 'Reader and Story, Viewer and Film: On Transference and Interpretation', *International Journal of Psychoanalysis* 84 (2003):119-29.

[3] Huston, *Losing North*, n.p.

[4] Sigmund Freud, 'Beyond the Pleasure Principle', *The Complete Psychological Works of Sigmund Freud* XVIII, trans. James Stratchey (London: Hogarth Press, 1920-22), 1-64.

[5] Sigmund Freud, 'Beyond the Pleasure Principle', 288.

[6] Sigmund Freud, 'Mourning and Melancholia', *The Complete Psychological Works of Sigmund Freud*, XIV, trans. James Strachey (London: Hogarth Press, 1915), 237-58.

[7] Ibid.

[8] See Melanie Klein, 'Note on Some Schizoid Mechanisms', *Envy and Gratitude and Other Works 1946-1963* (London: Hogarth and the Institute of Psycho-Analysis, 1975), 1-24; Melanie Klein, 'On the Theory of Anxiety and Guilt', *Developments in Psycho-Analysis*, ed. Joan Rivière, preface Ernest Jones (London: Hogarth and the Institute of Psycho-Analysis, 1952), 271-291.

[9] For more information on psychic absence and the 'dead mother', see André Green, 'The Dead Mother', *Life Narcissism, Death Narcissism*, trans. Andrew Weller (London and New York: Free Associations Books, 2001), 170-200.

[10] Huston, *Losing North*, 88.

[11] Donald W. Winnicott, 'Ego Distortion in Terms of *True and False Self*', *The Maturational Process and the Facilitating Environment: Studies in the Theory of Emotional Development* (New York: International University Press, 1965), 140-152.

[12] Ibid.

[13] Donald W. Winnicott, 'The Theory of the Parent-Infant Relationship', *International Journal of Psycho-Analysis* 41 (1960): 585-95.

[14] Donald W. Winnicott, 'Mind and Its Relation to the Psyche-Soma', *Through Paediatrics to Psycho-Analysis* (London: The Hogarth Press and the Institute of Psycho-Analysis, 1975), 243-54.

[15] Wilfred R. Bion, 'Attacks on Linking', *International Journal of Psycho-Analysis* 40 (1959): 308-15.

[16] Julia Kristeva, *Strangers to Ourselves*, trans. Leon S. Roudiez (New York: Columbia U.P., 1991).

[17] Julia Kristeva, *Strangers to Ourselves*, 5.

[18] Julia Kristeva, *Strangers to Ourselves*.

[19] Freud, 'Mourning and Melancholia', 237-258.

[20] Julia Kristeva, *Strangers to Ourselves*.

[21] Ibid.

[22] Julia Kristeva, *Strangers to Ourselves*, 16.

[23] Huston, *Losing North*, 96.

[24] Julia Kristeva, *Black Sun: Depression and Melancholia*, trans. Leon S. Roudiez (New York: Columbia University Press, 1989).

[25] Julia Kristeva, *La haine et le pardon* (Paris: Fayard, 2005).

[26] Ibid.

[27] Julia Kristeva, *Black Sun*, 97.

[28] Julia Kristeva, *La haine et le pardon*, 373.

[29] Read in both its French and English versions (first the French in 1999, then the English in 2002), the text caused pleasure and laughter in me at some of the realities described and recognised as familiar. In 2001, when embarking on a preliminary critical pursuit that required translation of some parts, I started perceiving patterns of erasure left unnoticed at the first reading. Engaging deconstructively with both the text and its translation stressed the disappearance of the emotional, confirmed today with new readings for this specific project.

[30] Jacqueline Rose, 'Negativity in the Work of Melanie Klein', *Reading Melanie Klein*, eds. Lindsey Stonebridge and John Phillips (London and New York: Routledge, 1998. 127-59), 128.

[31] Derrida's word play and tracing oppose an essentialist view of identity. He considers any aspect of human experience in comparison and connection to related others and finally encompasses the opposites to the original proposition. The breaking down and crossing of boundaries enable exchanges that embrace contraries instead of seeking to exclude or 'solve' them. See Jacques Derrida, 'Freud et la scène de l'écriture', *L'Ecriture et la différence* (Paris: Seuil: 1967). 293-340; Jacques Derrida, 'La structure, le signe et le jeu dans le discours des

sciences humaines', *L'Ecriture et la différence*, (Paris: Seuil, 1967), 409-28; and Jacques Derrida, 'La différance', *Théorie d'ensemble* (Paris: Seuil, 1968), 43-68.

[32] Indirect statements corroborate the impression that the original text keeps the maternal, or the emotional, at bay: 'For my part, I prefer French to English in intellectual conversations, interviews, colloquia—linguistic situations which call upon concepts and categories learned during my adult life' (Huston, *Losing North*, 47). French is 'less emotion-fraught, and therefore less dangerous, than my mother tongue. It was cold, and I approached it coldly. It was a smooth, homogeneous, neutral substance, with no personal associations whatsoever' (Huston, *Losing North*, 149). Huston's choice of French allows her to erase emotions regarding traumatic events.

[33] For more information on Jauss' approach, see Hans Robert Jauss, 'Literary History as a Challenge to Literary Theory', *New Literary Theory* 2 (1970): 7-37.

[34] As Jauss saw any text as subject to the cultural perception of readership at the time of conception and as always more than the readership would make of it at any point in time, he would have understood deconstruction as the results of a particular interpreter's tracing, not as the indication of the potential for deconstruction in a word. See Jauss, 'Literary History', 7-37.

[35] Towards the end of the narrative, though, the speaker does elaborate on a lively fantasy addressing sensual and affective planes, discussed later on.

[36] See Derrida, 'La différance', 43-68.

[37] Huston, *Losing North*, 1.

[38] Huston, *Nord perdu*, 11. Incidentally, the text does allude to the child being sent with her future stepmother to Germany where she experienced estrangement reinforcing the original loss.

[39] On account of her western approach to child-raising, Klein states that the 'fundamental fear of loss' is 'predetermined . . . in the infant from the experience of birth' [Melanie Klein, 'The Emotional Life and Ego-Development of the Infant with Special Reference to the Depressive Position', *Freud-Klein Controversies 1941-45*, eds. Pearl King and Riccardo Steiner (London and New York: Routledge in Association with the Institute of Psycho-Analysis, 1991. 752-97), 763-764. The child soon begins to associate the absence of the mother first with frustration and hatred [Melanie Klein, 'On Observing the Behaviour of Young Infants', *Developments in Psycho-Analysis*, ed, Joan Rivière, preface Ernest Jones, (London: Hogarth and the Institute of Psycho-Analysis, 1952. 237-70), 237]. The child then relates the absence to guilt and anxiety that leads to self-hatred (Klein, 'On the Theory of Anxiety and Guilt', 281-189).

[40] Freud, 'Mourning and Melancholia', 237-258.

[41] For melancholic self-hate, see Freud, 'Mourning and Melancholia', 237-258. For the evolution into exile, see Kristeva, *Stranger to Ourselves*. In her chapter on

Beckett's *Not* I, Antropova observes the same type of approach when the tears that Mouth sheds signal 'loneliness, suffering and pain' understandable 'as a voluntary exile from life and from memory or as a kind of self-punishment for her non-existent sins'.

[42] Huston, *Losing North*, 2.

[43] Bion, 'Attacks on linking'.

[44] Traditionally, the North of the human being stands for the head, the intellect, the orderly directions of consciousness and Chetwynd relates the North to indifference, lack of warmth and love [Tom Chetwynd, *A Dictionary for Dreamers* (London, Glasgow, Toronto, Sidney, Auckland: Collins, 1972), 130]. According to Ackroyd, it even connotes frigidity, the very negation of passion, the South, the body [Eric Ackroyd, *A Dictionary of Symbols* (London: Blanford, 1993), 234].

[45] Winnicott, 'Ego Distortion in Terms of *True and False Self*', 140-152.

[46] All grammar rules in French point to the trivialisation of the feminine. Given two nouns in a sentence, one feminine, the other masculine, the male gender governs the verb and all the adjectives; even if the nouns in the feminine outnumber those in the masculine, the rule applies. In a like manner, the indefinite pronoun *on* (one) tends to signify a masculine referent even if technically it can refer to a feminine subject. Arguing the same trivialisation of the female in the English language, Casey Miller and Kate Swift noted in their 1990 speech to the Association of American University Professors, entitled 'Who's in Charge of the English Language?', that the generic terms for nouns and pronouns are male, bonding with the male terms against the female ones [Casey Miller, and Kate Swift, 'Who's in Charge of the English Language', *Norton Reader: An Anthology of Nonfiction Prose*, eds. Linda H. Peterson et al, Shorter tenth edition, (New York and London: Norton, 2000. 289-94), 291-292]. They also remarked on the 'female-negative-trivial' versus 'male-positive-important' syndrome (290). Both considerations hold for French as well, not to speak of numerous other languages. For an ample discussion of trivialisation, see Casey Miller, and Kate Swift, *Words and Women*, (Garden City: Anchor Books, 1977),16-35.

[47] Huston, *Nord perdu*, 12; 'une chose qui ne se fait pas' translates literally as 'a thing that is not done'.

[48] Klein, 'On the Theory of Anxiety and Guilt', 281.

[49] Derrida, 'La structure, le signe et le jeu dans le discours des sciences humaines', 410-411.

[50] Tom Chetwynd, *A Dictionary for Dreamers* (London, Glasgow, Toronto, Sidney, Auckland: Collins, 1972), 150.

[51] Ibid.

[52] Eric Ackroyd, *A Dictionary of Dream Symbols* (London: Blanford, 1993), 305.

[53] Bion, 'Attacks on Linking'; Winnicott, 'Mind and its Relation to the Psyche-Soma'.

[54] Rivière, Joan Rivière, 'On the Genesis of Psychical Conflict in Earliest Infancy', *Developments in Psycho-Analysis*, ed. Joan Rivière, preface Ernest Jones, (London: Hogarth and the Psycho-Analytical Institute, 1952. 37-66), 45.

[55] Winnicott, 'Ego Distortion in Terms of *True and False Self*', 140-152.

[56] Ibid.

[57] Kristeva, *Strangers to Ourselves*, 39.

[58] Though the author's own translation of the text into English allows itself to slip into diglossia, it does so only occasionally where the translation of a French term into English would not convey the French counterpart or reality.

[59] Kristeva, *Strangers to Ourselves*, 32.

[60] Huston, *Losing North*, 2-3.

[61] Bion, 'Attacks on Linking'.

[62] *Robert et Collins: Dictionnaire français-anglais/français-anglais*, 5th edition (Paris: Dictionnaires Le Robert / Glasgow: HarperCollins, 1985.

[63] Winnicott, 'Ego Distortion in Terms of *True and False Self*'.

[64] Huston, *Losing North*, 3.

[65] Freud, 'Mourning and Melancholia'.

[66] Huston, *Losing North*, 3.

[67] Huston, *Losing North*, 31.

[68] Bion, 'Attacks on Linking'.

[69] Huston's circumscription or erasure of the traumatic bears similarity with the impulse to give a beautified representation of Polyxena's corpse in spite of its gruesome vision of it that Hughes refers to in her chapter on *Hecuba*. In this context, Hughes mentions LaCapra's caution against beautifying the traumatic.

[70] Huston, *Losing North*, 19; Winnicott, 'Ego Distortion in Terms of *True and False Self*'.

[71] Eva Hoffman, *Lost in Translation: A Life in a New Language* (New York and London: Penguin, 1989), n.p.

[72] Derrida, 'La structure, le signe et le jeu dans le discours des sciences humaines', 410.

[73] The relevant passage mentioning the narrator's children, for the first and virtually only time, reads as follows: '. . . everyone in the family is French, but some of us are more French than others. (Thanks to the relatively low amount of melanin in the pigmentation of their skin, the French-born offspring of a Canadian female and a Bulgarian male find it easy to be French)'. Huston, *Losing North*, 6.

[74] Huston, *Losing North*, 8. This quotation must be counterbalanced by another that stresses the disadvantage of the richness: 'That's what exile is about.

Mutilation. Guilt. Self-Censorship. You communicate with others by using either the child or the adult part of yourself. Never both'. Huston, *Losing North*, 12.

[75] Huston, *Losing North*, 6-7.

[76] The text notes, 'I often have the feeling that they 'sleep apart' in my brain. . . . distinct, hierarchized'; the mother tongue 'enfolds and envelops' the child; the second language must be tamed, appropriated as a second identity. Huston, *Losing North*, 47.

[77] Aritha van Herk, 'Writing the Immigrant Self: Disguise and Damnation', *In/Visible Ink: Crypto-Frictions*, The Writer as Critic Series 3 (Edmonton: NeWest, 1991), 174.

[78] The passage reads as follows: 'You quit the "tourist" when, in a foreign country, you experience new forms of despondency and distress. (One December in Paris, having just had my heart broken, I purchased a giant Suchard chocolate bar in a bakery and ate every square of it as I wandered tearfully through the freezing grey streets of the thirteenth *arrondissement*). Huston, *Losing North*, 70.

[79] Huston, *Losing North*, 49-50; Melanie Klein, *Envy and Gratitude and Other Works 1946-1963* (London: Hogarth and the Institute of Psycho-Analysis, 1975).

[80] Huston, *Losing North*, 50.

[81] Kristeva, *Strangers to Ourselves*.

[82] Huston, *Losing North*, 50.

[83] Huston, *Losing North*, 50.

[84] Klein's theory of speech production highlights the process followed: internalising the loss and separation from the mother, the child expresses its first affective responses in the mother tongue, for affections earn their symbols in it. See Melanie Klein, 'The Emotional Life and Ego-Development of the Infant with Special Reference to the Depressive Position', 222; Klein, 'On Observing the Behaviour of Young Infants' 258-259. Permanent loss of the mother results in distanciation from the mother tongue and the emotions it encourages. Such distanciation bears similarity with the aesthetic distance Hughes records in the choice of mythic elements to allude to distressing events that would otherwise affect the audience too much.

[85] Suzette A. Henke, *Shattered Subjects: Trauma and Testimony in Women's Life-Writing* (New York: St. Martin's Press, 2000), xiii. Akin to bibliotherapy, therapy with the help of texts, the scripto-therapeutic value of *Losing North* calls to mind the impact of *Hecuba* in affecting the audience turned into witnesses of trauma as Hughes remarks. In the same fashion, *Losing North* allows the exiles of the heart to experience the impact of their own trauma at a remove, and in so doing decoding their own patterns of erasure.

[86] Huston's essay thus calls to mind *Hecuba* that, in her chapter, Hughes also considers 'a first step toward working through' trauma through repetition.

[87] Nancy Huston, *Slow Emergencies* (Boston, New York, Toronto and London: Little, Brown and Co, 1996).

[88] Huston, *Losing North*, 82, 83.

[89] Huston, *Losing North*, 6, 83, 87.

[90] Sigmund Freud, 'Beyond the Pleasure Principle', 13.

[91] Shoshana Felman, 'Education and Crisis', *Trauma: Explorations in Memory*, ed. Cathy Caruth (Baltimore and London: John Hopkins University Press, 1995. 13-60), 19, 15.

[92] Huston, *Losing North*, 87.

[93] Huston, *Losing North*, 87-88.

[94] Kristeva, *Strangers to Ourselves*; Huston, *Losing North*, 89.

[95] Huston, *Losing North*, 89.

[96] Kristeva, *Strangers to Ourselves*, n.p.

[97] Huston, *Losing North*, 11.

[98] Huston, *Losing North*, 91.

[99] Huston, *Losing North*, 94-95.

[100] Huston, *Losing North*, 96.

[101] This calls to mind Antropova's and Hughes' findings with respectively Mouth and Hecuba. In their chapters, Antropova and Hughes note the disempowering character of language that fails to convey the traumatic. Hughes marks that Hecuba compensates for the failure of language by opting for action.

[102] The consideration about negation refers to Sigmund Freud, 'Negation', *The Complete Psychological Works of Sigmund Freud* XIX, trans. James Strachey. London: Hogarth Press, 1925), 235-239.

[103] Nancy Huston, *The Goldberg Variations* (Montreal: Nuage Editions, 1996); Nancy Huston, Interview with Catherine Argand [in French], *L'express France,* 2001, Accessed April 2010, http://www.lexpress.fr/culture/livre/nancy-huston_804287.html. The scope of this work does not allow to compare, let alone elaborate on the differences of, the French and English versions. Suffice it to say that by freeing the English narrator of specific linguistic constraints, *Losing North* loses some of the intricacies inherent in cultural adjustment. However, the reverberating echo the French text has found in so many exiles would have been lost to many non-Francophones if the author had not translated it into English. Though the speaker in Huston shuns the first-person pronoun extensively, she does not so throughout in the alienating manner that Antropova records in her chapter on Beckett's *Not I*.

[104] Huston's omissions and negations call to mind Antropova's consideration of the omissions, 'gaps, holes, and porosity' in her chapter on Beckett's *Not I*, whose title I agree with her offers a clear example of negation that shouts out trauma.

[105] Shoshana Felman, 'Education and Crisis', 17.

[106] Henry Krystal, 'Trauma and Aging: A Thirty-Year Follow-Up', *Trauma: Explorations in Memory*, ed. Cathy Caruth (Baltimore and London: John Hopkins Press, 1995. 76-99), 83.
[107] Huston, *Losing North*, 51.
[108] Huston, *Losing North*, 53.

# Bibliography

Ackroyd, Eric. *A Dictionary of Dream Symbols*. London: Blanford, 1993.

Berman, Emanuel. 'Reader and Story, Viewer and Film: On Transference and Interpretation'. *International Journal of Psychoanalysis* 84 (2003):119-29.

Bion, Wilfred R. 'Attacks on Linking'. *International Journal of Psycho-Analysis* 40 (1959): 308-15.

Chetwynd, Tom. *A Dictionary for Dreamers*. London, Glasgow, Toronto, Sidney, Auckland: Collins, 1972.

Derrida, Jacques. 'Freud et la scène de l'écriture'. *L'Ecriture et la différence*. Paris: Seuil: 1967.

———. 'La structure, le signe et le jeu dans le discours des sciences humaines'. *L'Ecriture et la différence*. Paris: Seuil, 1967.

———. 'La différance'. *Théorie d'ensemble*. Paris: Seuil, 1968.

Felman, Shoshana. 'Education and Crisis'. *Trauma: Explorations in Memory*, edited by Cathy Caruth, 13-60. Baltimore and London: John Hopkins University Press, 1995.

Freud, Sigmund. 'Beyond the Pleasure Principle'. *The Complete Psychological Works of Sigmund Freud* XVIII. Translated by James Strachey. London: Hogarth Press, 1920-22.

———. 'Mourning and Melancholia'. *The Complete Psychological Works of Sigmund Freud*, XIV. Translated by James Strachey. London: Hogarth Press, 1915.

Green, André. 'The Dead Mother'. *Life Narcissism, Death Narcissism*. Translated by Andrew Weller. London and New York: Free Associations Books, 2001.

Henke, Suzette A. *Shattered Subjects: Trauma and Testimony in Women's Life-Writing*. New York: St. Martin's Press, 2000.

Hoffman, Eva. *Lost in Translation: A Life in a New Language*. New York and London: Penguin, 1989.

Huston, Nancy. *Slow Emergencies*. Boston, New York, Toronto and London: Little, Brown and Co, 1996.

———. The *Goldberg Variations*. Montreal: Nuage Editions, 1996.

———. *Nord perdu* suivi de *Douze France*. Arles: Actes Sud/Léméac, 1999.

———. Interview with Catherine Argand [in French]. *L'express France*. 2001. Accessed April 2010.
http://www.lexpress.fr/culture/livre/nancy-huston_804287.html/.

———. *Losing North: Musings on Land, Tongue and Self.* Toronto: MacArthur & Co, 2002.

Jauss, Hans Robert. 'Literary History as a Challenge to Literary Theory'. *New Literary Theory* 2 (1970): 7-37.

Klein, Melanie. 'Note on Some Schizoid Mechanisms'. *Envy and Gratitude and Other Works 1946-1963*. London: Hogarth and the Institute of Psycho-Analysis, 1975 [1946].

———. 'On Observing the Behaviour of Young Infants'. *Developments in Psycho-Analysis*, edited by Joan Rivière, 237-70. London: Hogarth and the Institute of Psycho-Analysis, 1952a.

———. 'On the Theory of Anxiety and Guilt'. *Developments in Psycho-Analysis*, edited by Joan Rivière, 271-291. London: Hogarth and the Institute of Psycho-Analysis, 1952b.

———. 'The Emotional Life and Ego-Development of the Infant with Special Reference to the Depressive Position'. *Freud-Klein Controversies 1941-45*, edited by Pearl King and Riccardo Steiner, 752-797. London and New York: Routledge in Association with the Institute of Psycho-Analysis, 1991 [1944].

─────. *Envy and Gratitude and Other Works 1946-1963*. London: Hogarth and the Institute of Psycho-Analysis, 1975.

─────. 'Some Theoretical Conclusions Regarding the Emotional Life of the Infant'. *Developments in Psycho-Analysis*, edited by Joan Rivière, 198-236. International Psycho-Analytical Library Series, 43. London: Hogarth and the Institute of Psycho-Analysis, 1952c.

Kristeva, Julia. *Black Sun: Depression and Melancholia.* Translated by Leon S. Roudiez. New York: Columbia University Press, 1989.

─────. *La Haine et le pardon*. Paris: Fayard, 2005.

─────. *Strangers to Ourselves*. Translated by Leon S. Roudiez. European Perspectives series. New York: Columbia U.P, 1991.

Krystal, Henry. 'Trauma and Aging: A Thirty-Year Follow-Up'. *Trauma: Explorations in Memory*, edited by Cathy Caruth, 76-99. Baltimore and London: John Hopkins Press, 1995.

Miller, Casey, and Kate Swift. 'Who's in Charge of the English Language'. *Norton Reader: An Anthology of Nonfiction Prose*, edited by Caesar R. Blake, Hubert M. English, Joan E. Hartman, Alan B. Howes, Robert T. Lenghan, Leo F. MacNamara, Linda H. Peterson, and James Rosier, 289-294. 10th edition. New York and London: Norton, 2000.

─────. *Words and Women*. Garden City: Anchor Books, 1977.

Rose, Jacqueline. 'Negativity in the Work of Melanie Klein'. *Reading Melanie Klein*, edited by Lindsey Stonebridge and John Phillips, 127-159. London and New York: Routledge, 1998.

van Herk, Aritha. 'Writing the Immigrant Self: Disguise and Damnation'. *In/Visible Ink: Crypto-Frictions.* The Writer as Critic Series 3, 173-88. Edmonton: NeWest, 1991.

Winnicott, Donald W. 'Ego Distortion in Terms of *True and False Self*'. *The Maturational Process and the Facilitating Environment: Studies in the Theory of Emotional Development*. New York: International University Press, 1965 [1960].

————. 'Mind and Its Relation to the Psyche-Soma'. *Through Paediatrics to Psycho-Analysis.* London: The Hogarth Press and the Institute of Psycho-Analysis, 1975 [1949].

————. 'The Theory of the Parent-Infant Relationship'. *International Journal of Psycho-Analysis* 41 (1960): 585-95.

**Danielle Schaub** is Associate Professor at Oranim, the Academic College of Education in Israel (where she teaches, among others, Canadian Literature) and Adjunct Professor at the University of Alberta in Canada. Her publications include *Precarious Present, Promising Future? Ehtnicity and Identities in Canadian Literature* (1996), a monograph on Mavis Gallant (1998), *Mapping Canadian Cultural Space: Essays on Canadian Literature* (2000), *Identity, Community, Nation: Essays on Canadian Literature* (2004), *Reading Writers Reading: Canadian Authors' Reflections* (2006), *Interior Views: Photopoetry* (2009) and *Tissage et métissage dans l'oeuvre de Gérad Etienne* (2013). Influenced by her training in bibliotherapy, her research currently focuses on literary representations of trauma and psychoanalytic interpretations of filmic works.

# 'Stigmatized body in pain...what?...who?...no!...she!' Samuel Beckett's *Not I*

## Svetlana Antropova

**Abstract**

A faintly lit tiny mouth hovering above the stage in darkness, and talking incessantly, is the stage image of Beckett's most traumatic play *Not I* (1972). The mouth/language becomes the protagonist of this short play, where even the title (*Not I*) reflects the impossibility of coming to terms with one's identity. Mouth never uses the first-person singular pronoun in her disturbed narration, but uses the pronoun 'she' as a device of alienation from something dreadful that happened to her. Sexual abuse brings about the worst trauma of all – the loss of identity. Here, Mouth may be considered a fragmentary identity suspended in the nightmarish stage presence, as both an organ of speech and an organ of sex. The language of trauma records a traumatic event not on a linguistic, but on a somatosensory level. Unable to reconstruct such an event coherently, she is compelled to tell it again and again, since she can only survive through narration. Different elements of trauma come into view here: failure of personalization, dissociation, regression, prevalence of images and sensations, and continuous flashbacks of memory. Mouth's continuous logorrhoea affects the audience's perception and forces them to witness the trauma of sexual abuse, also inscribed in the physical stage language: a disembodied mouth may resemble a vagina. In analysing the language of trauma I apply the recent teachings on memory and trauma to the analysis of traumatic memories in *Not I*.

**Key Words:** Identity, ABM, temporal landmarks, failure of personalization, PTSD, diachronic disunity, postmodern theatre, body fragmentation.

\*\*\*\*\*

## 1. Introduction

Many of Samuel Beckett's plays embody memory and specifically trauma but probably the most traumatic in both form and content is *Not I*. Even the title of the play points to trauma with the negation of self and the impossibility or reluctance to see or to remember, making pun on the same pronunciation of 'eye' and 'I'. The act of seeing gains extreme importance in the play on multiple levels. The vicarious trauma of watching affects the audience.[1] In *Not I*, Samuel Beckett intends to shock and bereave the audience with Mouth's logorrhoea:

> I hear [Mouth] breathless, urgent, feverish, rhythmic, panting along, without undue concern with intelligibility. Addressed less

to the understanding than to the nerves of the audience which
should in a sense *'share her bewilderment'*.[2]

The image of a flickering mouth, a shadowed figure of a silent Auditor and the
theatre submerged in darkness — all contribute to the enhanced feeling of
confusion and, probably, fear on part of the audience. Furthermore, the
minimalistic setting of the play creates a claustrophobic atmosphere in the theatre:
we cannot but watch the fragmented mouth uttering words at neck-breaking speed.
In several of his plays Beckett staged fragmented bodies, but Mouth in *Not I* is the
highlight of fragmentation, the play an enigma in itself: no questions asked and no
answers provided. As always with Samuel Beckett various readings of the play
exist, one of which psychological/psychoanalytical, taking into consideration that
Mouth tries to make her chaotic confession to silent Auditor. I propose to treat this
play as a theatrical psychoanalytic session. As Samuel Beckett himself had to
undertake psychoanalytical sessions with Dr. Bion in London in 1937,[3] he was
familiar with the whole procedure. And Mouth appears on stage to tell her never-
narrated story, which starts with the moment of her birth.

In order to prove the aforementioned, the current analysis deals with the
following aspects of the play: the visual image of Mouth, the language of troubled
self/ves as the result of diachronic disunity, and the artistic representation of
sexual abuse. A phenomenological method applies to the analysis of the stage
language and images just as the theory of trauma and its impact on memory (Freud,
Caruth, Mollon, Felman and Laub, etc.), as well as the recent findings on memory,
discussed in Beike, Lampinen and Behren's edition.

## 2. The Analysis of Visual Onstage Image

As far as the physical language of the play, there are only three elements
present: darkness enveloping Mouth and the audience, Mouth and a silent Auditor
backstage wearing a djelaba, which makes all of them prominent and significant to
the understanding of the play. Nevertheless, Mouth is the centre of attention, for
two major reasons. Firstly, it stands out against the stage darkness, illuminated by
the spotlight from below; and secondly, Mouth is the only speaker of the play.
Ruby Cohn writes, 'Words come to and through She only in the dark, and in a
darkened theatre the spotlit mouth offers us an unparalleled experience'.[4] The
fragmented body image shocks the audience and inevitably holds their gaze,
making them aware of their own intact bodies. And during the whole performance
the spectators are bewildered at Mouth's lack of body and her incoherent stream of
words. So what is Mouth: a character or a prop? What is she supposed to mean if
any meaning can be attached? The analysis of the visual onstage image clarifies
this.

Deprived of body, sight and movement, Mouth becomes a grotesque figure
onstage: the lips move, trying to articulate words and spitting saliva; the mouth

gulps for air, which obviously suggests a human breathing body (a part of the body) and therefore a character. Mouth is too aware of 'all those contortions without which . . . no speech possible'.[5] This excruciatingly physical image of Mouth becomes a body in pain.[6] She cannot but talk non-stop, tortured by the flashbacks of her memories and by constant buzzing, presumably, of 'something she had to tell' in her skull. Even acting out Mouth seems to be a terrifying experience. Billie Whitelaw, who performed Mouth at the Royal Court production in 1972, said: 'The play had touched terrors within me that I have never come to terms with'.[7] Mouth in turn is fragmented both physically and psychically, transformed into a bleeding wound onstage. From the very beginning the onstage image rejects any possibility of cure. Therefore, in *Not I*, Mouth may be perceived as the symbol of trauma and body disintegration.

As a static onstage mouth forms part of the physical stage language and acquires more meanings in *Not I*, we may consider it a prop. Visually a mouth may represent a hole, opening and closing relentlessly. So the audience face omission from the very beginning of the play; and the play itself is more concerned with gaps, holes and porosity both in the visual image and in the speech.[8] Mouth's staccato speech defies the very notion of autobiographic memory; 'I' erased from the speech disappears as a doer or constituter of memory, and instead the memories of the impersonal 'she' are offered in the form of flashbacks of emotions and sensations. Consequently, Mouth becomes the form and content of this play. Suspended in the air and lit from below, it brings forth several associations: a tiny hole, vagina, which links it to the trauma of sexual abuse, and even anus — all of these associations supported by the text of the play.

Lacking a body, the mouth takes on other compensatory bodily functions: in this play it becomes a fragment of identity (representing whole), the organ of breathing, speech expulsion organ (the preposition 'out' made prominent in the play) and since the whole play has to do with remembering, it takes on the role of a memory organ. But the process of remembering seems to entail the process of self-mutilation and even self-consumption. Mouth may be devoured by the surrounding darkness: when Mouth closes her mouth she disappears into the darkness of the stage. Consequently, Mouth's presence is already made absence, a kind of 'god-forsaken hole'[9] onstage.

From a psychoanalytical point of view, the mouth serves as an important organ from the time of our very birth, normally associated with the process of eating, thus with nutrition and life *per se*. Psychoanalysts deal with the eating process in relation to the self and memory. Ellmann points out that 'through eating the subject learns to take control over what can be taken into the body from outside and to demarcate the boundaries of his or her own body'.[10] Therefore, eating marks a difference between the inside and the outside of a body; it points to a distinction between self and other. By digesting food we assimilate what is other to the self. On the contrary, the image of a constipated body points both to the blockage of communication and to the almost physical need to allow repressed emotions to emerge, to pass through openings and holes. Robson suggests that 'Psychoanalysis mobilizes a leaky body, a body from which uncontrolled words and feelings can pour, in a different sort of narrative of self'.[11] If we take Mouth for a fragment of an identity, we may talk about both memory repression and her almost physical need to spit out memories 'undigested', her speech becoming a constant logorrhoea of memory fragments. And since her whole body has vanished, Mouth depends on what is left – the words. She admits that speaking constitutes her existence: 'the whole being ... hanging on its words'.[12] Mouth needs words for her existence as much as breathing to exist. Rodriguez-Gago writes that 'Beckett's late plays create a single aural visual body which is the product of a remembered, or misremembered, story told usually by a decrepit, or malfunctioning body'.[13]

The visual image of Mouth highlights a process of digestion gone awry; it points to the impossibility of remembering the past in narrative, and to the simultaneous impossibility of forgetting. The mouth is turned into a speech expulsion organ unable of assimilation.

## 3.  The Language of Troubled Self/ves

> In Plato, speech or *logos* gives us access to Truth; in Rousseau, speech or *parole* gives us access to nature [...]; and in Husserl speech or *phone* gives us access to the Self.[14]

In the play, where Mouth is an 'absolute speaker',[15] her voice occupies the soundscape of the theatre and is the centre of attention. Although the voice comes from Mouth, at first she cannot recognize the voice as her own: 'realized ... words were coming ... imagine! ... words were coming ... a voice she didn't recognize ...'.[16] During the whole play Mouth stubbornly rejects the pronoun 'I', substituting it by the impersonal 'she.' The failure of personalization destabilizes our perception, but at the same time, 'she' also gives stability to the narration and roots Mouth in femininity. We understand that the whole story deals with a girl/woman and something dreadful that happened to her. Narrating in the third person singular functions as an alienation device, used by people with post-traumatic stress disorder (PTSD). Mouth is pathologically incapable of accepting the pronoun 'I' and therefore her memories and her self. She feverishly repeats during the whole performance: 'what? ... who? ... no! ... she!'.[17] Furthermore, the failure of personalization may also serve as a self-negation technique, since it is definitely easier to talk about our past traumas as an observer than as a participant. Mouth tries to distance herself from what she used to be. Paradoxically, the effect of distancing does not help Mouth to remember and to assimilate her memories; the failure of personalization only further shatters her understanding of the self. Thus, her speech is pregnant with unanswered questions. The interrogative pronouns, a stable presence in her speech, may be attributed to an internal dialogue going on within her and, consequently, to her split identity:

> *Not I* further widens the distance between self-narration and identity by focusing on the gap between the enunciating subject and the enunciated subject and the uncertainty about who is saying what to whom.[18]

At the same time the recurring interrogative pronouns conjure up a possibility of invisible and non-heard voices, with which Mouth communicates. In *Beyond the Pleasure Principle*, Freud attributes the ability to hear voices to the symptoms of trauma or as he calls it 'traumatic neurosis',[19] later defined as PTSD. Moreover, the enveloping darkness gives way to our imagination and to the possibility of other hallucinatory presences onstage. Mouth doubts all the way what she says, as though another voice in her brain constantly corrects her: 'nothing of any note till coming up to sixty when- ... what? ... seventy? good God! ... coming up to seventy...'.[20] Jeanette Malkin proposes an internal dialogue between her 'involuntary confessional voice and the voice of resistance, refusing to reveal or denying the memories being offered'.[21] The traces of this internal dialogue are present throughout the performance. I would like to put forward the hypothesis that Mouth has various conflicting voices or fragmented traumatic identities 'inside'. These ghost voices belong to different periods of Mouth's life and instead of reconciling Mouth's memory, these past fragments disrupt her already unstable self and probably drive her mad. I suggest that repetitions-regressions of past events in Mouth's speech hold the key to these identities and form the temporal landmarks of her autobiographic memory. Skowronski, Walker and Benz[22] discuss the importance of assimilating certain important events and integrating them into our life-story in the formation of autobiographic memory (ABM). These landmarks are the periods of transition that place our identity in time and provide a unity: 'Temporal landmarks tend to form when events are both experienced in time and have personal significance';[23] thus they attribute the importance of ABM to the development of identity. Consequently, lack of temporal landmarks and chronology in our life-story lead to diachronic disunity, according to Lampinen, Odegard, and Leding.[24]

Mouth's narration rejects both unity and chronology. She cannot utter one complete sentence and constantly leaps from one memory to another. Discontinuous, all her memories overlaps and she cannot anchor them in any certain time of her life. As a result, time markers, such as reference to certain years, disappear from her speech. The latter challenges the formal concept of time. For Mouth, time as such does not exist, the concept too slippery to grasp; she uses the word 'time' in different word combinations, such as 'before its time',[25] 'just as the odd time',[26] 'that time she cried',[27] etc. Instead she uses prepositions and adverbs to anchor her memories in time. And this gives an impression of unstable memory; Mouth cannot provide temporal landmarks for her past events and therefore she scatters her memories in time. Instead of chronology, discontinuity and overlapping invade her speech:

> As is typical of many Beckett's works, each reference to biography becomes more rapid and increasingly more nebulous, making the inchoate origins of speech more discernible.[28]

Nevertheless, as during the whole play Mouth stubbornly repeats the same episodes from her past, we may consider them turning points or landmarks in her life-story. Each of these turning points represents a different Mouth, uprooted from her own unique self. Her self is shattered to pieces, the memories of which come in flashes to haunt Mouth. All of these identities are created linguistically and the words introduce them into the stage hallucinatory present. The importance of these landmarks lies in the circular structure of their remembrance. Besides, with the zooming-in effect, every time Mouth returns to one particular layer of memory she enlarges it with new memories from this life period, which Malkin defines as 'additional moments of remembrance'.[29] For instance, 'always winter some strange reason ...',[30] which has to do with Mouth's old age at Croker's Acres, later in her speech is remembered more in detail: 'once or twice a year ... always winter some strange reason ... long hours of darkness'.[31] These 'additional moments of remembrance' point to the process of remembering going on in Mouth's brain.

The play starts with the memory of birth:

> ... out ... into this world ... this world ... tiny little thing ... before its time ... in a godfor– ... what? ... girl? ... yes ... tiny little girl ... into this ... out into this ... before her time ... godforsaken hole called ... called ... no matter ... parents unknown ... unheard of ... he having vanished ... thin air ... no sooner buttoned up his breeches ... she similarly ... eight months later ... almost to the tick ... so no love ... spared that ... no love such as normally vented on the ... speechless infant ... in the home ... no ... nor indeed for that matter any of any kind ... no love of any kind ....[32]

Birth seems the most painful turning point in her life and constitutes her first identity. Rank's trauma of birth appears in the play from the very beginning; the preposition 'out' negatively points to the act of 'getting rid of'. Mouth's date of birth is actually the day of her doom. From the darkness of a womb she transforms from a tiny little girl into another tiny hole in the darkness onstage and/or the darkness of her memory. 'Spared of love' with 'just the birth cry to let her going' and born prematurely – a child was dragged out into this world. As Rank states in *El Trauma del Nacimiento*, the condition of being born a woman is not well accepted and preconditions her to the life of suffering.[33] Danielle Schaub discusses the 'loss of the child' in connection to Nancy Huston's *Losing North*, where she argues for a relationship between self-hatred and separation from the mother. Sent away 'like a neatly packed parcel'[34] and uprooted from her family and her origins, Huston experiences the childhood trauma and has an unresolved identity conflict. A child rejected by parents cannot accept her own self, which leads to self-hatred and further to disorientation and confusion mirrored by the textual voice that states: 'Your childhood stays with you all your life, no matter where you go'.[35] It seems to me that Otto Rank's trauma of birth already appears in this narrative. And Mouth, unwanted from her very birth, cannot accept her own self and the originary trauma has been haunting her for her whole life. Self-hatred and the feeling of permanent guilt may explain her dissatisfaction with her former selves and also memory repression.

The second turning point in Mouth's life is her Catholic upbringing in the orphanage, since her references to God and 'merciful waifs', as well as punishment repeat endlessly in the play: 'brought up as she had been to believe ... with the other waifs ... in a merciful...'.[36] Mouth remembers very little from that life – mostly abrupt quotes from the Bible. She has no emotional memory about this period in her life either due to its insignificance or possible memory repression. Most likely brought up sternly following God's faith, Mouth experienced the hard life in the orphanage 'spared of love'. At this period she used to believe in God and his 'tender mercies',[37] accepting punishment and penance. The allusion to punishment recurs constantly in the play: 'first thought was ... oh long after ... sudden flash ... she was being punished ... for her sins ...'.[38] But about what sins does Mouth talk? There are no memory traces of any sins in the play. I may only presume that her major sin is to be born into this world. Instead of the promised 'tender mercies' and love her life turns into a nightmare. Twice Mouth laughs at merciful God, the god who punished her at the very moment of her birth.

Then comes the moment of 'April morning', the most traumatic memory of all, which I consider must have brought about her speechlessness and suffering, and disrupted her already split self. The next turning point concerns the memory of shame and speechless resistance; and then in a flash comes her memory at court. She remembers next starting to talk again in the supermarket – her verbal rebirth. But she herself describes her new too-verbal identity as something that she cannot control. And her whole brain begs it to stop:

> now can't stop ... imagine! ... can't stop the stream ... and the whole brain begging ... something begging in the brain ... begging the mouth to stop ... pause a moment ... if only for a moment ... and no response ... as if it hadn't heard ... or

> couldn't ... couldn't pause a second ... like maddened ... all that
> together ... straining to hear ... piece it together ... and the brain
> ... raving away on its own ... trying to make sense of it ... or
> make it stop ... or in the past ... dragging up the past ... flashes
> from all over ... .[39]

The words mercilessly pour from Mouth and the brain desperately tries to silence the voice. A certain tension emerges between the words/speech and Mouth's brain/memory, as they seem to constitute two separate entities. Mouth cannot control what she says and cannot make sense of her past, since the spontaneous process of remembering comes in flashes.

Her last memory concerns old age. 'Tears on her palm'[40] in Croker's Acres create the image of loneliness, suffering and pain, taken as a voluntary exile from life and from memory or a kind of self-punishment for her non-existent sins.[41]

Whether due to the originary trauma or another traumatic experience or most probably both, Mouth has lost her own unique identity and her narrative mirrors the ongoing confusion and conflict between her multiple personalities. The latter may also constitute the landmarks of Mouth's ABM. Taking into consideration the lack of either chronology in remembrance or linking between them, we may say that the rather painful transition periods prevented an agreement between her former selves. And since ABM glues the self together, I may propose that Mouth is not only refused wholeness in body, but also deprived of selfhood.. Fragmented into many overlapping voices/identities, Mouth becomes an alien to her own self.

### 4. The Trauma of Sexual Abuse

The memory of 'April morning' predominates in Mouth's narration. Mouth constantly returns to its narration (five times), which takes on a circular form, as 'psychotic urges to return to, and eternally repeat, the traumatic moment'.[42] After each narration of this memory Mouth asks in confusion 'who?... what?... no!... she!', as though this memory shatters the deep foundations of her identity. The framing device of pauses signals the importance of this memory: this memory makes Mouth stop her speech in a frustrated attempt to look backwards. This memory is the last to go together with the fall of the curtain. Besides, after each chaotic narration of this memory, the silent Auditor helplessly raises his hands as a gesture of compassion or frustration. Moreover, Mouth cannot translate this numbing, senseless memory into words. This memory deprived her of her voice and of her body, bringing her back to darkness, inducing the feeling of shame and her body rejection. This memory seems to have split her already unstable and unwanted identities. All these lead me to discuss this trauma in the light of sexual abuse. I quote some of these memory repetitions in the endnotes.[43]

The results of the trauma of sexual abuse may have life-lasting effects and produce both psychological and physical impacts. Paralyzing fears, femininity rejection, loss of faith, identity disorder, nightmarish existence are only some of the symptoms brought about by sexual abuse. Its victims come to feel ashamed, insecure, guilty, afraid, and angry. The trauma of sexual abuse, especially in childhood, may also induce partial or total amnesia in a victim. Nevertheless, the painful event is not erased from the memory forever, but stored in the subconscious and painful memory flashbacks and/or nightmares may accompany a victim for years.

The impossibility 'to piece' the memory of sexual abuse together involves the mechanisms of traumatic memory storage. On a neuropsychological level, when a traumatic event occurs, a person cannot store this event coherently in their memory, as they cannot locate it in time or create the temporal landmark for it. Phil Mollon writes:

> If a traumatic experience is not processed into autobiographic memory, then it is not available to intentional and explicit recall. This kind of memory cannot easily be described in words – it is not verbally accessible.[44]

According to Mollon, the traumatic experience may be encoded on a motor-sensory level in the form of visual images, sensations, emotions and motor acts.[45] This explains why emotions difficult to translate into words and images prevail in traumatic memory narration. Therefore, as the result of traumatic event storage, the impossibility to narrate the event coherently leads to unreal existence and loss of identity. A traumatic experience exists outside temporal landmarks and a victim loses the perception of time.

The 'April morning' memory differs from other memories, as Mouth remembers it in the present, as though in frozen time. While speaking, Mouth cannot utter one complete sentence; all the memories come in flashes:

> wandering in a field ... looking aimlessly for cowslips ... to make a ball ... a few steps then stop ... stare into space ... then on ... a few more ... stop and stare again ... so on ... drifting around ... when suddenly ... gradually ... all went out ... all that early April morning light ... and she found herself in the – ... what? ... who? ... no! ... she![46]

Though this memory is generally placed in the 'when' (some April morning) and the 'where' (the fields), it remains deprived of a 'what' (an event). The victims of trauma normally remember the settings and small details of the event, but they try to alienate themselves from its painful content by blocking it. And Mouth remembers the larks' song, the distant sound of the bells, the morning sun and the grass, but the rest of this memory is wrapped up in darkness; 'what' always buzzes in her subconscious, but Mouth stubbornly repeats - '... nothing she could tell'.[47] Always there, the buzzing forever haunts her: 'all the time buzzing ... so-called ... in the ears ... though of course actually ... not in the ears at all ... in the skull ... dull roar in the skull ...'.[48] The unborn words or her memory, still to be told, torture Mouth. The buzzing in her skull constitutes her present and makes her talk incessantly; several times in the play Mouth repeats 'all silent but for the buzzing', as though the buzzing sound maintains her alive and makes her remember.

The narration of the 'April morning' memory occurs on a motor-sensory level through images, sounds, movement and perception. Most importantly, Mouth's lacking body is present in the first three memory flashbacks through physical action of 'picking flowers', 'standing', 'sitting', 'wandering', etc. But when the event happens, there are only references to her mouth.

The act of picking flowers to make a ball shows her innocence when, wandering in the fields as a girl. We may understand the act of picking flowers on a metaphorical level: 'deflower' means to deprive of virgin hood. The distant sound of the bells and the larks' song are remembered on the level of sounds and constitute Mouth's auditory memory. The sound of the bells indicates Mouth's proximity to a church together with the remote possibility that she was on her way to morning mass. A lark has a very rich symbolism in literature. Its crescent shape often signifies lunar qualities, and the moon often connects with the concept of self and with a woman's image. Therefore, the 'lark' reflects the inward journey often associated with self-discovery. Paradoxically, Mouth takes this inward journey, though incapable of reflexivity. In *Not I*, the 'lark' transforms into a textual symbol of 'doom' and 'mourning',[49] since something dreadful happened on this April morning, when she was 'like numbed ... couldn't make the sound ... not any sound ... no sound of any kind ... no screaming for help for example ...'.[50]

The constant references to 'eyes' and 'light' may possibly indicate memory retrieval processes. During the whole play, Mouth feverishly alludes to a 'sudden flash'[51] or 'flashes from all over'.[52] These references to sudden flashes may relate to sudden moments of memory return, possibly caused by a beam of light, on and off in her mind. As Mouth says, the beam is only 'poking around',[53] and is 'painless ... so far ... ha! ... so far ... all that ... keep on ... not knowing what ... what she was ...'.[54] That may mean that the beam is not there to search her mind, for it lacks any objective. This light has not found her most painful of memories yet. The 'April morning' event itself is shielded by the darkness of her forgetting: she recreates the sensation 'when suddenly ... gradually ... all went out',[55] as if she was suddenly blindfolded. The traumatic event was erased from her memory or she was literally blinded.

The first sensation that she remembers, that of numbness concerns trauma . Sometimes at the moments of danger, a victim of trauma tries to numb her feelings as a mental protection and becomes an observer of her pain. Mouth seems to be uncertain of her real position at that moment, although the position itself has sexual characteristics: the sequence of standing, sitting, kneeling and lying recreates the scene of someone manipulating her body together with 'grabbing of the straw'[56] as if in pain. At the same time the sequence of these movements calls to mind a regression towards Mouth's being an infant, depriving her of maturity and returning her to a defenceless state of 'lying', which brings forth the trauma of birth.

Mouth's exclamation 'what position she was in!'[57] may refer to the woman's morality, since Mouth makes references to her Catholic upbringing, and a possibility of further judgment and punishment, as if it were her fault of being raped. Thereafter comes the sense of shame and impotence. The shame comes also from her inability to call for help and to defend herself: 'couldn't make the sound ... not any sound ... no sound of any kind ... no screaming for help for example ...'.[58] Rape brings on the shame of one's own body, and Mouth literally loses her body after this dreadful experience. Once abused, the body becomes a container and a reminder of trauma, causing the victims of sexual abuse to reject their bodies. I might only suppose that it resulted in Mouth's pregnancy and consequently her abortion, judged and condemned for, though the text gives no clear evidence of this. So her phrases later – 'guilty or not guilty ... stand up woman ... speak up woman ...'[59] – may actually refer to her speechlessness at court and further self-punishment and reclusion.

The trauma of sexual abuse marks a person for life, and the question of survival comes into light. Mouth wonders how she managed to survive – survive her pain. The answer to this is, probably, her period of speechlessness, probably considerable as latency. For Caruth latency does not consist in forgetting, 'but in an inherent latency within the experience itself'.[60] Both Caruth and Felman and Laub[61] coincide about the period of speechlessness as essential for survival. According to Felman and Laub, this silence occurs both internally and externally. Internally because a victim represses the recall in order not to relive the nightmare; and externally, because, on the one hand, a victim prefers silence as she is uncertain whether others will believe her, and, on the other hand, because she cannot translate the events into words. Felman and Laub stress that although 'silence is defeat, it serves them [victims] both as a sanctuary and as a place of bondage'.[62]

The moment, when Mouth recovered that 'other' voice, is not as important as the fact that she started to talk. Nevertheless, speaking for her has to do with the bowel movements. Mouth wanted to get the release – the release from her memory. The stage image may also remind us of an anus as words of excretion abound in the play ('sudden flash', 'sudden urge', 'steady stream', 'all went out', etc.). Mouth parallels her sudden talking to going to the lavatory: '... sudden urge to ... tell ... then rush out stop the first she saw ... nearest lavatory ... start pouring it out ... steady stream ... mad stuff ...'.[63] Language ceases to express meaning to her; she only feels the urge of a release. But this verbal rebirth has a side-effect. All her bottled-up feelings of pain, suffering and shame flood her and Mouth is not ready to accept her memories. And since she does not want to recognize her former identities, stubbornly refusing the 'I' in her speech, Mouth denies her physical onstage body: 'the whole machine ... but no ... spared that ... the mouth alone ... so far ... ha!'[64] She fears recovering the feelings of her body, preferring physical and emotional numbness to remembering. Ruby Cohn writes that Mouth 'finds the return to words so fearful because they may trail a rebirth of feeling'.[65]

## 5. Conclusions

Memory and trauma become the protagonists in postmodern theatre, as exemplified by *Not I*. Therefore, new staging techniques are invented. The stage acquires a new hallucinatory quality, and in *Not I* the stage darkness may represent both Mouth's subconscious (the dominium of the unheard voices) and the void of time. Body disconnectedness and mutilation are other techniques to stage trauma, resulting from unresolved psychic conflicts and traumas. Furthermore, staging a disembodied orphic mouth links *Not I* with the trauma of sexual abuse. The loss of the body results from shame and consequent rejection of femininity. Moreover, the failure of personalization constitutes another device of trauma narration. Sexual abuse affects Mouth's past and present, making her reject her other selves and inducing a continuous state of latency. Her total seclusion from the world results from this trauma. Although narration of trauma should enhance survival, Mouth cannot remember. Remembrance comes only in the form of flashes, with the fragmentation of speech driven to the extreme. And since Mouth's identity had already split before this traumatic event (lack of love and the feeling of being unwanted had been haunting her since birth), I consider it practically impossible for her to come to terms with this trauma and Mouth continues speaking after the fall of the curtain. Sexual abuse overwhelmed her too much for her already unstable self.

# Notes

[1] In her chapter, Lisa B. Hughes points out the importance of catharsis in watching Euripides' *Hecuba:* 'The audience, like Hecuba, remain physically intact, though assailed with painful images, and possibly psychically wounded.'
[2] Beckett to Shneider, quoted in Ruby Cohn, *A Beckett Canon* (Ann Harbor: University of Michigan Press, 2001), 316.
[3] James Knowlson, *Damned to Fame: The Life of Samuel Beckett* (UK: Bloomsbury, 1997), 178. In this most complete biography of Samuel Beckett, Knowlson demonstrates Beckett's interest in, and thorough study of, psychology.
[4] Ruby Cohn, *A Beckett Canon*, 319.

[5] Samuel Beckett, *The Complete Dramatic Works* (London: Faber & Faber, 1986), 379.

[6] In her chapter, Lisa B. Hughes discusses the concept of 'a body in pain' in relation to Hecuba, who although, somatically intact, is 'shown to be the most psychically fragmented, to receive the most wounds'.

[7] Linda Ben-Zvi, *Women in Beckett: Performance and Critical Perspective* (Urbana and Chicago: University of Illinois Press, 1992), 131.

[8] In her chapter on Nancy Huston's *Losing North*, Danielle Schaub writes, 'Trauma filters in through linguistic turns of phrases and, particularly, through omissions and negations in the text'.

[9] Beckett, *Complete Dramatic Works*, 376.

[10] Maud Ellmann, *Psychoanalytic Literary Criticism* (London: Longman, 1994), 8.

[11] Katheryn Robson, 'Bodily detours: Sarah Kofman's Narrative of Childhood Trauma', in *The Modern Language Review* (London: Modern Humanities Research Association, 2004), Viewed 12 October 2011.

[12] Samuel Beckett, *The Complete Dramatic Works* (London: Faber & Faber, 1986), 379.

[13] Antonia Rodriguez-Gago, 'The Embodiment of Memory (and Forgetting) in Beckett's Late Women's Plays', in *Drawing in Beckett: Portraits, Performances and Cultural Contexts,* ed. Linda Ben-Zvi (Tel Aviv: Assaph Books Series, 2003), 114.

[14] Richard Begam, 'Beckett and Postfoundationalism, or, How Fundamental are those Fundamental sounds?', in *Beckett and Philosophy*, ed. Lane R. (New York: Palgrave, 2002), 16.

[15] Jeannette R. Malkin, *Memory-Theatre and Postmodern Drama* (Ann Harbor, MI: University of Michigan Press, 1999), 47.

[16] Beckett, *Complete Dramatic Works,* 379.

[17] Beckett, *Complete Dramatic Works,* 377, 379.

[18] Malkin, *Memory-Theatre and Postmodern Drama*, 74.

[19] Sigmund Freud, *Beyond the Pleasure Principle,* trans. James Stratchey (New York and London: W.W Norton, 1961). In chapter 3, Freud describes the occurrence of traumatic memories. The persistent pattern of sufferings comes in the form of nightmares and painful re-enactments totally outside the control of the victim. Freud gives an example of a romantic love story told by Taso in *Gerusalemme Liberata.* When Tancred accidentally kills his beloved Clorinda in a duel, after the funeral he goes into a magic forest and stabs a tree with his sword. Unexpectedly, blood runs from the tree, which seems to hold the soul of his beloved one, and her voice tells him that he has wounded her again. The second episode with the tree actually repeats the event, but on the other level. It seems that

the knight cannot control the voice and the visual image, the catastrophe replaying in his head again and again. Freud calls this experience 'traumatic neurosis'.

[20] Beckett, *Complete Dramatic Works*, 376.

[21] Malkin, *Memory-Theatre and Postmodern Drama,* 48.

[22] John J. Skowronski, W. Richard Walker, and Andrew L. Benz, 'Who was I when That Happened? The Timekeeping Self in Autobiographical Memory', in *The Self and Memory*, ed. Denise B. Beike et al. (New York: Hove Psychology Press, 2004), 183-207.

[23] Skowronski, Walker, and Benz, 'Who was I when That Happened? The Timekeeping Self in Autobiographical Memory', 201.

[24] James M. Lampinen, Timothy N. Odegard, and Juliana K. Leding, 'Diachronic Disunity', in *The Self and Memory*, ed. Denise R. Beike et al. (New York: Hove Psychology Press, 2004), 231.

[25] Ibid., 376.

[26] Ibid., 377.

[27] Ibid., 380.

[28] Linda Ben-Zvi, 'The Schismatic Self in *A Piece of Monologue*', *Journal of Beckett Studies* 7 (1982): 12.

[29] Malkin, *Memory-Theatre and Postmodern Drama*, 50.

[30] Beckett, *Complete Dramatic Works*, 379.

[31] Ibid., 372.

[32] Ibid., 376.

[33] Otto Rank, *El Trauma del Nacimiento.* Trans. H. F. de Saltzmann (Buenos Aires: Editorial Paidos, 1961), 46.

[34] Danielle Schaub, in this volume.

[35] Nancy Huston, *Losing North*, quoted in Danielle Schaub, in this volume.

[36] Beckett, *Complete Dramatic Works*, 377.

[37] Ibid., 377.

[38] Ibid., 376.

[39] Ibid., 378.

[40] Ibid., 380.

[41] This calls to mind the comment that Danielle Schaub makes about the character's self-guilt and loneliness affecting the text of *Losing North*: 'An overwhelming disruption with the separation from the maternal and the ensuing loneliness and self-guilt lead to the narrative voice's marginalizing and even effacing records of any past unitary sense.'

[42] Malkin, *Memory-Theatre and Postmodern Drama*, 29.

[43] 'that April morning ... she fixing with her eye ... a distant bell...as she hastened towards it ... fixing it with her eye ... what? ... who? ... no! ... she! ...'. Beckett, *Complete Dramatic Works*, 378.

'keep an eye on that too…corner of the eye … all that together … can't go on … God is love … she'll be purged … back in the field … morning sun … April … sink face down in the grass . . . nothing but the larks . . . so on . . . grabbing at the straw … straining to hear … the odd word … make some sense of it … whole body like gone … just the mouth … like maddened … and can't stop … no stopping it … something she– … something she had to– … what?…who?…no! … she! … something she had to–… what?'. Ibid., 381.

'April morning … face in the grass … nothing but the larks … pick it up there … get on with it from there … another few– …what?…not that?…nothing to do with that?…nothing she could tell?… all right…nothing she could tell … try something else … think of something else … oh long after … sudden flash…[...] what?… who?…no!…she!' Ibid., 382.

[44] Phil Mollon, *Remembering Trauma: A Psychotherapist's Guide to Memory and Illusion* (London: Whurr Publishers, 2002), 30.

[45] Ibid., 28.

[46] Ibid., 377-376.

[47] Beckett, *Complete Dramatic Works*, 382.

[48] Ibid., 378.

[49] Michael Ferber, *A Dictionary of Literary Symbols* (Cambridge, England: Cambridge University Press, 2001), 104-105. 'Lark' as the symbol of 'mourning' appears in Shakespeare's *Romeo and Juliet*. It symbolises Romeo's leaving.

[50] Beckett, *Complete Dramatic Works*, 378.

[51] Samuel Beckett, *The Complete Dramatic Works*, 377, 379, 382.

[52] Ibid., 380.

[53] Ibid., 382.

[54] Ibid., 382.

[55] Ibid., 377.

[56] Ibid., 381.

[57] Ibid., 377.

[58] Ibid., 378.

[59] Ibid., 381.

[60] Cathy Caruth, *Unclaimed Experience: Trauma, Narrative and History* (Baltimore and London: Johns Hopkins University Press, 1996), 17. Caruth's definition of trauma was extremely important to the present research: 'The wound of the mind – the breach in the mind's experience of time, self, and the world – is not, like the wound of the body, a simple and healable event, but rather an event that [...] is experienced too soon, too unexpectedly, to be fully known and is therefore not available to consciousness until it imposes itself again, repeatedly, in the nightmares and repetitive actions of the survivor' (4).

[61] Shoshana Felman and Dori Laub, *Testimony: Crisis of Witnessing in Literature, Psychoanalysis, and History* (New York and London: Routledge, 1992).
[62] Ibid., 58.
[63] Beckett, *Complete Dramatic Works*, 382.
[64] Ibid., 378.
[65] Ruby Cohn, *A Beckett Canon* (Anne Harbor, MI: University of Michigan Press, 2001), 318.

## Bibliography

Beckett, Samuel. *The Complete Dramatic Works.* London: Faber & Faber, 1986.

Beike R. Denise, James M. Lampinen and Douglas A. Behrend. *The Self and Memory.* New York: Hove Psychology Press, 2004.

Ben-Zvi, Linda. *Women in Beckett: Performance and Critical Perspective.* Urbana and Chicago: University of Illinois Press, 1992.

Caruth, Cathy. *Unclaimed Experience: Trauma, Narrative and History.* Baltimore and London: Johns Hopkins University Press, 1996.

Cohn, Ruby. *A Beckett Canon.* Ann Harbor, MI: University of Michigan Press, 2001.

Culbertson, Roberta. 'Embodied Memory, Transcendence, and Telling Recounting Trauma, Re-establishing the Self'. In *New Literary History*, edited by Rita Felski, 165-195. Baltimore: Johns Hopkins University Press, 1995.

Ellmann, Maud. *Psychoanalytic Literary Criticism.* London: Longman, 1994.

Felman, Shoshana and Laub, Dori. *Testimony: Crisis of Witnessing in Literature, Psychoanalysis, and History.* New York and London: Routledge, 1992.

Ferber, Michael. *A Dictionary of Literary Symbols.* Cambridge, England: Cambridge University Press, 2001.

Freud, Sigmund. *Beyond The Pleasure Principle.* Trans. Stratchey, James. New York and London: W.W. Norton, 1961.

Knowlson, James. *Damned to Fame: The Life of Samuel Beckett.* London: Bloomsbury, 1997.

Lampinen, James M., Timothy N. Odegard and Juliana K. Leding. 'Diachronic Disunity'. *The Self and Memory*, edited by Denise Beike, James M. Lampinen, and Douglas A. Behrend, 227-255. New York: Hove Psychology Press, 2004.

Malkin, Jeannette. *Memory-Theatre and Postmodern Drama.* Ann Harbor, MI: University of Michigan Press, 1999.

McNally, Richard. *Remembering Trauma.* Cambridge, MA: Harvard University Press, 2003.

Mollon, Phil. *Remembering Trauma: A Psychotherapist's Guide to Memory and Illusion.* London: Whurr Publishers, 2002.

Rank, Otto. *El Trauma del Nacimiento.* Trans. H. F. de Saltzmann. Buenos Aires: Editorial Paidos, 1961.

Robson, Katheryn. 'Bodily Detours: Sarah Kofman's Narrative of Childhood Trauma'. *The Modern Language Review.* London: Modern Humanities Research Association, 2004.

Rodriguez-Gago, Antonia. 'The Embodiment of Memory (and Forgetting) in Beckett's Late Women's Plays'. In *Drawing in Beckett: Portraits, Performances and Cultural Contexts*, edited by Linda Ben-Zvi, 113-127. Tel Aviv: Assaph Books Series, 2003.

Skowronski, John J., Richard W. Walker and Andrew L. Benz. 'Who Was I When That Happened? The Timekeeping Self in Autobiographical Memory'. In *The Self and Memory*, edited by R. Denise Beike, James M. Lampinen, and Douglas A. Behrend, 183-207. New York: Hove Psychology Press, 2004.

**Svetlana Antropova** graduated from Moscow State Pedagogical University where she taught for two years. In 1993 she immigrated to Spain and continued her teaching career at the Centro Universitario Villanueva. She took up post-graduate studies at the Universidad Autónoma de Madrid, Madrid, Spain and soon became one of Samuel Beckett's fans. She defended her thesis on 'Staging Memory and Trauma: Past Voices and Bodies Haunting the Present in the Theatre of Samuel Beckett' in 2011. While interested in the English Literature, especially theatre, her research and writing currently focus on the artistic representation of memory and trauma in postmodern theatre.

# Part 3

# Trauma Spaces and Places

# Representing a Trauma Space and Rendering the Real of the Spanish Civil War in Carlos Saura's *La caza*

## Jeremy Kasten

**Abstract**
In trauma theory, temporal relations (past, present, future) have taken precedence in the exploration of a traumatic event while the significance of the geographical space where the event occurred has received much less attention. This requires re-evaluation because space plays an equally decisive role in individual and collective memory, feelings, symptoms, and the eventual possibility of working through the experience. A space becomes extremely significant after a traumatic event for both the victims and the communities affected by the incomprehensible occurrences that *took place* there. Such a space I term 'trauma space,' one whose meaning was transformed by a traumatic experience and subsequently affects those wounded (physically and/or psychically) by the event. In this chapter, I use the example of Castile – a territory that hosted some of the bloodiest battles of the Spanish Civil War and the subject of various literary and cinematic representations of the war and its posterior effects. Castile offers an especially interesting example because at the beginning of the 20th century, it had been a space associated with nostalgia for Spain's glorious past and hope for the nation's future. Not surprisingly, the war transformed the feelings associated with the territory from hope, nostalgia, and pride to grief, guilt, fear, and solitude. Castile remains a 'trauma space' long into the post-War period as represented cinematically in the 1960s and 1970s. Thus Castile was transformed into a symbol of the loss, anxiety, and generational divide in post-War Spain, all of which are reflected in Carlos Saura's 1965 film, *La caza*. This portrayal of Castile renders it a cultural memorial of the war's lingering effects in the present that must be worked through in order to look toward an improved future in which the historical trauma is recognized, respected, and remembered properly.

**Key Words:** Anxiety, Castile, *La caza*, film, space, Spanish Civil War, trauma.

*****

## 1. Introduction

In 2009, a non-profit organization, 'Arqueologia del punt de vista,' created the 'Passejant Centelles,' a route of Barcelona which revisited the exact locations of iconic photographs taken during the Spanish Civil War by Agustín Centelles – a photographer who captured some of the most well-known images of the conflict. Some of the photographs enlarged to life-size were even placed at the site where the events occurred, thus recreating the very moment of their photographic immortalization. This itinerary attests to the lasting effect that the war has had on the Spanish imaginary and demonstrates the continued need to revisit memories and psychological wounds *in situ*, at their originating locations. In this way, the 'Passejant

Centelles' highlights the significance of space and of revisiting certain locations which become important sites after painful events – painful for both the victims and the communities affected by the incomprehensible occurrences that *took place* there.

The term 'trauma space' exposes the double relationship between a traumatic event and the location where it took place. Therefore, a trauma space is both *traumatized* – with ruins or other vestiges of the past event – and *traumatic* – in that it may evoke symptoms and anxiety in trauma victims. The representation of a space can point back to the trauma that affected it in various ways. This appears in the case of the Spanish territory focused on in this study: Castile. Finally, cultural production set in trauma spaces may have an effect within a repressive culture that denies the country's psychological wounds through censorship in art as well as in public discourse. Thus cultural production set in a trauma space may render psychological wounds to work through in order to look toward a future in which the historical trauma is re-inscribed into an individual or collective experience. Carlos Saura's 1965 film, *La caza*, an exemplary work that deals with the relationship between a battlefield in Castile, the psychological consequences of the war, and the evocation of anxiety as a cinematic working-through of Spanish Civil War trauma.

In the second chapter of this section, Emina Hadziosmanovic and Nigel Hunt discuss the findings from a study of the effects of displacement in relation to PTSD in victims of the war in the former Yugoslavia. They examine how Bosnian refugees now living in the United Kingdom process traumatic experience in comparison with those victims who remained in Bosnia throughout the post-war period. My study, in contrast, focuses solely on Spaniards who remained in the country for over thirty years of Francoist rule. I will examine how the places where a trauma occurred – trauma spaces – become both a trigger for symptoms as well as a potentially lasting memorial to the incomprehensible events that occurred there.

While Hadziosmanovic and Hunt use a psychologistic methodology, I take a psychoanalytic approach to the relationship between trauma, the traumatized individual(s), and the space where a trauma takes place. Hal Foster provides a clear explanation of the distance between the two frameworks, stating that 'strictly in a psychoanalytic register there is no subject of trauma – the position is evacuated' while a psychologistic approach elevates the subject to absolute authority because their trauma cannot be challenged by others. The psychoanalytic view of the subject-less trauma accounts for the presence of trauma in cultural production without discussing a traumatized subject/victim (author, director, etc.). In fact, the work itself should be understood as symptomatic of trauma: this occurs in *La caza* through narrative, *mise-en-scène*, sound, camera-work, and the selection of a trauma space as the setting of the action.

From a psychoanalytic perspective, the effect of trauma is not a question of displaced and non-displaced but one of *here* (trauma) and *return* (the return of the trauma or to the trauma space). In other words, the safety of the geographical distance from the trauma space results from misrecognition: an unconscious formation that the traumatized individual constructs to avoid an encounter with the real (trauma). Slavoj

Žižek explains that a return can only allow the traumatic past to 'become what it always was'.[1] In other words, this amounts to a movement from reality to the real (the traumatic materials). Cultural production at times *re-presents* a return to trauma spaces and, at other times, renders as real certain elements of the traumatic event otherwise concealed or manipulated by the dictatorship that gained control after the conclusion of the war.

Trauma theory, a cultural studies approach to psychological trauma, has enjoyed popularity since the early 1990s. One trauma theorist, Holocaust historian Dominick LaCapra, discusses the processes by which traumatized individuals deal with their experiences. Like many trauma theorists, LaCapra understands trauma primarily as a relationship between traumatized individuals and their temporal experiences. He characterizes 'acting out' as a phenomenon in which an individual becomes unknowingly trapped in repetition of the past, 'to be haunted by ghosts or even to exist in the present as if one were still fully in the past, with no distance from it.'[2] He goes on to describe the term 'working through' as a countervailing process to acting out in which an individual gains critical distance from the historical trauma and is 'able to distinguish between past, present and future.'[3] Thus 'acting out' and 'working through' are characterized in terms of the capacity – or incapacity – to distinguish between past, present, and future.

While the temporal dimension is undoubtedly a crucial aspect of the traumatic experience and of its symptoms, space also plays an important role in the way that the traumatized deal with and remember the event. This stems from a traumatic experience taking place at a specific location and, as Ruth Ginsberg tells us, 'time is frozen in space [...] in an untouchable memory, in a long, hesitant, present moment in front of "nothingness".'[4] Even time can be understood in terms of space, which is paramount when discussing the experience of an individual who faced an overwhelming and violent shock. In psychoanalysis, the unconscious is likewise conceived in terms of space. Jacques Lacan explains that it must 'be apprehended in its experience of rupture, between perception and consciousness, in that non-temporal locus [...] the idea of another locality; another space, another scene, the between perception and consciousness.'[5] The unconscious being a kind of liminal space of an individual, the imaginary materials associated with a geographical space become repressed in the unconscious space of the psyche. The discourse of space can thus contribute to a more thorough understanding of the effects trauma has and how certain artistic representations of spaces can affect their audiences and potentially play a role in the collective working through of historical trauma.

## 2. Trauma and Space

After the Nationalist force emerged victorious from the Spanish Civil War, the Francoist regime implemented an institutional history comprised of a single version of events that systematically denied the wounds that the war had caused. This repressive government and its censorial machine refused to allow those defeated in the war to participate in the construction of the 'official' Francoist account of the events. In his historiographical contribution to this current section, Mireno Berrettini discusses the role that the church had in this process of silencing and abusing the trauma of the conflict for ideological motives during the war, under the repressive Francoist dictatorship, during the transition to democracy, and are even expressing dislike for the recent attempts to 'uncover' many silenced atrocities committed during the war and dictatorship. As Berrettini's convincing chapter illustrates, the church played a decisive role in the Nationalist victory and helped the dictatorship to maintain power for thirty-six years. Moreover – and, perhaps, more remarkably – the church has continued to resist current historical memory endeavours in Spain in the past decade. However, as I will show here, some of the cultural production created during the Francoist dictatorship was already uncovering and exposing the historical trauma caused by the war despite the social, political, and religious repression that held a stronghold over the country. These works were participating in the construction of a new historical memory in Spain in which the trauma of the war and its effect on the nation are being acknowledged and reconsidered.

In her study of Spanish cinema and its relation to the construction of the nation, Anne-Marie Jolivet refers to Spain as 'that hunting ground where the memory of the civil war and the latent repressed and deadly feeling of guilt remain buried.'[6] This statement attests to the impact of the Spanish Civil War on the country and how the geographical territory is invested with memory and trauma of the violent event that left an open wound in the collective psyche. More specifically, certain locations that hosted extraordinarily violent events take on a traumatic meaning that reveals the space's erasure but also its potential to preserve the memory of the difficult experience.

In his article, 'The Place of Trauma', Dylan Trigg applies the word 'site' to the post-traumatic geographical location due to its connotation of 'being levelled-out, divested of its specificity and reduced to a non-place [which] serves to distance the remoteness and fragmentation of trauma with the felt experience of place.'[7] Site is a place virtually erased by a traumatic event – along with the subjectivity of those affected by it. A 'ruin,' on the other hand, resists erasure by maintaining visible marks of the event. The term 'ruin' refers to any environment whose identity is marked by an event which 'effectively undercuts a claim of temporal continuity and, instead, offers a counter-narrative in which testimony becomes guided by voids rather than points of presence.'[8] Ruins draw our attention to the remains and the absent: they spatially construct the story of the missing pieces caused by the trauma.

In the case of the Spanish Civil War, the Francoist treatment of ruins paralleled the regime's repressive treatment of historical memory. Bruce Wardropper compares the British and Spanish treatment of war ruins: in England,

> when Coventry Cathedral was bombed in the Second World War, a
> new cathedral was built beside the ruins. When the Alcázar of
> Toledo was bombarded by artillery in the Spanish Civil War, it was
> [...] reconstructed in its original form.[9]

This replacement of ruins with a replica of the original structure leaves no vestiges to demarcate the reality or occurrence of the event. Thus the Francoist regime attempted to physically erase – or, at the very least, control – the memory of the traumatic past. Perhaps the term 'control' works more appropriately when discussing the Francoist handling of ruins, because other structures damaged by the Republican side were left *as ruins* to serve as a reminder of the barbarities committed by the irreverent anti-Spanish invaders. In the case of the Alcázar in Toledo reconstructed in its original form, the spatial ruins are denied the spectral qualities that could have otherwise opposed the one-sided story that the strategically-preserved ruins told. Similarly, Francoist censorship attempted to manipulate and silence the testimonies of the trauma that contradicted the institutionalized, Francoist version of the events.

If ruins function to remind and potentially to help victims deal with past atrocities, some artistic productions also serve as ruins, a monument to the silenced trauma. Julian Bonder suggests that monuments and memorials are not just objects. Rather, 'instead of a form, a shape, or an image, monumentality may well be a quality: the quality that some places or objects have to make us recall, evoke, think, and perceive something beyond themselves.'[10] The trauma spaces analysed in this study are not constructed monuments nor are they memorials designed to pay homage to the victims. Nevertheless, these trauma spaces share some monumental qualities in that they evoke a response in those who witness the site. Thus this monumentality may forge a connection between the space and the unspeakable events that occurred there. In the case of Spain's repressive post-War policies, the monumental space may even challenge the problematic manner of handling the memory of the war for the decades that followed.

In addition to the physical spaces, cultural production which evokes the real of trauma spaces also displays a monumental quality which may lead the audience to recall or confront the painful history of that place and, perhaps, recognize the distressing nature of the Spanish Civil War and its lasting effect on the current society. These 'monumental' works do not represent the experience conventionally in the plot (i.e. they are not mimetic of the traumatic experience) but rather render the memories and traces of a painful event that has been erased, manipulated, or repressed. In fact, both physical ruins and cultural production can render the real of a traumatic event. Walter Benjamin asserts that 'allegories are, in the realm of thoughts, what ruins are in the realm of things'[11]. In this way, artistic works may represent a trauma and others may render the traumatic materials. Both may become cultural 'ruins' that evoke the otherwise buried stories of trauma. Moreover, when works that render the real are set within a trauma space, sites of trauma may be reinscribed into the experience of the painful period in Spanish history in large part erased from the institutionalized, official memory.

## 3. Representations and Renderings of (Trauma) Spaces

In order to fully understand the significance of the relationship between cultural production, affects, and trauma space, one must stress that the diverse post-Spanish

Civil War works are not limited by their meanings. In fact, a work's meaning is determined by the experience of the reader or viewer because a work's true *meaning* comes from what it *does*. I will use Stanley Fish's concept of 'affective stylistics' as well as Slavoj Žižek's application of Michel Chion's notion of *rendu*, both of which focus on stylistic and formal idiosyncrasies that *affect* the audience. 'Affective stylistics' describes the textual peculiarities that break the audience out of his or her complacent reading experience. When the reader is not given answers in a text, s/he is forced to fill in the gaps. Fish states that 'rather than following an argument along a well-lighted path [...] he is now looking for one.'[12] This results in questioning what a work does 'and the execution involves an analysis of the developing responses of the reader in relation to the words as they succeed one another in time.'[13] By thinking about affective stylistics, we can question the effects of post-Spanish Civil War cultural production on the audience because irregular elements at the level of the plot and narrative can *affect* readers or viewers moved by certain works.

Another tool to delineate the effects of an artistic work on its audience concerns Slavoj Žižek's elaboration of *rendu*: the disruptive artistic element that 'does not imitate or symbolize anything, but that "seizes" us immediately, "renders" immediately the thing' which is 'the real of the "psychic reality".'[14] Accordingly, Žižek describes formal experimentations which cannot be explained logically and, therefore, render real (i.e., traumatic) elements. The term *rendu* comes from Michel Chion's use of the word in the context of audio-visual aspects that do not have a diegetic purpose and, due to their unsettling presence, render reality instead of representing it.

*Rendu* does not remind the audience of aspects of reality; it forces the audience to confront the real. This ensues from 'the prohibition of a formal element that is central constituent of the "normal" narrative procedure of a sound film.'[15] *Rendu* is fundamental in the relationship between cultural artefacts and a trauma. This effect on the audience is not caused by the

> psychotic contents of these films, but in the way the content, far from being simply 'depicted,' is immediately 'rendered' by the very form of the film – here, the 'message' of the movie is immediately the form itself.[16]

According to these two concepts, through the significance of trauma space and through certain formal elements, some aspects of post-Spanish Civil War cultural production evoke memories of trauma. This matters especially when the entire narrative takes place in a trauma space that contains many unsettling scenes and disturbing objects that point back to a historical trauma.

The specific work chosen for this study set in Castile becomes a crucial aspect, for the decision to use this significant trauma space that also renders silenced and forgotten wounds of the past. Castile was an emblematic territory in early 20th-century literature, especially with the group of Spanish modernists referred to as 'The

Generation of 1898'. The authors belonging to this 'Generation' looked toward the Castilian plains in an attempt to restore the Spanish splendour of the conquest over the Moors, the height of the Spanish Empire, and the subsequent Golden Age. This influx of literary and other artistic representations of Castile made the territory a recurring cultural *topos* in Spanish literature that lasted even after the turn of the century.

At least partly due to its emblematic status and its frequent role as a metonym for the entire nation, the territory continued to be an important space in cultural production after the war; however, in these new representations, the region takes on very different meanings. First, both sides of the war attempted to appropriate Castile as a symbol of *their* Spain. On both sides, many of these representations contained strong socio-political and ideological content. For example, in Federico de Urrutia's *Romance a Castilla en armas*, Castile symbolizes the Fascist cause and the Spanish glory that demands restoration at the hands of its loyal Castilian sons. Castile becomes the symbol of a strong, unified Spain and the site of a successful hierarchical system. For its part, José Herrera Petere's 'Si por el amor movidos...' describes a 'Castile without castles,' de-aristocraticizing the territory and linking it to the communist cause of a classless, castle-less Spain. Many other works treat Castile as a significant space for ideological purposes, however tacitly or explicitly articulated.

Leaving aside its ideologized usage, Castile also became a symbol for the absences and trauma of the war. Castile hosted some of the bloodiest battles of the Spanish Civil War, making it replete with painful memories of violence and loss. A traumatic event breaks the identity of a subject into two 'selves' – before and after. As a result, 'the void [between the two] gained the privileged, but wholly fragmented position of forming an intercession between time and place.'[17] In the case of the Spanish Civil War, this split manifests itself in the cultural artefacts of the time. The Chilean poet Pablo Neruda explains how the war changed the way poets wrote because 'there has not been an equally fertile essence for poets in intellectual history as the Spanish war. Spanish blood exercised a magnetism that made the poetry of a great epoch tremble,' going as far as to claim that that this change was even more powerful than the Second World War.[18] This break appears in traumatized individuals, cultural production, and in the representation of spaces which have taken on new meanings as a result of the events which occurred there. The 'before' and 'after' also affected the way that certain spaces were remembered in the context of the Spanish Civil War. In *Senses of Place*, Keith Basso and Steven Feld tell us that 'place is the most fundamental form of embodied experience – the site of a powerful fusion of self, space and time'.[19] The region, like the rest of Spain, became marked by the war – as manifested in the transformed artistic portrayals of Castile.

The territory remains a trauma space into the late Francoist period, as evidenced by Castile remaining an important *topos* in prose, photography, painting, poetry, and film: the region continues to have the ability to evoke repressed memories and symptoms in traumatized individuals. This occurs in the cinematic depiction of three war veterans' return to Castile in *La caza*. However, the trauma of the war veterans and their hunting experience in the Castilian battlefield finds further expression in certain aspects of cinematography. Through the representation and rendering of this trauma space as a site of silenced, but dangerous memories, *La caza* may lead its audience to an encounter with the country's trauma, which gives rise to anxiety.

## 4. Anxiety and Working through Historical Trauma in *La caza*

Anxiety, in psychoanalysis, refers to the feeling of fear whose object-cause escapes the individual. Sigmund Freud explains that 'anxiety is the affect for which all "repressed" affects are exchanged'[20] and Jacques Lacan further claims that anxiety amounts to 'the central affect, the one around which everything is organized'[21] and 'the only affect that does not deceive.'[22] It indicates approaching the Real of one's own trauma and may allow the subject to begin to understand his or her own place in the past. According to Lacan, working through brings the trauma to completion; anxiety makes its appearance 'once this image which had been rendered incomplete is completed, once the imaginary facet which was non-integrated, suppressed, repressed, looms up.'[23] In this way, *La caza* deals with memories and the trauma of the war in a manner that exposes the anxiety in the characters upon their return to Castile. However, the film's presentation may also provoke anxiety through the *re-presentation* of painful memories and reappearances of the buried past.

In the film, three Nationalist veterans and a younger man, Enrique, embark on a rabbit hunt in the Castilian countryside. I accept the general interpretation of the film as an allegory of the war. However, I ask what the film *does* in 1965 Spain under Franco's repressive dictatorship that lasted for over 35 years. Through its allegorical references to the war, its overwhelming use of violence and fear, and its affective and traumatic narrative, *La caza* resists official, institutional history by representing the experiences of the war and its damaging effects on those affected by it in the past. I will briefly summarize four of the film's main points about Castile, the disturbing events that take place on this former battlefield, and the symbolic objects located within this space.

The film, staged at a Spanish Civil War battlefield in Castile, points back to the historical trauma of the time. With memory situated in a space, trauma victims tend to avoid the place where the traumatic event occurred.[24] Moreover, the return to the geographical space and the repetition of similar situations can reactivate the symptoms in a victim.[25] This happens to the veterans in the film returning to the Castilian site that triggers shocking symptoms. When they arrive, Enrique asks if the caves are from the war. Luis answers, 'Here many people died, piles of people died here, and now all that remains are these holes' and later exclaims that 'the best hunt is that of man'; these lines reaffirm the site as a battlefield and also foreshadow the final massacre. This obsession with violence persists throughout the film, demonstrating that the war has left a psychological wound on these men. However, the film also violently transports the audience to this trauma space and forces them to witness the site, its ruins, and its damaging effect on the characters.

The battlefield is not only significant for the men who experienced the war; it also takes on a trans-generational aspect when Enrique looks around the Castilian plains and reflects, 'I have the impression that I've been here before. I like it. The heat. The smell of thyme. How strange! When have I been in a place like this?' This attests to the meaning of the space in the present for the new generation that did not experience the war. Enrique, who did not participate in the conflict and who had not even visited the land, senses an unexplainable connection to this hunting ground and, therefore, to the country's trauma that took place there. In other words, Castile becomes an important element of the Spanish imaginary that transcends the generational divide. This recalls Ron Eyerman's definition of a cultural trauma, 'a dramatic loss of identity and meaning, a tear in the social fabric, affecting a group of people who have achieved some degree of cohesion.'[26] In other words, the war affected not only the veterans, but also the entire Spanish population – including the next generation of Spaniards – because of its profound impact on, and fragmentation of, the country. Enrique's disturbing feeling of *déja vu*, perhaps connected to the anxiety calling to mind the country's hidden trauma, indicates the cultural and trans-generational traumatization embodied in this former battlefield.

In addition to the significance of the battlefield setting itself, cinematography plays an important role in connection with the painful experience of this space. This is most notable in the rabbit-hunt scenes, which do not simply remind the viewers of the violence of the war; in fact, these scenes also affect the audience and may evoke certain memories or traumatic materials caused by the violent episode of Spanish history. The excessive realism of the rabbit hunts prohibits the audience from simply considering these scenes just another part of the film's fiction. In fact, the shots of the rabbits being slaughtered are actual videos of the animals being killed, then represented on the screen in a close-up, accompanied by the dying animals' shrieks. As a result, the violence of the rabbit-hunts renders the trauma by forcing the audience to witness real deaths, which results in a break from the fictional world of the film. Sally Faulkner states that the hunt scenes 'violently interrupt the narrative and shake us out of our viewing complacency [...] and force us to maintain a critical distance from the film.'[27] These scenes force the viewer to react, thus marking a rupture in the narrative.

The violent interruption in the film's narrative exemplifies Slavoj Žižek's concept of *rendu*. In the case of *La caza*, the disruptive images as well as the sound of the rabbit slaughter affect the viewer. In fact, Michel Chion's original conception of *rendu* relates to sound – specifically those sounds which render reality by involving two senses that do not replicate the experience exactly but rather manipulates the experience using nonconventional combinations of audio and camera-work. This idiosyncratic combination recreates the impact of the experience instead of mimetically representing the experience itself.[28] This further connects to the hunt scenes, as Chion identifies the sound of physical blows or gunshots as 'the canonical example of a rendering.'[29] Thus gunshots in a film are not necessarily faithfully represented auditorily or visually; rather, they attempt to replicate the impact of a gunshot and render the real elements using multiple senses simultaneously. This happens with the hunt scenes in *La caza*, which are much more complex than a simple representation of war veterans embarking on a recreational hunt.

The sound in the rabbit-hunts is as disturbing as the *mise-en-scène* of the dying animals. This not only refers to the sounds of the mortally wounded rabbits, but also to the extradiegetic music that renders the real of the event and resists any attempt to deny the connection between the hunt and the Spanish Civil War. Gwynne Edwards explains that in the hunt scenes of *La caza*, 'the soundtrack has a vital role to play. The sequence begins with an insistent kettle-drum, and, as it develops, drum and piano combine to produce an increasingly jarring, discordant and frenetic rhythm.'[30] Thus camera work and soundtrack combine to become an example of *rendu* in the film that makes *La caza* one of the most intriguing and disturbing works produced in Spain in the 1960s. The seemingly unnecessary close-ups of the mortally wounded rabbits in their final moments, their loud shrieks while shot and the extradiegetic military music playing throughout the scenes force the viewer to forget the fictitious world of the film and to confront some of the real elements that pervade the film. Therefore, these hunts render a type of narrative trauma – a trauma to the narrative, even – in that they unsettle the viewing of the otherwise conventional narrative. Once shaken out of their complacent viewing, the audience may form connections between trauma, the battlefield, and the symbols of fear and anxiety.

Throughout the film, the men complain about the discomfort and misery caused by the scorching, Spanish sun. In a voice-over, Paco thinks: 'this god-forsaken sun is making me nervous.' Shortly thereafter, Luis' thoughts are also interrupted as he looks up at the sun and thinks, 'This heat is unbearable.' Similarly, as Paco contemplates how he and his old friends have changed over the years, he stops and laments to himself, 'We're being roasted alive.' As seen in these voice-over scenes, the sun becomes an incessant and torturous presence in the film that causes anxiety in the characters. Anxiety constitutes the key affect in identifying the presence of a repressed trauma. Other examples of the sun's role as an anxiety-evoking object result from camera work, constantly capturing close-ups of the men's miserable, sweating faces as they look for rabbits. An undulating background creates the effect of nausea or even of heat-stroke, intensifying multiple close-up scenes. While this latter example of *mise-en-scène* communicates to the viewer that the heat causes this undulation, it also unsettles the audience. I argue that the ever-present, inescapable sun manifests the men's anxiety – which has no avoidable object (in the same way that they cannot escape the sun, tormenting them). More precisely, the object of anxiety remains unidentifiable because of its location in the Real, the same register where trauma originates.

Finally, the men find a physical remnant of the war: the skeleton of a dead Republican soldier. This reminds both the characters and the viewers of the 'forgotten' war losses. José takes Paco to the cave where he has discovered the skeleton and Paco quickly leaves. As I have noted, anxiety amounts to the fear of an unknown object, an indication of one's dangerous closeness to recollecting something from the Real; this appears to happen to José, who experiences discomfort and perhaps guilt at too close a reminder of the historical trauma. However, the film presents an avoidable object, thus converting anxiety into phobia. In psychoanalysis, 'should one manage to locate the object so eagerly sought, another dimension is reached and one is in the presence of fear.'[31] The fear caused by the skeleton links to the country's repressed and/or silenced hidden past. José even asks, 'Why don't you bury him as God intended? […] I won't stay here one more minute.' The skeleton *embodies* the cause of anxiety, allowing the objectification of the historical trauma cinematically. Thus disruptive scenes (the rabbit-hunt sequences) and trauma space (the agonizing yet inescapable sun, the undulating backgrounds) evoke anxiety, while the discovery of the skeleton articulates the consequences of a return to Castile for both the characters and the audience.

In the end, *La caza* erupts into a bloodbath between the three veterans on the Castilian battlefield. Enrique, in a panic, sprints away from the scene as the film ends on a freeze-frame of his terrified face. This violence, occurring in a matter of minutes, explodes out of the tension building throughout the film. A few scenes prior to the triple murder, Paco states 'I don't know what has happened to us today'. The answer lies in the overwhelming influence of the memories that these men have managed to keep repressed but which the return to Castile has caused.

## 5. Conclusion

*La caza* – as well as an allegory for the Spanish Civil War – can read as a cinematic working through of the nation's repressed and silenced trauma of the war. The characters do not work through their trauma but rather act it out, lashing out against each other. However, the film itself exposes the presence of trauma in the Spanish collective memory and the potential danger of the repressed materials in relation to a site of trauma. Thus *La caza* – the film itself and not the characters within the film – works through the historical trauma with its allegorical representation of the war and its unsettling narrative and cinematography that renders traumatic materials. Trigg explains that

> the return to a space between identities emerges as an attempt to give back a presence, both spatial and temporal, to a non-experience. To give back a presence to an event means, above all, to *place* the event in time, an event that […] has no place in time.[32]

Space constitutes a significant component in working through as Castile is endowed with memories and feelings previously repressed or displaced, marked by the appearance of anxiety and fear. The men's tragic return to Castile becomes the film's vehicle to place the trauma in time, thereby confronting the effect of the war and dictatorship on the country. This cinematographic return to a trauma space allows for the re-inscription of space within the story of Spanish Civil War and the historical events that occurred there.

Space in cultural production can re-present memories and effects that a trauma has had on the individual and collective imaginary. While many displaced trauma survivors of the Spanish Civil War were attempting to work through the difficult experience from abroad – which poses distinct problems in dealing with trauma, as shown in Hadziosmanovic's study e– those who remained in the country had to live among trauma spaces. Thus the place where a traumatic event occurred plays an important role in coming to terms with the reality of the trauma. By situating the action of the film in a trauma space such as Castile and by rendering the trauma, a cultural artefact becomes a cultural ruin or monument that may connect the voids in the historical memory for both those displaced Spaniards as well as those who remained in the country under Franco. Analogous to the 'Passejant Centelles,' this work takes its audience on an itinerary back to painful, erased or forgotten memories of a traumatic event to revisit and recognize as a trauma space in order to place the event in time. Revisiting the site of repressed memories and the resulting anxiety are conditions of possibility for a cultural artefact to become a counter-narrative and help its audience work through aspects of historical trauma.

# Notes

[1] Slavoj Žižek, *The Sublime Object of Ideology* (London: Verso 1989), 57.
[2] Dominick LaCapra, *Writing History, Writing Trauma* (Baltimore: John Hopkins UP, 2001), 143.
[3] Ibid., 143.
[4] Ruth Ginsberg, 'Ida Fink's Scraps and Traces: Forms of Space and the Chronotope of Trauma Narratives,' *Partial Answers: Journal of Literature and the History of Ideas* 4.2 (2006): 216.
[5] Jacques Lacan, *The Four Fundamental Concepts of Psychoanalysis* (New York: W.W. Norton, 1998), 56.
[6] Anna-Marie Jolivet, 'El "otro" y su representación fílmica. Hacia nuevos planteamientos nacionales.' *Cine, nación y nacionalidades en España*, ed. Nancy Berthier and Jean-Claude Seguin (Madrid: Casa de Velazquez, 2007), 40.
[7] Dylan Trigg, 'The Place of Trauma: Memory, Hauntings, and the Temporality of Ruins,' *Memory Studies* 2 (2009): 89.
[8] Ibid., 89.
[9] Bruce Wardropper, 'The Poetry of Ruins in the Golden Age,' *Revista Hispánica Moderna* 35.4 (1969): 305.
[10] Julian Bonder, 'On Memory, Trauma, Public Space, Monuments, and Memorials,' *Places* 21.1 (2009): 64.
[11] Walter Benjamin, *The Origin of German Tragic Drama* (London: Verso, 1977), 178.
[12] Stanley Fish, 'Literature in the Reader: Affective Stylistics,' *New Literary History* 2 (1970): 124.
[13] Ibid., 127.

[14] Slavoj Žižek, *Looking Awry: An Introduction to Jacques Lacan through Popular Culture* (Cambridge, Mass: MIT Press, 1991), 41.

[15] Ibid., 41.

[16] Ibid., 43.

[17] Trigg, 'Place of Trauma,' 94.

[18] Pablo Neruda, *Confieso que he vivido* (Santiago, Chile: Pehuén, 2005), 174.

[19] Steven Feld and Keith H. Basso, eds., *Senses of Place* (Santa Fe: SAR Press, 1997), 9.

[20] Sigmund Freud. *The Standard Edition of the Complete Psychological Works of Sigmund Freud, Volume XIV (1914-1916): On the History of the Psycho-Analytic Movement, Papers on Meta-Psychology and Other Works* (London: Vintage, 2001), 179.

[21] Jacques Lacan, *The Other Side of Psychoanalysis* (New York: Norton, 2007), 144.

[22] Lacan, *The Four Fundamental Concepts*, 41.

[23] Jacques Lacan, *Freud's Papers on Technique, 1953-1954* (New York: W.W. Norton, 1988), 187-188.

[24] Deborah Langstaff and Jane Christie, *Trauma Care: A Team Approach* (Oxford: Reed Educational Publishing, 2000), 153.

[25] Ibid., 153.

[26] Ron Eyerman, 'The Past in the Present: Culture and the Transmission of Memory,' *Acta Sociologica* 47.2 (2004): 160.

[27] Sally Faulkner, 'Ageing and Coming of Age in Carlos Saura's *La caza*,' *MLN* 120.2 (2005): 461.

[28] Michel Chion, 'Quiet Revolution... and Rigid Stagnation,' *October* 58 (1991): 71.

[29] Ibid., 71

[30] Gwynne Edwards, 'The Persistence of Memory in Carlos Saura's *La caza* and *La prima Angélica*,' *Journal of Iberian and Latin American Studies* 3.2 (1997): 194.

[31] Roberto Harari. *Lacan's Seminar on Anxiety: An Introduction* (New York: Other Press, 2001), 31.

[32] Trigg. 'Place of Trauma,' 97.

# Bibliography

Benjamin, Walter. *The Origin of German Tragic Drama*. Translated by Charles Rosen. London: Verso, 1977.

Bonder, Julian. 'On Memory, Trauma, Public Space, Monuments, and Memorials.' *Places* 21.1 (2009): 62-69.

Eyerman, Ron. 'The Past in the Present: Culture and the Transmission of Memory.' *Acta Sociologica* 47.2 (2004): 159-169.

Feld, Steven and Keith H. Basso, eds. *Senses of Place.* Santa Fe: SAR Press, 1997.

Fish, Stanley. 'Literature in the Reader: Affective Stylistics'. *New Literary History* 2 (1970): 123-160.

Freud, Sigmund. 'The Unconscious.' *The Standard Edition of the Complete Psychological Works of Sigmund Freud, Volume XIV (1914-1916): On the History of the Psycho-Analytic Movement, Papers on Meta-psychology and Other Works.* Translated by James Strachey. London: Vintage, 2001.

Ginsburg, Ruth. 'Ida Fink's Scraps and Traces: Forms of Space and the Chronotope of Trauma Narratives'. *Partial Answers: Journal of Literature and the History of Ideas* 4.2 (2006): 205-218.

Jolivet, Anne-Marie. 'El "otro" y su representación fílmica. Hacia nuevos planteamientos nacionales.' *Cine, nación y nacionalidades en España*, edited by Nancy Berthier and Jean-Claude Seguin, 37-50. Madrid: Casa de Velazquez, 2007.

Lacan, Jacques. *Freud's Papers on Technique, 1953-1954.* New York: W.W. Norton, 1988.

———. *The Four Fundamental Concepts of Psychoanalysis.* New York: W.W. Norton, 1998.

———. *The Other Side of Psychoanalysis.* New York: Norton, 2007.

LaCapra, Dominick. *Writing History, Writing Trauma.* Baltimore: Johns Hopkins University Press, 2001.

Langstaff, Deborah and Jane Christie. *Trauma Care: A Team Approach.* Oxford: Reed Educational Publishing, 2000.

Trigg, Dylan. 'The Place of Trauma: Memory, Hauntings, and the Temporality of Ruins.' *Memory Studies* 2 (2009): 87-101.

Wardropper, Bruce. 'The Poetry of Ruins in the Golden Age.' *Revista Hispánica Moderna* 35.4 (1969): 295-305.

Žižek, Slavoj. *Enjoy Your Symptom: Jacques Lacan in Hollywood and Out.* 3rd ed. New York: Routledge, 2008.

―――. *Looking Awry: An Introduction to Jacques Lacan through Popular Culture.* Cambridge, Mass: MIT Press, 1991.

―――. *The Sublime Object of Ideology*, London: Verso, 1989.

**Jeremy Kasten** is a PhD candidate at The Florida State University, currently working on his dissertation reconsidering the role of some canonical works in Francoist Spain that, through the tacit expression of trauma, are working through some of the events that were silenced or manipulated under the authoritarian regime. His primary research interests are post-Spanish Civil War cultural production, trauma theory, film, psychoanalysis, queer theory, and affect theory.

# Towards Narrating Trauma: The Impact of the Civil War in Former Yugoslavia

*Emina Hadziosmanovic and Nigel Hunt*

**Abstract**
This chapter seeks to investigate social, psychological, and environmental consequences of the war in former Yugoslavia for individuals that became displaced from their homes as a result. It explores difficulties facing refugees who have undergone traumatic experiences in Bosnia, how they have processed these difficulties in the context of social and political developments, and the ways in which they are affected by them today. A cross-country comparison study was undertaken in Bosnia and Herzegovina and in the United Kingdom with 225 Bosnian residents in the UK and 172 in Bosnia completing self-administered questionnaires. All adult participants identified themselves as Bosnian Muslims. The questionnaire assessed personal and second-hand experiences of trauma, mental health post-war, including symptoms of PTSD and general health and wellbeing, explored alongside social relations with the perpetrator group, considering the likelihood of forgiving members of the out-group and the differential influence of living in Bosnia or the UK. The study assessed the importance of everyday living conditions or the immediate environment and the extent to which anxiety proved provoking for individuals across the two countries. The chapter also discusses how individuals cope following traumatic experiences and whether the immediate environment or country of current residence affects them. Implications arising from the results will emerge in the context of using narratives in a potentially therapeutic sense.

**Key Words:** PTSD, war, Bosnia, refugees, trauma, forgiveness, inter-group relations.

*****

## 1. The Bosnian War

This chapter focuses on the war in former Yugoslavia, namely Bosnia & Herzegovina and the social, psychological, and environmental effects which it had upon survivors and continues to have today, more than 20 years since it began. The war, which lasted from April 1992 until the signing of the Dayton Peace Agreement in December 1995, took the lives of over 156,000 individuals, injuring around 175,000 and left many of these permanently disabled.[1] More recent estimates suggest that as many as 200,000 were killed.[2] Bodies from mass graves are still being discovered today, which makes it difficult to obtain precise statistics documenting the number of war casualties. The war also forced more than two million people out of their homes, either internally displaced or displaced as refugees in other countries.[3]

## 2. Short-Term Psychological Impact of the Bosnian War

In the immediate aftermath of the war, the estimates of war trauma and its shorter term impact varied considerably. The studies conducted in Bosnia have reported prevalence rates of PTSD ranging from 26% to 71% and depression at around 40%.[4] In comparison, Hans Thulesius and Anders Hankanssan (1999) found a PTSD prevalence rate of 18-30% in Bosnian refugees living in Sweden.[5] Others have suggested that intergenerational effects may come into play[6] and that the adverse consequences of war could affect subsequent generations.[7] For these reasons, it is all the more important to consider the longer-term psychological impact of the Bosnian War.

## 3. Long-Term Impact of the Bosnian War

In the longer-term, these adverse psychological effects have been demonstrated with internally displaced individuals up to 10 years after the war.[8] Manuel Carballo and his colleagues (2004) suggested that up to 5,000 people were thought to be attending mental health clinics across Bosnia and Herzegovina[9] and roughly 60% of these for serious mental health issues related to the war.[10]

The effects of losing one's home and becoming displaced may have more severe consequences on subsequent mental health than war experiences alone. Studies have found poorer self-rated health in women internally displaced in Lebanon compared to those not displaced[11] and poorer overall mental health in resettled children compared to those not internally resettled in Turkey.[12] Additionally, more depressive symptoms have been observed in children who became displaced within Croatia during the war years[13] and higher levels of PTSD in individuals more directly involved in the Bosnian War, who subsequently became externally displaced to Australia.[14] The prevalence of PTSD and symptoms of depression, anxiety and psychological disorders in Bosnian women displaced during the war to Sweden appeared significantly greater than Swedish-born women.[15]

The effects of war upon individuals can also be manifested in a number of different ways and seen to affect their social perceptions of the world and more specifically the environment around them. This especially holds true in terms of inter-group relations post-war and the ability to reconcile with or forgive the perceived perpetrator. Sabina Cehajic, Rupert Brown and Emanuele Costano used a sample of Bosniak (Muslim) university students to look at the social psychological effects of inter-ethnic conflict by assessing the quality and quantity of contact taking place between the Bosnian and Serb ethnic groups.[16] Their results indicated that positive inter-group contact and higher in-group identification led to greater forgiveness and a lower degree of social distance from Serbs. A large majority of the population reported a low inclination to forgive the Serbs for their past misdeeds. This matters greatly because forgiveness can act as an interventional tool to bring about reconciliation.[17] The authors allege that this could result from the tendency to associate forgiveness with forgetting owing to the frequent interchangeability of these two concepts in human perception.[18] Thus low scores on forgiveness may actually reflect a resistance to forget the past, rather than to forgive it, a distinction important to make.

This particular social psychological concept matters all the more because of its link to mental health. Using a survey-based sample of randomly selected Catholic and Protestant adults from Northern Ireland, Elissa Myers, Miles Hewstone and Ed Cairns discovered that inter-group forgiveness was positively correlated with general health, as measured by the general health questionnaire (GHQ-12).[19] This means that individuals more willing to forgive also experienced better mental health (and lower rates of psychiatric morbidity). Forgiveness acted to mediate the relationship between group identification and psychiatric morbidity. The likelihood of developing mental health problems following conflict was reduced in individuals who exhibited a greater degree of forgiveness. Evidence from other studies further suggests that forgiveness positively associates with mental health.[20]

Other social and environmental changes within Bosnia & Herzegovina during and after the war also need considering in the context of mental health developments. The violations in basic human rights and the atrocities on all sides led to the breakdown in societal values, rules, predictability, norms of behaviour, and everything that had come before.[21] Mere feelings of betrayal on the part of neighbours may have remained strong even after the war and shifted the value systems to developing pessimistic world views. Dean Ajdukovic and Dinka Corkalo observed this in finding strong feelings of distrust between Serb and Croat adolescents after the war.[22] Such feelings could detrimentally cause negative effects upon the health of individual's and one should take the measurement of factors related to reconciliation, such as forgiveness, in post-war mental health research.

This contrasts to the Spanish Civil War, which Mireno Berrettini examines in his chapter looking at the Catholic Church, the Spanish Civil War, and collective memory.[23] Berrettini notes that the Catholic Church leaders advocated forgetting the past in order for reconciliation and forgiveness to take place. Based on the following research in post-war Bosnia, this concept seems inconceivable as mental health is linked to the willingness to forgive and simply forgetting the past could to lead to further traumatisation in survivors of war. Whilst some argue that Franco's coup was not a political one and the Civil War became a Crusade to free Spain from atheism, many Bosnian war survivors believe the war had a predominant religious aim; unlike the Francoists seeking to free Spain from atheism and Republican values, the Orthodox Serbs fought to free Bosnia from its Muslim inhabitants.

The experience of changing the environment in which one lives could have contributed to further traumatisation. This holds especially true if one considers the reasons that the majority of individuals became externally displaced – they were rescued from concentration camps and taken to safety abroad or were medical evacuees after suffering extensive injuries in the war. This means they already came to their host country with trauma and maladaptive experiences, and sometimes the initial months of refugee-hood led to further traumatisation. Those who become displaced following war have a higher overall dose of trauma, making them predisposed to experiencing increased levels of PTSD and other associated psychological disorders. This concept widely endorsed within the literature to date was studied by Catherine Nicholl and Andrew Thompson in their review of psychological treatments for adults with PTSD. The association between war experiences and increased levels of mental health disorders years after the war has been documented in relation to the Bosnian War[24] and termed the 'dose-response' relationship in which a greater degree of involvement in the war brings about more pronounced adverse psychological effects.

An effect of place contributing to this poorer general health overall may also exist because forced displacement leads to greater loses than material possessions and a roof over one's head. Individuals become deprived of place bonds, which result in cultivation of collective identities,[25] which hold together their identity, gender, social class, ethnic background, occupation, and religion.[26] Once these become broken, the self is disjointed, identity unclear, and the boundaries of human interactions and capabilities deleted. Therefore, the disintegration of place could have long-lasting effects on the health of displaced peoples.[27]

In addition to these effects, the importance of place can also appear in acts that link trauma and place, such as burials. The restoration of health might come through such acts. The burial site chosen in Srebrenica for victims of genocide in this region introduced an important concept: the breakage of attachment through place, but also the healing of trauma through place. Potocari was chosen as the burial site for mass victims because there the Serbs massacred over 8,000 Bosnian men and boys in July 1995. It represented the ultimate site of the horror connected to the individual's sense of home.[28] However, Potocari also holds immense hope for people, encouraging collective grieving to take place and the outward display of emotions to act as a warning and deterrent for future generations of the genocide effects.

This might suggest that greater healing takes place more likely in the country of origin with its physical boundaries connected to trauma and place as the level of exposure to them will also be significantly higher. This further factor might lead to individuals who become externally displaced during the war to experience more mental health problems because of the restricted opportunity for healing caused by the broken bonds with the place of trauma, in addition to the resettlement issues faced by refugees. These may include worry about family members left behind, unemployment and economic difficulties, and acculturative stressors.[29]

In the previous chapter, Jeremy Kasten also discussed the links between trauma and place, terming this 'trauma space', a space both traumatised (with historical ruins to portray past events) and traumatic (which may evoke particular feelings or anxieties in victims).[30] Where Kasten uses Carlos Saura's film *La Caza* to cinematically represent a trauma space following the Spanish Civil War, the present chapter focuses on current or real life portrays of trauma and its effects following the aftermath of the Yugoslavian Civil War. Whilst the representations of trauma in Kasten's work nicely fit psychoanalytical frameworks, trauma in the present chapter proves a somewhat 'messier' and more complicated psychological concept, incorporating the social, environmental, and mental wellbeing of an individual — very much a fluid concept changing from person to person and time to time.

In *La caza,* the space in which a traumatic event took place has historical significance for the country itself and the continuation of that history. In Castile some of the bloodiest fighting in the Spanish Civil War took place, which brings about painful memories of both violent events but also loss. As discussed earlier in this chapter with regards to Srebrenica (where genocide happened), place can also trigger a process of healing and processing the events. In the same way that Castile brings back memories, places where war atrocities took place in Bosnia might re-activate otherwise dormant memories and neural pathways in the brain. This process in itself could lead to healing trauma through exposure. The impact of the environment in this way — an important construct — will be considered in the present study.

## 4. Social, Psychological and Environmental Impact of the Bosnian War

The present chapter compares the effects of war for those who became refugees to the UK, with those who remained in Bosnia and Herzegovina and live there today. It aims to examine the relationship between key variables, including mental health post-war, the capacity to forgive the perpetrator group, and everyday concerns or anxieties surrounding the environment one resides in. In line with previous literature, which found poorer mental health in individuals displaced to the UK compared to those who remained within Bosnia and Herzegovina,[31] we hypothesise that the externally displaced group in the UK will suffer more severe mental health consequences, with higher rates of PTSD symptoms and poorer overall general health, than those currently living in Bosnia and Herzegovina. Consequently, they will less likely forgive the other ethnic groups for the atrocities carried out against their in-group. In contrast, they are predicted to have less concern for their everyday environment in the UK because of the somewhat more stable social, political, and economical situation in the UK than that in Bosnia and Herzegovina.

A. Method

A study compared 172 individuals living in Bosnia and Herzegovina and 225 living in the United Kingdom between October 2011 and May 2012. The study implemented a questionnaire design, with participants required to answer questions relating to the Bosnian War, their personal physical and mental health post-war, as well as their views on forgiveness, and any anxieties about everyday environmental factors, such as housing, healthcare or jobs. Comparisons in the study are made in relation to these factors.

B. Participants

Participants aged between 19 and 84, with a mean age 44.43 had either been displaced from their pre-war homes to the UK or they had remained within their pre-war homes in Bosnia and Herzegovina. The study comprised 194 male participants and 203 female participants. Employment status was not measured for all the participants. Out of the 290 that did complete this question, 112 identified as employed, 118 unemployed, 7 were housewives, and 53 pensioners. Some participants chose to leave this question unanswered. This happened with the further 107 participants. Participants all had some kind of experience of war, even if they subsequently left the country. The level of war exposure differed, with some individuals enduring longer periods in Bosnia, and perhaps increased sustained trauma, but this was not measured. Of those that came to the UK, some had been medical evacuees after sustaining life-threatening injuries in the war, whilst others had been rescued from concentration or detention camps. The precise number of such individuals is not known. All participants ethnically described themselves as Bosnian Muslims (Bosniaks) and the study focuses only upon the effects of the conflict for the Bosniak group.

C. Design and Procedure

Participants were required to complete a questionnaire relating to their experiences during the civil war in former Yugoslavia 1992-1995, their personal reactions, and subsequent interpretations of these experiences. Each participant was given an information sheet and required to verbally consent to the study, prior to signing the consent form. The conditions of participation were clearly explained and participants were given the opportunity to have questions answered prior to completing the questionnaire. The anonymity of responses was fully explained as was the fact that they could withdraw their participation from the study at any point. This did not happen in any case. Participants sometimes preferred to sign the consent form with a 'false' name, which they believed would give them the freedom to answer without thinking about cultural, social, or political repercussions the answers might yield. This gave them greater comfort to be more open with their answers.

The majority of participants were given questionnaires that were returned in person, or collected by the first author. Some were completed in the presence of the first author, but without any author input. Others were actively completed with participants, where questions were read through and explained, before answers were selected. This was particularly so with older individuals. Questionnaire completion time varied considerably, due to the factors noted above. Self-completed ones took approximately 20 minutes, whereas assisted ones took up to an hour.

D. Measures

Questionnaires were constructed in English, translated into Bosnian (the first language of the majority in the study), and back-translated into English. Questionnaires relating to 5 central concepts were completed. All the measures displayed good reliability and validity.

The 5 measurements included the following:

> **General Health Questionnaire (GHQ-12):** a measure to assess general psychological wellbeing. It is a short questionnaire developed by David Goldberg (originally in 1978 as a 60 item instrument) assessing psychiatric morbidity and has largely been used in the literature as a unidimensional instrument to measure common mental health problems, to indicate signs of depression, anxiety, somatic symptoms, and social withdrawal. The longer version was modified by David Goldberg and Paul Williams (1988) as a 12-item questionnaire focusing on the inability to complete normal everyday tasks and the presence of new and distressing experiences.[32] It can be used in both clinical and non-clinical populations which is a further advantage of using this measure.

> **Impact of Event Scale-Revised (IES-R):** developed by Mardi Horowitz, Nancy Wilner and William Alvarez in 1979,[33] the IESR remains to be one of the most widely used measures of self-reported trauma available in the literature.[34] The IES-R consists of 22 items and measures subjective reporting of traumatic events in the adult population. It can be used for any traumatic event and repeated over time to measure progress. Demonstrating reliability and validity, it has been utilised across a wide range of populations and traumatic events.

> **Brief Cope:** developed by Charles Carver in 1997, brief cope is a 28-item measure designed to assess effective and ineffective

coping strategies in health-related research.[35] It is taken from a longer 60-item measure called the COPE Inventory developed by Charles Carver, Michael Scheier and Jagdish Weintraub in 1989[36] and has previously been tested in a study of 168 American adults in the process of recovery after Hurricane Andrew[37] where it demonstrated good internal reliability. The Brief Cope-28 was designed to measure 14 conceptually differentiable coping strategies or reactions to stressful life events; some of which are adaptive and others which are known to be problematic. Two items are used to measure each of the 14 strategies, which include: active coping; planning; positive reframing; acceptance; humour; religion; using emotional support; using instrumental support; self-distraction; denial; venting; substance use; behavioural disengagement; self-blame.

**Forgiveness:** assessed using a new 9-item scale adapted for Bosnia from Tam and colleagues (2007).[38] Questions looked at the likelihood of Bosniaks forgiving the Serbs for past misdeeds committed against their in-group under various conditions (i.e., if war criminals were to be caught).

**Environmental/Everyday Life Anxiety**: A new 11-item scale was developed specifically to measure the level of anxiety an individual has towards their everyday environment, whether living in Bosnia or the United Kingdom. Questions assessed how anxious or worried individuals were about aspects in their daily lives, such as healthcare, government, ethnic tensions, housing, jobs etc. According to previous research conducted, there was no existing scale available to test these particular constructs.

## 5. Differences between Displaced and Non-Displaced War Populations?

The results from the present study have determined 3 main differences between the group of individuals displaced to the UK and those who remained within Bosnia and Herzegovina during, and after, the war years. These include the following:

1. Poorer overall general health in the group externally displaced to the UK.
2. Higher levels of PTSD symptoms in the externally displaced to the UK group.
3. More anxiety towards the environment in the group currently living in Bosnia and Herzegovina.

No differences in forgiveness between the groups nor in coping styles appeared. The group displaced to the UK exhibited higher levels of PTSD symptoms and poorer mental health functioning overall. Significant differences also surfaced in environmental factors, with individuals in Bosnia and Herzegovina experiencing more anxiety towards their everyday conditions of life in comparison to those living in the UK. No differences in the coping styles (levels of processing or avoidance) came to light between the two groups neither in forgiveness, as previously reported in other populations and conflicts.[39]

The study replicated other research in depicting poorer mental health for displaced compared to non-displaced individuals. Nigel Hunt and Maha Gakenyi found poorer mental health functioning and higher levels of traumatic symptomatology in externally displaced individuals compared with those residing in Bosnia and Herzegovina, including those internally displaced.[40]

Other studies conducted in Sweden and Australia (for example Kristina Sunquist and colleagues [41] and Shakeh Momartin and colleagues [42]) have all found high rates for refugees externally displaced, when compared with individuals permanently resident in those countries or with those not displaced from Bosnia and Herzegovina. This includes larger scale studies using mixed methodologies that have measured the incidence of PTSD in over 3,000 participants from the Balkans and almost 900 displaced to other Western European countries such as Germany and Italy.[43]

In more general terms, the estimates for refugees suffering from PTSD symptoms oscillate between 12% to 91%.[44] This may result from post-migration factors and the various challenges faced, such as lack of language-knowledge, the loss of social identity, unemployment, social isolation, and acculturation. The time of measurement and cultural factors might also come into play in determining these effects. If an individual has only just become displaced to another country following war or conflict, their primary concerns likely relate to settling into their new surroundings as opposed to their immediate psychological health. Once their everyday environments are relatively stable, individuals will begin to process traumatic events that might have occurred in their lives. Culturally speaking, Bosnians tend to respond to adverse events by keeping busy and keeping themselves occupied with other everyday activities as a means of self-distraction. Thus taking measurements of PTSD might temporally differ, with a lower likelihood to report immediately following the trauma and an increased likelihood to report such events after a period of time has elapsed and has helped process this information. If individuals experience other life difficulties during this 'processing' (such as unemployment or bereavement), this might worsen their overall outlook on life and thus cause heightened reactions and subsequent reporting of PTSD symptoms.

For these reasons a new questionnaire emerged for the purpose of this study to examine environmental and everyday living stressors and the extent to which they were anxiety provoking for those living in two different environments: Bosnia and the UK. The results demonstrated significant differences between environments' post-war, with those in Bosnia and Herzegovina having more concerns about their living conditions than those in the UK. This finding makes sense when one considers the political and economic situation in Bosnia and in the UK. There exists much greater stability for individuals living in the UK in comparison to Bosnia with the common concern to have enough money to feed the children or pay the bills. The UK has minimised this worry for many individuals through the welfare and benefit system. The instability in Bosnia caused by the economic collapse after the war resulted in greater inequalities, poverty, and unemployment,[45] which still continues today.

Whilst this finding makes theoretical sense, it contradicts those from other studies that have examined specific environmental traits post-war for refugees, such as employability in their host country. Karin Blight and her colleagues found that Bosnian refugees in Sweden experience higher rates of unemployment overall, particularly if they have poorer general mental health.[46] The study also indicated that job occupancy mattered particularly to men and that those employed in Sweden fared better in terms of mental health than those unemployed. This correlational finding does not clarify the causal nature of the relationship. Individuals less traumatised and in better health when they came to Sweden may be more likely find employment or the mental health of refugees may improve once they become employed.

Socialisation could also contribute to this. When displaced to another country, an individual loses most social ties and friendships. It is a well-known fact that social support can act as a buffer against some of the adverse effects following traumatic experiences, as found in soldiers for example[47] and also more generally.[48] Therefore, when an individual becomes displaced from their homes, they not only lose their physical possessions but also experience the severing of ties and relationships they had with others. Their main support base tends to become lost through the displacement experience. By starting a new job and becoming employed, they might gain a new social support structure to put in place of the one they have lost in Bosnia. With increased social support through their difficulties, their mental health issues might begin to improve. Becoming employed might facilitate this through the new social support system, rather than anything else relating to the new job status more directly. This warrants additional investigation, but studies have already established unemployment as one of the most frequently occurring stressors in resettlement for refugees.[49]

In terms of social reconciliatory factors post-war, particularly with regards to forgiveness, no differences came to light between externally displaced refugees and those who remained within Bosnia and Herzegovina. This means that forgiveness can be considered as particularly person-specific as opposed to varying according to place of residence. It might be influenced by factors that relate more to personal experiences with Serbs before, during, and after the war. This could relate to the number of friendships Bosniaks had with Serbs before the war and the nature in which they continued such friendships during or after the war. For example, one individual may have had many Serbian friends before the war, maintained good contact with them during the war, the same Serbian friend may have fought for the Bosnian Army and been on the same 'side' as them. Such a person is likely to have kept contact with their Serbian friend and might be more likely to forgive all Serbs for atrocities committed against the Bosniak in-group due to the positive relations they have with their own Serbian friends. This could be in direct contrast to another individual who never had contact with Serbs prior to the war, then witnessed the killing of 10 family members by Serbs in the war, and faces prejudice on a daily basis whilst living in Serbian-owned territory. Someone in this situation may be less likely to forgive the Serbs because they have been more negatively affected by them and have not seen the positive qualities of Serbs. These concepts can be explained using Allport's 'contact hypothesis' whereby with the establishment of positive good quality and frequent contact with the opposing group, forgiveness is more likely to take place.[50]

A negative correlation with environment, however, occurred, which suggests that individuals, more concerned with and anxious about their everyday surroundings, less likely forgive people for past misdeeds committed against their in-group. This could connect to growth in that individuals who feel comfortable in their surroundings, and have attained a certain level of 'economic growth' are more inclined to focus upon inter-group relations and think about forgiveness, in comparison to those fighting with their everyday living conditions to feed their children, for example, or build a new home for themselves. This can be linked to Maslow's concept of growth and self-actualisation.[51] Until basic needs at the lower level are met, such as food and shelter, those at that top, concerned with self-actualisation and betterment, cannot be met.

The other non-significant difference observed between the groups concerns coping and the nature in which individuals process traumatic events. This does not differ according to displacement factors and the post-war environment does not have an effect upon this. Coping may be a factor linked to the personality style of individuals, which neither partaking of, nor dictated by the war. Coping style may be person-specific which could explain why no differences were observed. Previous literature supports this assumption, such as that conducted by Robert McCrae and Paul Costa[52] as well as Igor Kardum and Nada Krapic.[53]

Clearly, refugees who are externally displaced outside of their homelands fare worse in terms of mental health post-displacement and may need a longer recovery/rehabilitation period. Differences appeared in PTSD symptoms and general health and wellbeing scores between the groups. This effect was also observed for anxiety towards the environment and everyday living conditions, with those in Bosnia and Herzegovina expressing greater concerns than individuals living in the UK. No differences were found in forgiveness and coping styles, which seems to suggest other factors than displacement need to be taken into consideration if differences between the groups exist.

This is the first study of its kind examining the interactions between psychological, social, and environmental factors for the long-term effects of war on externally displaced and non-displaced individuals post-war. It also uses a large sample size (n = 397), comprising different categories of people (e.g., ex-soldiers, pensioners, young adults) who undertook varied roles during the war. Such a diverse sample was deliberately chosen in order to encompass breadth of experiences and roles undertaken during the war.

## 6. Limitations

This study presents one limitation, namely that the sample was not randomly selected nor representative of the population, since it focused solely on Bosniaks (Bosnian Muslims). This opportunistic sample resulted from snowballing and the willingness of external organisations to collaborate in this research and on personal contacts of the first author. This includes organisations working with Bosnian refugees in the UK, in addition to organisations representing the rights of ex-soldiers in Bosnia and Herzegovina. The nature of the recruitment procedure means that the sample could be non-representative of the general population and only those individuals most or least affected by the war were approached or included to take part to begin with. This makes producing comparisons across the wider population more difficult.

## 7. Conclusion

The study links social, psychological, and environmental constructs in looking at the long-term effects of war. More studies of this kind are needed to elicit which factors contribute to social rehabilitation and the potential improvement of inter-group relations post-conflict. What matters is the incidence of PTSD symptoms and poor general health in these populations, even sixteen years since the end of the war. This depicts the long-lasting effects of war and the need for assistance to heal the traumatic experiences individuals have faced.

The importance of talking about traumatic war experiences came across clearly throughout this study. Whilst completing the questionnaires, participants would begin to go into depth to explain the reasons why they had selected certain answers or to give examples in their lives for their selections. This clarifies why some of the questionnaires took up to an hour to complete. Participants had something to say about each of the constructs used and wanted to tell their own personal stories. Many of them discussed 'feeling better' after talking about their experiences, which gives rise to the notion of using narrative as a potentially therapeutic technique to facilitate such changes in individuals. The use of Narrative Exposure Therapy (NET) introduced by Maggie Schauer, Frank Neuner and Thomas Elbert as a non-specialist therapy or technique in achieving this with both adults and children is becoming more popular over recent years.[54] Its short-term use with refugees in African settlements has led to reductions in PTSD symptoms.[55] Based on information about this technique, it potentially could facilitate Bosnian refugees in the UK, in addition to those living in Bosnia, to tell their war stories whilst feeling better at the same time and overcoming some of the negative past experiences. This direction will enable the present research to progress in the future.

# Notes

[1] Amer Smajkic, Vernes Bekric, and Ilijas Bosnjovic, 'Genocide, Ethnic Cleansing and Annihilation of People in Bosnia and Herzegovina,' *Health and Social Consequences of the Bosnian War and Herzegovina: Rehabilitation Proposal* ed. Amer Smajkic (Sarajevo, Svjetlost: Institute of Public Health of B&H, 1996).
[2] Eric. D Weitz, *A Century of Genocide: Utopias of Race and Nation* (Princeton: Princeton University Press, 2003).
[3] UNHCR Report, 'Jolie Highlights the Continuing Suffering of the Displaced in Bosnia', 6 April 2010. Viewed on 19 October 2010, http://unhcr.org.
[4] Solveig Dahl, Atifa Mutapcic and Berit Schei, 'Traumatic Events and Predictive Factors in Posttraumatic Symptoms in Displaced Bosnian Women in a War Zone,' *Journal of Traumatic Stress* 11 (1998): 137-145.
[5] Hans Thulesius and Anders Hankanssan, 'Screening for Posttraumatic Stress Disorder Symptoms among Bosnian Refugees,' *Journal of Traumatic Stress* 12 (1998): 167-174.
[6] Derek Summerfield, 'A Critique of Seven Assumptions behind Psychological Trauma Programs in War-Affected Areas,' *Social Science and Medicine* 48 (1999): 1449-1462.
[7] Chantelle A. M. Richmond and Nancy A. Ross, 'The Determinants of First Nation and Inuit Health: A Critical Population Health Approach,' *Health and Place* 15. 2 (2009): 403-411.
[8] Maria E. Kett, 'Internally Displaced Peoples in Bosnia-Herzegovina: Impacts of Long-Term Displacement on Health and Wellbeing,' *Medicine, Conflict and Survival* 21 (2005): 199-215.
[9] Manuel Carballo et al., 'Mental Health and Coping in a War Situation: The Case of Bosnia and Herzegovina,' *Journal of Bio-Social Science* 00 (2004): 1-15.
[10] Bernard Lagerkvist et al., 'Assessment of Community Mental Health Centres in Bosnia and Herzegovina as Part of the Ongoing Mental Health Reform,' *Medicinski Arhiv* 57.1 (2003): 31-38.

[11] Nathalie Choueiry and Marwan Khawaja, 'Displacement and Health Status in Low Income Women: Findings from a Population-Based Study in Greater Beirut,' *Journal of Migrant and Refugee Issues* 3 (2007): 1-13.

[12] Neşe Erol et al., 'Effects of Internal Displacement and Resettlement on the Mental Health of Turkish Children and Adolescents,' *European Psychiatry* 20 (2005): 152-157.

[13] Andreja Brajsa-Zganec, 'The Long-Term Effects of War Experiences on Children's Depression in the Republic of Croatia,' *Child Abuse & Neglect* 29 (2005): 31-43.

[14] Shakeh Momartin et al., 'Comorbidity of PTSD and Depression: Associations with Trauma Exposure, Symptom Severity and Functional Impairment in Bosnian Refugees Resettled in Australia,' *Journal of Affective Disorders* 2 (2004): 231-238.

[15] Kristina Sundquist et al., 'Posttraumatic Stress Disorder and Psychiatric Co-Morbidity: Symptoms in a Random Sample of Female Bosnian Refugees,' *European Psychiatry* 20 (2005): 158-164.

[16] Sabina Cehajic, Rupert Brown and Emanuele Costano, 'Forgive and Forget? Antecedents and Consequences of Intergroup Forgiveness in Bosnia and Herzegovina,' *Political Psychology* 29.3 (2008): 351-367.

[17] Mícheál D. Roe, 'Intergroup Forgiveness in Settings of Political Violence: Complexities, Ambiguities, and Potentialities,' *Peace and Conflict: Journal of Peace Psychology* 13.1 (2007): 3-9.

[18] Desmond Tutu, *No Future without Forgiveness* (London: Rider, 1999).

[19] Elissa Myers, Miles Hewstone and Ed Cairns, 'Impact of Conflict on Mental Health in Northern Ireland: The Mediating Role of Intergroup Forgiveness and Collective Guilt,' *Political Psychology* 30. 2 (2009): 269-290.

[20] Alfred Allan et al., 'Exploration of the Association between Apology and Forgiveness amongst Victims of Human Rights Violations,' *Behavioural Sciences and the Law* 24 (2006): 87-102. Berton H. Kaplan, 'Social Health and the Forgiving Heart: The Type B Story,' *Journal of Behavioural Medicine* 15 (1992): 3-14. Michael E. McCullough, Everett L. Worthington and Chris K. Rachel, 'Interpersonal Forgiving in Close Relationships,' *Journal of Personality and Social Psychology* 73 (1997): 321-336. Edward Scobie and Geoffrey Scobie, 'Damaging Events: The Perceived Need for Forgiveness,' *Journal for the Theory of Social Behavior* 28 (1998): 373-401. Charlotte vanOyen Witvliet, Thomas Ludwig and Kelly L. Vander Laan, 'Granting fForgiveness or Harboring Grudges: Implications for Emotions, Physiology, and Health,' *Psychological Science* 12.2 (2001): 117-123. Charlotte vanOyen Witvliet et al., 'Posttraumatic Mental and Physical Health Correlates of Forgiveness and Religious Coping in Military Veterans,' *Journal of Traumatic Stress* 17 (2004): 269-273.

[21] Stefan Priebe et al., 'Experience of Human Rights Violations and Subsequent Mental Disorders: A Study Following the War in the Balkans,' *Social Science and Medicine* 71 (2010): 2170-2177.

[22] Dean Ajdukovic and Dinka Corkalo, 'Trust and Betrayal in War,' *My Neighbor, My Enemy: Justice and Community in the Aftermath of Mass Atrocity*, eds. Eric Stover and Harvey Weinstein (Cambridge: Cambridge University Press, 2004), 287-302.

[23] Mireno Berrettini in this volume.

[24] Metin Basoglu et al., 'Psychiatric and Cognitive Effects of War in Former Yugoslavia: Association of Lack of Redress for Trauma and Posttraumatic Stress Reactions,' *Journal of the American Medical Association* 294 (2005): 580-90. Miro Klaric et al., 'Psychological Consequences of War Trauma and Postwar Social Stressors in Women in Bosnia and Herzegovina,' *Croatian Medical Journal* 48 (2007): 167-176.

[25] Helmut Anheier and Jeremy Kendall, 'Interpersonal Trust and Voluntary Associations: Examining Three Approaches,' *British Journal of Sociology* 53.3 (2002): 343–362.

[26] Lee Cuba and David Hummon, 'A Place to Call Home: Identification with Dwelling, Community, and Region,' *The Sociological Quarterly* 34.1 (1993): 111-131.

[27] Nihaya Daoud et al., 'Internal Displacement and Health among the Palestinian Minority in Israel,' *Social Sciences and Medicine* 74 (2012): 1163-1171.

[28] Craig Evan Pollack, 'Burial at Srebrenica: Linking Place and Trauma,' *Social Science and Medicine* 56 (2003): 793-801.

[29] Jan Sundquist, Alija Behmen-Vincevic and Sven-Erik Johannsson, 'Poor Quality of Life and Health in Young to Middle-Aged Bosnian Female War rRefugees: A Population-Based Study,' *Public Health* 112.1 (1998): 21-26.

[30] Jeremy Kasten in this volume.

[31] Nigel Hunt and Maha Gakenyi, 'Comparing the Refugees and Non-Refugees: The Bosnian Experience,' *Anxiety Disorders* 19 (2005): 717-723.

[32] David Goldberg and Paul Williams, *A Users Guide to the General Health Questionnaire* (Slough: NFER Nelson, 1988).

[33] Mardi Horowitz, Nancy Wilner and William Alvarez, 'Impact of Events Scale: A Measure of Subjective Stress,' *Psychosomatic Medicine* 41 (1979): 209-218.

[34] Daniel Weiss and Charles R. Marmar, 'The Impact of Event Scale-Revised,' *Assessing Psychological Trauma and PTSD: A Practitioner's Handbook*, eds. John P. Wilson and Terence M. Keane (New York: Guilford Press, 1999), 399-411.

[35] Charles C. Carver, 'You Want to Measure Coping but Your Protocol's too Long: Consider the Brief COPE,' *International Journal of Behavioural Medicine* 4 (1997): 92-100.

[36] Charles C. Carver, Michael F. Scheier and Jagdish Kumari Weintraub, 'Assessing Coping Strategies: A Theoretically-Based Approach,' *Journal of Personality and Social Psychology* 56 (1989): 267-283.

[37] Daniella David et al., 'Psychiatric Morbidity following Hurricane Andrew,' *Journal of Traumatic Stress* 9 (1996): 607-612. Gail Ironson et al., 'Post-Traumatic Stress Symptoms, Intrusive Thoughts, Loss, and Immune Function after Hurricane Andrew,' *Psychosomatic Medicine* 59 (1997): 128-141.

[38] Tania Tam et al., 'The Impact of Inter-Group Emotions on Forgiveness in Northern Ireland,' *Group Processes and Intergroup relations* 10 (2007): 119-135.

[39] Myers, Hewstone and Cairns, 'Impact of Conflict on Mental Health in Northern Ireland,' 269-290.

[40] Hunt and Gakenyi, 'Comparing the Refugees and Non-Refugees,' 717-723.

[41] Kristina Sundquist et al., 'Posttraumatic Stress Disorder and Psychiatric Co-Morbidity: Symptoms in a Random Sample of Female Bosnian Refugees,' *European Psychiatry* 20 (2005): 158-164.

[42] Momartin et al., 'Comorbidity of PTSD and Depression,' 231-238.

[43] Priebe et al., 'Experience of Human Rights Violations' 2170-2177.

[44] Howard Johnson and Andrew Thompson, 'The Development and Maintenance of Posttraumatic Stress Disorder (PTSD) in Civilian Adult Survivors of War Trauma and Torture: A Review,' *Clinical Psychology Review* 28 (2006): 36-47.

[45] David J. Pevalin and Karen L. Robson, 'Social Determinants of Health Inequalities in Bosnia & Herzegovina,' *Public Health* 121 (2007): 588-595.

[46] Karin J. Blight et al., 'Mental Health, Employment, and Gender: Cross-Sectional Evidence in a Sample of Refugees from Bosnia-Herzegovina Living in tTwo Swedish Regions,' *Social Science and Medicine* 62 (2006): 1697-1709.

[47] Robert H. Pietrzak et al., 'Psychosocial Buffers of Traumatic Stress, Depressive Symptoms, and Psychosocial Difficulties in Veterans of Operations Enduring Freedom and Iraqi Freedom: The Role of Resilience, Unit Support, and Post Deployment Social Support,' *Journal of Affective Disorders* 120 (2010): 188-192.

[48] Krzysztof Kaniasty, 'Social Support and Traumatic Stress,' *PTSD Research Quarterly* 16.2 (2005): 1-8.

[49] Morton Beiser and Feng Hou, 'Language Acquisition, Unemployment and Depressive Disorder among Southeast Asian Refugees: A 10-Year Study,' *Social Science and Medicine* 53 (2001): 1321-1334.

[50] Gordon Allport, *The Nature of Prejudice* (Cambridge, MA: Perseus Books, 1954).

[51] Abraham Maslow, 'A Theory of Human Motivation,' *Psychological Review* 50.4 (1943): 370-96.

[52] Robert R. McCrae and Paul T. Costa, 'Personality, Coping, and Coping Effectiveness in an Adult Sample,' *Journal of Personality* 54 (1986): 385-405.

[53] Igor Kardum and Nada Krapic, 'Personality Traits, Successful Life Events, and Coping Styles in Early Adolescence,' *Personality and Individual Differences* 30 (2001): 503-515.

[54] Maggie Schauer, Frank Neuner, and Thomas Elbert, *Narrative Exposure Therapy: A Short-Term Treatment for Traumatic Stress Disorders* (Gottingen Germany: Hogrefe Publishing, 2011).

[55] Martina Ruf et al., 'Narrative Exposure Therapy for 7- to 16-Year Olds: A Randomised Controlled Trial with Traumatized Refugee Children,' *Journal of Traumatic Stress* 23.4 (2010): 437-445.

# Bibliography

Ajdukovic, Dean, and Dinka Corkalo. 'Trust and Betrayal in War.' *My Neighbor, My Enemy: Justice and Community in the Aftermath of Mass Atrocity*, edited by Eric Stover and Harvey Weinstein, 287-302. Cambridge: Cambridge University Press, 2004.

Allan, Alfred, Maria Allan, Debra Kaminer, and Dan Stein. 'Exploration of the Association between Apology and Forgiveness amongst Victims of Human Rights Violations.' *Behavioural Sciences and the Law* 24 (2006): 87-102.

Allport, Gordon. *The Nature of Prejudice*. Cambridge, MA: Perseus Books, 1954.

Anheier, Helmut, and Jeremy Kendall. 'Interpersonal Trust and Voluntary Associations: Examining Three Approaches.' *British Journal of Sociology* 53.3 (2002): 343–362.

Basoglu, Metin, Maria Livanou, Cvetana Crnobaric, Tanja Franciskovic, Enra Suljic, Dijana Duric, and Melin Vranesic. 'Psychiatric and Cognitive Effects of War in Former Yugoslavia: Association of Lack of Redress for Trauma and Posttraumatic Stress Reactions.' *Journal of the American Medical Association* 294 (2005): 580-90.

Beiser, Morton, and Feng Hou. 'Language Acquisition, Unemployment, and Depressive Disorder amongst Southeast Asian Refugees: A 10-Year Study.' *Social Sciences and Medicine* 53 (2001): 1321-1334.

Blight, Karin, Solvig Ekblad, Jan-Olov Persson, and Jan Ekberg. 'Mental Health, Employment, and Gender: Cross-Sectional Evidence in a Sample of Refugees from Bosnia-Herzegovina Living in Two Swedish Regions.' *Social Science and Medicine* 62 (2006): 1697-1709.

Brajsa-Zganec, Andreja. 'The Long-Term Effects of War Experiences on Children's Depression in the Republic of Croatia.' *Child Abuse and Neglect* 29 (2005): 31-43.

Carballo, Manuelle, Arif Smajkic, Damir Zeric, Monika Dzidowska, Joy Gebre-Medhin, and Joost Van Halem. 'Mental Health and Coping in a War Situation: The Case of Bosnia and Herzegovina.' *Journal of Bio-social Science* 00 (2004): 1-15.

Carver, Charles C. 'You Want to Measure Coping but Your Protocol's too Long: Consider the Brief COPE.' *International Journal of Behavioural Medicine* 4 (1997): 92-100.

Carver, Charles C, Michael Scheier, and Jagdish Kumari Weintraub. 'Assessing Coping Strategies: A Theoretically Based Approach.' *Journal of Personality and Social Psychology* 56 (1989): 267-283.

Cehajić, Sabina, Rupert Brown, and Emanuele Castano. 'Forgive and Forget? Antecedents and Consequences of Intergroup Forgiveness in Bosnia and Herzegovina.' *Political Psychology* 29.3 (2008): 351-367.

Choueiry, Nathalie, and Marwan Khawaja. 'Displacement and Health Status in Low Income Women: Findings from a Population-Based Study in Greater Beirut.' *Journal of Migrant and Refugee Issues* 3 (2007): 1-13.

Cuba, Lee, and David Hummon. 'A Place to Call Home: Identification with Dwelling, Community, and Region.' *The Sociological Quarterly* 34.1 (1993): 111-131.

Dahl, Solveig, Atifa Mutapcic and Berit Schei. 'Traumatic Events and Predictive Factors in Posttraumatic Symptoms in Displaced Bosnian Women in a War Zone.' *Journal of Traumatic Stress* 11 (1998): 137-145.

Daoud, Nihaya, Ketan Shankardass, Patricia O'Campo, Kim Anderson and Ayman Agbaria. 'Internal Displacement and Health among the Palestinian Minority in Israel.' *Social Sciences and Medicine* 74 (2012): 1163-1171.

David, Daniella, Thomas Melman, Lourdes Mendoza, Renee Kulick-Bell, Gail Ironson and Neil Schneiderman. 'Psychiatric Morbidity following Hurricane Andrew.' *Journal of Traumatic Stress* 9 (1996): 607-612.

Erol, Nese, Zeynep Sqimsek, Ozgur Oner, and Kerim Munir. 'Effects of Internal Displacement and Resettlement on the Mental Health of Turkish Children and Adolescents.' *European Psychiatry* 20 (2005): 152-157.

Goldberg, David and Paul Williams. *A Users guide to the General Health Questionnaire.* Slough: NFER Nelson, 1988.

Horowitz, Mardi, Nancy Wilner and William Alvarez. 'Impact of Events Scale: A Measure of Subjective stress.' *Psychosomatic Medicine* 41 (1979): 209-218.

Hunt, Nigel, and Maha Gakenyi. 'Comparing the Refugees and Non-Refugees: The Bosnian Experience.' *Anxiety Disorders* 19 (2005): 717-723.

Ironson, Gail, Christina Wynings, Neil Schneiderman, Andrew Baum, Mario Rodriguez, Debra Greenwood, Charles Benight, Michael Antoni, Arthur LaPerriere, Hue-Sheng Huang, Nancy Klimas and Mary Ann Fletcher. 'Post-Traumatic Stress Symptoms, Instrusive Thoughts, Loss, and Immune Function after Hurricane Andrew.' *Psychosomatic Medicine* 59 (1997): 128-141.

Johnson, Howard, and Andrew Thompson. 'The Development and Maintenance of Posttraumatic Stress Disorder (PTSD) in Civilian Adult Survivors of War Trauma and Torture: A Review.' *Clinical Psychology Review* 28 (2006): 36-47.

Kaniasty, Krzysztof. 'Social Support and Traumatic Stress.' *PTSD Research Quarterly* 16.2 (2005): 1-8.

Kaplan, Berton. 'Social Health and the Forgiving Heart: The Type-B Story.' *Journal of Behavioural Medicine* 15 (1992): 3-14.

Kardum, Igor, and Nada Krapic. 'Personality Traits, Successful Life Events, and Coping Styles in Early Adolescence.' *Personality and Individual Differences* 30 (2001): 503-515.

Kett, Maria. 'Internally Displaced Peoples in Bosnia-Herzegovina: Impacts of Long-Term Displacement on Health and Wellbeing.' *Medicine, Conflict and Survival* 21 (2005): 199-215.

Klaric, Miro, Branka Klaric, Aleksandra Stevanovic, Jasna Grgovic and Suzana Jonovska. 'Psychological Consequences of War Trauma and Postwar Social Stressors in Women in Bosnia and Herzegovina.' *Croatian Medical Journal* 48 (2007): 167-176.

Lagerkvist, Bernard, Reima Ana Maglajilic, Vesna Puratic, Aleksandar Susic and Lars Jacobson. 'Assessment of Community Mental Health Centres in Bosnia and Herzegovina as Part of the Ongoing Mental Health Reform.' *Medicinski Arhiv* 57.1 (2003): 31-38.

Maslow, Abraham. 'A Theory of Human Motivation.' *Psychological Review* 50.4 (1943): 370-96.

McCrea, Robert, and Paul Costa. 'Personality, Coping, and Coping Effectiveness in an aAdult Sample.' *Journal of Personality* 54 (1986): 385-405.

McCullough, Michael, Everett Worthington, and Chris Rachel. 'Interpersonal Forgiving in Close Relationships.' *Journal of Personality and Social Psychology* 73 (1997): 321-336.

Momartin, Shakeh, Derrick Silove, Vijaya Manicavasagar, and Zachary Steel. 'Comorbidity of PTSD and Depression: Associations with Trauma Exposure, Symptom Severity and Functional Impairment in Bosnian Refugees Resettled in Australia.' *Journal of Affective Disorders* 2 (2004): 231-238.

Myers, Elissa, Miles Hewstone, and Ed Cairns. 'Impact of Conflict on Mental Health in Northern Ireland: The Mediating Role of Intergroup Forgiveness and Collective Guilt.' *Political Psychology* 30.2 (2009): 269-290.

Nicholl, Catherine, and Andrew Thompson. 'A Psychological Treatment of Post Traumatic Stress Disorder (PTSD) in Adult Refugees: A Review of the Current State of Psychological Therapies.' *Journal of Mental Health* 13 (2004): 351-362.

Pietrzak, Robert, Douglas Johnson, Marc Goldstein, James Malley, Alison Rivers, Charles Morgan and Steven Southwick. 'Psychosocial Buffers of Traumatic Stress, Depressive Symptoms, and Psychosocial Difficulties in Veterans of Operations Enduring Freedom and Iraqi Freedom: The Role of Resilience, Unit Support, and Post Deployment Social Support.' *Journal of Affective Disorders* 120 (2010): 188-192.

Pollack, Craig Evan. 'Burial at Srebrenica: Linking Place and Trauma.' *Social Science and Medicine* 56 (2003): 793-801.

Richmond, Chantelle, and Nancy Ross. 'The Determinants of First Nation and Inuit Health: A Critical Population Health Approach'. *Health and Place* 15.2 (2009): 403-411.

Roe, Micheal. 'Intergroup Forgiveness in Settings of Political Violence: Complexities, Ambiguities, and Potentialities.' *Peace and Conflict: Journal of Peace Psychology* 13.1 (2007): 3-9.

Ruf, Martina, Maggie Schauer, Frank Neuner, Claudia Catani, Elizabeth Schauer and Thomas Elbert. 'Narrative Exposure Therapy for 7- to 16-Year Olds: A Randomised Controlled Trial with Traumatized Refugee Children.' *Journal of Traumatic Stress* 23.4 (2010): 437-445.

Schauer, Maggie, Frank Neuner, and Thomas Elbert. *Narrative Exposure Therapy: A Short-Term Treatment for Traumatic Stress Disorders.* Hogrefe Publishing: Gottingen, Germany, 2011.

Scobie, Edward, and Geoffrey Scobie. 'Damaging Events: The Perceived Need for Forgiveness.' *Journal for the Theory of Social Behavior* 28 (1998): 373-401.

Summerfield, Derek. 'A Critique of Seven Assumptions behind Psychological Trauma Programs in War-Affected aAreas.' *Social Science and Medicine* 48 (1999): 1449-1462.

Sundquist, Jan, Alija Behmen-Vincevic and Svem-Erik Johansson. 'Poor Quality of Life and Health in Young to Middle-Aged Bosnian Female War Refugees: A Population-Based Study.' *Public Health* 112.1 (1998): 21-26.

Thulesius, Hans, and Anders Hakansson. 'Screening for Posttraumatic Stress Disorder Symptoms among Bosnian Refugees.' *Journal of Traumatic Stress* 12 (1999): 167-174.

Tutu, Desmond. *No Future without Forgiveness.* London: Rider, 1999.

Weitz, Eric. *A Century of Genocide: Utopias of Race and Nation.* Princeton: Princeton University Press, 2003.

Witvliet, Charlotte, Thomas Ludwig, and Kelley Vander Laan. 'Granting Forgiveness or Harboring Grudges: Implications for Emotions, Physiology, and Health.' *Psychological Science* 12.2 (2001): 117-123.

Witvliet, Charlotte, Karen Phipps, Kenneth Feldman, and Joseph Beckman. 'Posttraumatic Mental and Physical Health Correlates of Forgiveness and Religious Coping in Military Veterans.' *Journal of Traumatic Stress* 17 (2004): 269-273.

**Emina Hadziosmanovic** is a PhD candidate in clinical psychology at the University of Nottingham. In her work she examines the social, psychological, and environmental impact of the Bosnian War & Herzegovina for survivors who remained in Bosnia and those displaced to the United Kingdom. She has an interest in using narratives in trauma therapy and was awarded The Rayne Fellowship for Refugees to run a project administering narrative exposure therapy with war trauma survivors from Bosnia, for the first time in the UK. Emina won Young Woman of the Year 2013 (Honorary Award) for her contribution to improving the lives of refugee and migrant communities in the UK.

**Nigel Hunt** is Associate Professor at the University of Nottingham specialising in traumatic stress. He also has a post as Docent in Social Psychology at the University of Helsinki. His PhD focused on the impact of war on World War Two veterans; he has since researched veterans of other wars, and many other traumatised and distressed populations around the world, such as earthquake victims in China, civilians in Iraq, and South Sudanese humanitarian aid workers. He has written a number of books on the subject, such as *Memory, War and Trauma* (Cambridge).

# From Accomplice to Victim: Catholic Church, Spanish Civil War and Collective Memory

*Mireno Berrettini*

**Abstract**
Most of the studies analysing historical memory of the Spanish Civil War, post-war political repression and Franco's dictatorship, focus on narratives developed by political parties or on politics of memory promoted by Governments. No studies about the memory of the Catholic Church exist due to the lack of interest in Spanish Catholicism shown by historiography. This significant lack may surprise considering various factors. First, the Catholic Church, by its very nature, is a religion in which the collective memory plays a central role. Second, Bishops had a vital role in legitimizing Franco's *golpe* and war, and a relevant social role during the dictatorship. Third, in the last years the *Conferencia Episcopal Española*, the assembly of the Spanish Bishops, criticized the Historical Memory Law (2007) proposed by the Government of José Luis Rodríguez Zapatero. It is therefore interesting to know the narrative construction of political cleavages of the Spanish twentieth-century offered by Catholic hierarchy. I will analyse the collective documents of the episcopate and the individual Bishops' pastoral letters, while also paying attention to the ecclesiastical policies of memory. In particular, my analysis will focus on beatifications and canonizations of the priests killed by anticlerical Republicans during the Civil War: the so-called 'martyrs of the twentieth century'. These are true 'agents of memory' and an instrument of political controversy with which Bishops have participated in a real struggle for memory which is still in progress.

**Key Words:** Spanish Civil War, Spanish Church, collective memory, political violence, religious persecution.

*****

## 1. Introduction

In recent years in Spain there has been a proliferation of academic studies on collective memory as the controversy over the recovery of historical memory. Surprisingly, only few studies in literature assess the role of the Church in remembering (and proposing) the Spanish Civil War, the Francoist political repression and dictatorship, an unusual phenomenon, especially if considering the following factors. Bishops had a vital role in legitimizing Franco's *golpe* and war, and an important social role during the regime. After the Second Vatican Council and especially in the 1970s, the Catholics have contributed to the processes of democratic transition and its consolidation. In the last few years, the *Conferencia Episcopal Española* (CEE), the assembly of Spanish Bishops, has strongly criticized the so-called *Ley de Memoria Histórica* (Historical Memory Law) approved by Government of José Luis Rodríguez Zapatero in 2007. The Bishops have seen the HML as a symbol of socialist *revanche*, as a way for those Socialists, who lost out in the Civil War, to have their political and symbolic revenge. In 2006, during the negotiations for the law, the CEE issued *Orientaciones morales ante la situación actual de España* (A moral guideline for the present Spanish situation), a collective document that stated that HML served as a 'historical and civil regression that represents a clear risk in terms of tensions, discrimination and alterations to compromise the peaceful coexistence'. In the Bishops' opinion the new law was reopening 'old wounds of the Civil War', healed during the transition.[1] In the 1970s, during the democratization, the public discourse of the political élite (not that of the civil society) about the twentieth century political cleavages was marked by some silence,[2] to which the Catholic Church contributed actively.[3] The best strategy to overcome the trauma was to forget what had happened. This silence was considered as a sign of the reconciliation between the two sides of Spain that had fought in the Civil War.[4] Dismissing the Civil War from the public talks, however, did not mean erasing its existence and consequences. In the past years, a growing part of society has started to criticise the paradigm of silence.[5] In this new framework we can find the genesis of the HML, a law that recognizes new rights and helps the localization of mass grave sites where are buried the victims of Francoist repression.

As the Catholic hierarchy believed that reconciliation was threatened, the Church started to represent itself (and acts) as a real guardian of the memory constructed during the transition. After the approval of the law, the statements in controversy with those who wanted to promote the recovery of historical memory increased, and in 2008, Cardinal Antonio María Rouco Varela, Archbishop of Madrid and the real leader of the Spanish episcopate, affirmed: 'sometimes you have to forget. Not by ignorance or cowardice, but by virtue of a desire for reconciliation and forgiveness'.[6]

'Forget', 'forgive', 'reconciliation' are the keywords of the Bishops. However, the question seems more intricate. This chapter aims to analyse the way in which the Catholic Church has contributed to challenging the paradigm of silence: in other words, this chapter studies the memorialistic narrative of Spanish Bishops and the relationship of this narrative with the clerical historiography, a group of scholars that in recent years have tried to rewrite the history of twentieth-century Spain. Both of them are shaping a new memory, which can be considered the updating of the one the Church held during the Franco Regime. Like the narrative developed during the dictatorship, this new memory is asymmetrical, as it celebrates only the victims killed by the Republicans and not those Catholics killed by Francoists. Irrespectively, the Bishops presented it as a 'third space' not attributed to any side of the Civil War. In their discourse, they also deny (or forget) that the mild behaviour adopted by the clergy in the political repression carried out by the Francoists tends to represent the Church just as the real victim of the Civil War.[7] The new memory proposed by the Spanish Church is not only the product of Spanish socio-political dynamics, but it also responds indirectly to the shift towards the post-secular age. In this sense this constitutes not only a study of collective memory, but also a different way of analysing the relationship between the Church and the modern world. As Catholicism truly functions as a relevant actor even in secularised Western societies, religion and memory fit together insofar as the Church is still a provider of meanings, and not only to believers. Catholicism, by its very nature, is a religion in which the concept of collective memory has a central place.

## 2. 'Martyrs of the Twentieth Century', Guilt and Forgiveness

In 1986 Bishops issued *Contructores de la paz* (Builder of the peace) a collective document which stated 'the Church does not claim to be without error.' It was the swan song of the transition hierarchy, a moderately progressive episcopate which wanted to 'know the whole truth about the past'.[8] Indirectly, the theological and pastoral framework of this document came from Apostolic Constitution *Gaudium et spes* promulgated by the Second Vatican Council in 1965. This text reflected on the Catholics' faults in the genesis of atheism (and anticlericalism):

> Hence believers can have more than a little to do with the birth of atheism. To the extent that they neglect their own training in the faith, or teach erroneous doctrine, or are deficient in their religious, moral or social life, they must be said to conceal rather than reveal the authentic face of God and religion.[9]

At the same time, they retained the historical deficiencies of the believers in the way of living their faith: 'we cannot but deplore certain habits of mind, which are sometimes found too among Christians'.[10] However, the heirs of this hierarchy, the new Spanish episcopate, changed their pastoral strategy. Various endogenous and exogenous factors have enhanced those clerical areas that have preferred a more militant pastoral of memory. The Church started to follow a special path of victimization, if not martyrization: the first step occurred in Rome on March 29, 1987 when Pope John Paul II declared as blessed the Carmelite of Guadalajara killed in 1936. It was a decision of breakage, because one of his predecessors, Pope Paul VI, had decided to block the processes of canonization and beatification. During the years of the transition and the post-conciliar, the Church was looking for more compromise dialogue with the democratic society. Nevertheless the papacy of John Paul II was complicated. With the preparation of the Great Jubilee in 2000 started the afterthought (sometimes insufficient) of the Roman Church about its history. In 1994 the same Pope issued an Apostolic Letter *Tertio Millenio Adveniente* (As the Third Millennium Approaches) and stated:

> Hence it is appropriate that, as the Second Millennium of Christianity draws to a close, the Church should become more fully conscious of the sinfulness of her children, recalling all those times in history when they departed from the spirit of Christ and his Gospel and, instead of offering to the world the witness of a life inspired by the values of faith, indulged in ways of thinking and acting which were truly forms of counter-witness and scandal.[11]

In 1998, Holy See published *Incarnationis mysterium* (The Mystery of Incarnation), the bull of indiction of the Great Jubilee. This document serves as an invitation for the 'purification of memory':

> this calls everyone to make an act of courage and humility in recognizing the wrongs done by those who have borne or bear the name of Christian.[12]

In parallel, the International Theological Commission after a three-year discussion issued *Memory and Reconciliation: the Church and the faults of the past*. This document approved by Cardinal Joseph Ratzinger, later Pope Benedict XVI, functioned as the pastoral preparation for the first Catholic 'Day of Forgiveness', held in Rome on 12 March 2000. It affirmed that 'the recognition of the past faults of the Church's sons and daughters of yesterday can foster renewal and reconciliation in the present'. *Memory and Reconciliation* 'corrected' in the conservative sense the timid statements John Paul II, probably because 'some of the faithful are disconcerted and their loyalty to the Church seems shaken'.[13]

Between these disconcerted areas the Spanish hierarchy definitely made the best of a bad situation. Which was the reaction of the Bishops to the Pope's demand that the Church should apologise for its behaviour during and after the Civil War? In 2000, in response to the controversy raised by the beatification of almost 500 martyrs declared until then, Juan José Asenjo, the former spokesman of the CEE and Archbishop of Seville, stated that 'in the Civil War the Church was passive and just a victim'.[14] Some days later, Cardinal Rouco Varela reaffirmed that the clergy was a victim of the Civil War; for that reason no one need ask for forgiveness.[15]

Over the years the tone of the debate has radicalized. In March 2003, the Parliament of Navarre, a Spanish *Comunidad Autónoma*, approved a declaration condemning the Francoist execution of Republicans arguing that those shootings took place 'with the blessing of the Catholic Church [...] and in some cases [even] with the its direct participation'.[16] The former Archbishop of Pamplona, Fernando Sebastián Aguilar, reacted by pointing out that these words were 'not true and [were] really insulting'.[17] His answer is paradigmatic in so far as the Spanish Bishops do not accept being considered as compliant with the executers. The response is considered as insufficient by many Spanish organizations, principally by the *Asociación para la Recuperación de la Memoria Histórica* (ARMH), the *Federación Estatal de Foros por la Memoria*, or the *Asociación de Familiares de Fusilados, Asesinados y Desaparecidos* en Navarra en 1936 (AFFNA36). In the last years, many others controversies have been raised, especially in 2007 around the mass beatification,[18] and in 2010 on occasion of the inauguration of the *Santuario de los Beatos Mártires valencianos*,[19] the parish dedicated to the new martyrs. In November 2011, the *Comisión para la Recuperación da Memoria Histórica da Coruña* sent a public letter to Rouco Varela inviting him to visit a Galician mass grave,[20] and affirming that:

> it is time the Catholic Church asks for forgiveness for its role in the crimes against humanity and for his great sin to support a Fascist dictatorship.[21]

Indeed, the Bishops have asked for forgiveness in a very peculiar way, mostly through referring to past errors of all the Spaniards. *La fidelidad a Dios dura para siempre* (Faithfulness to God lasts forever), issued in November 1999, asked 'God's forgiveness' for the sin of all Spaniards 'of one side or the other' instead of the Spaniards' forgiveness for past errors of the Church.[22] The clergy escaped the judgment, because it was considered just as a victim (a special victim) in the conflict. In the new memory of the Bishops, the martyrs represent a metaphor of the entire Spanish clergy as the Church; in fact, the martyrs are considered external to the Civil War. In April 2007, *Vosotros sois la luz del mundo* (You are the light of the world), a pastoral document signed for the mass beatification of October 2007 by all the Bishops, affirmed that 'the martyrs are above the tragic circumstances that led to their death'.[23] Any dissent with respect to this narrative was isolated and neutralized. A few months after the Bishop of Bilbao, Ricardo Blázquez said that the Bishops had to 'ask for forgiveness [...], recognize limitations, sins, need for a change of attitude and the purpose of the repair'.[24] It was a moderate position rather than a request for forgiveness, and just an invitation to ask for it. However, some segments of the same CEE wasted no time to restrict the scope of the speech. A few days later, the spokesman of the Bishops and Secretary General of the CEE, Juan Antonio Martínez Camino, declared that the word of Blázquez had been 'taken out of context',[25] while the former Cardinal Carlos Amigo Vallejo, Archbishop of Seville, stated that the opinion of Bishop of Bilbao 'does not represent the entire Church'.[26] In substance, the great majority of prelates have specified the 'victim' position by saying that martyrs were not at all 'involved in the fight between brothers'[27] but 'above the factions or partisanship'[28] and further added that they 'neither sympathized with this or that ideology, nor were in the battlefield for one side or another in our Civil War'.[29] In the opinion of Cardinal Rouco Varela, the 'historical background' of the '30s was 'marked by radical materialism of some triumphant political ideologies: Fascism and Communism'.[30] The Civil War was fought by the Rightists and Leftists, one against the other, while the Church was left out of this 'game'.

This 'third space' position contributes to an axiological discrimination among the dead of the conflict. In 2007, the collective document *Beatificación de 498 mártires del siglo XX en España* (Beatification of 498 martyrs of the twentieth century in Spain) explained that:

> wars have fallen beings in one and the other side. Have political repression victims [...]. Only the religious persecutions have martyrs, whether of one or another ideology, of one or another other preference, or political affiliation, or even of different religions.[31]

That helps to explain why Spanish Bishops celebrate only those men (and women) killed by the anticlerical Republicans. The men (and women) killed by Francoists do not count as martyrs; ontologically different, they are 'just' victims. What if they were Catholics — believers and even priests who chose democracy for religious reasons and were killed by the Francoists? In 2009, the four Bishops of the Basque Dioceses issued *Purificar la memoria, servir a la verdad, pedir perdón* (Purifying the memory, serving the truth, asking for forgiveness), a document that exemplifies the flexibility of the Bishops' narrative on the Civil War. On the one hand the four Bishops officially recognized: 'the dignity of those who have been forgotten or excluded and ease the pain of their families and friends.' But on the other hand were celebrated only the Catholic ones, and only the Basque ones: the 'fourteen priests executed in 1936 and 1937 who won in that war.' Once again, the Church was again presented just as a victim of the conflict: 'the ecclesial community was absolutely not excluded from suffering'.[32] Church is still presented as a 'third space', continuing the equidistance and continuing to equating the two *bandos*: Basque hierarchy asked God's forgiveness for the sins of all Spain and did not request forgiveness for the collaboration of the Church in the anti-Republican repression.[33] This document, orthodox and heretical at once,[34] can be considered as a typical expression of Basque socio-religious context — a very different context from the historically more conservative Castillan (region of central Spain) clergy. In fact, in July 2011, the excavation of a mass grave near Gumiel de Izán (province of Burgos) has found the remains of a priest murdered by Francoists.[35] There were no comments from the Castillan hierarchy.[36]

## 3. Re-Writing History: Removing Francoist Responsibilities

Since the second half of the '80s, the Bishops have been sponsoring the publication of historiographical books or pamphlets. They claim the scientific validity of these; many result from doctoral dissertations and most of them use original documents or archival materials, have a critical apparatus of footnotes and have come out in academic publishing circuits. However, most of these books use concepts and expressions not exactly matching the classic tools of historians: 'the enemies of "our martyrs"'.[37] Some even retrieve expressions typical of the Francoist vocabulary, as 'the fallen for God and the Country',[38] or 'the defines of the eternal values: religion and Country'.[39]

These scholars have a peculiar relation with academic historiography, as the great part affirm bluntly that literature about the Civil War abound in 'historiographical falsehood'.[40] In the Spanish academy:

> everything is subjected to the typical methods of propaganda. [...]
> This [has] the absolute ideological control State Universities,
> [and practice] [...] and true intellectual terrorism.[41]

Due to 'the manipulative contamination in certain sectors of historiography',[42] the only credible one, scientifically trustworthy and ethically correct historiography is the one linked to the Catholic Church, namely a real alternative historiography that claims fairness but instead proves biased.

These scholars also conduct a controversy with another sector of Catholic historiography which has described the relationship between the Civil War and religion as something more complex. While the latter works criticize the pastoral, social and theological deficiencies of the Church in the 1930s, the clerical historiography defends that model, more conservative and more militant in the political sphere. In this sense, the controversy targets those Catholics who do not want to hear about martyrs and crusades anymore. In a bestseller issued in 2007 and entitled *La Cruz, el Perdón y la Gloria. La persecución religiosa en España durante la II República y la Guerra Civil* (The Cross, the Glory and Forgiveness. Religious persecution in Spain during the Second Republic and the Civil War), the author Ángel David Martín Rubio, then Professor of Church History at the Instituto Superior Ciencias Religiosas Santa María de Guadalupe (Cáceres) and linked to the Instituto Teologico 'San Pedro de Alcantara', denounced:

> the great discomfort caused, seventy years later, in talking about religious persecution in Spain, not so much among those who claim to follow the ideology of the executioners, but between those who should have picked up the legacy of heroes and martyrs inextricably linked to a Civil War that acquired the characteristics of a Crusade. A symbiosis that occurs not only in

the chronological coincidence but by an intimate communion of ideals in defines of the faith and of the Christian Western civilization.[43]

Two years later, in 2009, *La persecución religiosa del clero en Asturias, 1934, 1936 y 1937: Martirios y odiseas* (Religious persecution of the clergy in Asturias, 1934, 1936 and 1937: Martyrs and odysseys) was re-issued. This 855-page book written by another priest, Ángel Garralda García, in 1977, can be summarized in a formula: 'our Civil War was just'; it was a 'Crusade'.[44] The difference between this position and the leading position of Church during the first years of democracy seems clear. In 1986 the President of CEE, *Monseñor* Gabino Díaz Merchán, Archbishop of Oviedo, wrote that the

> exaltation done by one of the contending parties in the Civil War with the nickname Crusade was a mistake, because it was actually a fratricidal strife.[45]

To clerical historiographists, the Church 'seemed more embarrassed than proud […]. It was a wrong attitude',[46] due to 'the searching for "dialogue", "coexistence" or tolerance'.[47] For them, the present Church does not need this coexistence. In fact, those works criticize the Catholicism that sought dialogue with the Socialists in the years of the Zapatero Government (2004-2011). Some of them explained that in the 1930s, the moderation of the Church

> may have brought the left-wing parties to reconsider their politics and act with a more conciliatory spirit, but it did not happen.[48]

The Church of the Second Republic clearly serves as a metaphor for the actual Church: it sought dialogue with the Government but obtained persecution — a familiar pattern.

Analytically we can divide clerical historiography into two groups. Indeed, between them no incompatibility exists even though both are maintained at different levels and with different registers. The first group, neo-crusader historiography, interprets the war as a reaction of the Spaniards against those who tried to delete the Catholicism that represented the Spanish identity. It retakes the positions Aniceto de Castro Albarrán, who during the Civil War wrote a book entitled *Guerra Santa. El sentido católico del Movimiento Nacional* (Holy War. The Catholic meaning Nacional Movement):

> If we eliminate its religious significance, our uprising is no more a Crusade, because it downgrades it to the level of a coup, to a civil war and […] a class struggle.[49]

These words still resonate in the twenty-first century:

> The *Alzamiento Nacional* [National Uprising, old Francoist denomination of golpe] was inevitable, and emerged as a supreme reason of an entire people which risked extermination.[50]

The war began as a traditional military war, but 'left wing political parties turned it into a war against religion'.[51] Franco's coup was not a political *golpe* but a reaction against the Republican Government's radical secularism (so-called laicism), and religious persecution turned the Civil War into a Crusade fought 'for the cause of God and his Church, and, therefore, to free Spain from atheism'.[52] These works more or less have a good opinion of the dictator: Franco was an 'exceptionally shining personality';[53] after his victory 'a period of peace began that lasted 36 years, until the death of the general [...]. Catholicism, during those years, was freed from the Marxist oppression'.[54]

Another group of scholars separate the Civil War from religious persecutions, engaging in hierarchical historiography. The term came from the classical book *Historia de la persecución religiosa en España, 1936-1939* (History of religious persecution in Spain, 1936-1939) written by Antonio Montero Moreno, later Archbishop of Mérida-Badajoz, in 1961. While the Civil War related to 'the weight of religious reasons in the national front', the persecution 'focuses on the violence perpetrated against the Church in the red rear-guard'. That explains why he stated that religious persecution took place 'after the Civil War and before it; it consisted of a carefully planned persecution of the Church'.[55]

The Catholic Church used those books to support its memorialistic narrative, as between the two historiographies there can be a combination. While the Church was the victim of persecution, the Spaniards fought a Crusade in reaction. The clergy was neither with the Republic nor with Franco, but real Catholic Spaniards fought against the Republic. While some sectors of lower clergy, generally more militant, linked with the neo-crusader historiography, the Bishops linked with the hierarchical position, neither properly undemocratic, neither anti-Francoist.

During the first years of the Franco Regime, the clergy used the expression 'fallen for God and Spain' to indicate the victims of anticlerical violence. In the so-called late Francoism, the Bishops used a less bombastic formula instead, namely the 'martyrs of the Civil War'.[56] Changes occurred again after 1975 when the phrase 'martyrs of the twentieth century' became used. Using this expression, the Bishops affirm that in Spain the religious persecution began before the Civil War and it was particularly virulent during the Second Republic (1931-1936) with the deeply anticlerical governments. Extrapolating martyrs from their historical context, the Church removes the responsibilities of the anti-Republican rebels, because the most serious historians have shown that religious persecution was not only followed the Franco coup but was indirectly triggered by it. Clearly the new narrative of memory legitimates ideologically the rapprochement between Catholicism and the Spanish right-wing, the *Partido Popular* (PP), a post-Francoist political party. The Bishops often use a very radical language, describing the executioners with terms similar to those used during the Civil War,[57] and implicitly condemning the political heirs as 'Communists', 'Anarchists' or 'Liberals', who fought in the Civil War and are often associated to expressions like 'blood and fire',[58] 'anti-religious furor', 'evil gestures of the murderers',[59] 'treachery and violence of the false prophets of atheism'.[60] On the other hand, the universe of the political right-wing shares the vision of the past proposed by the Bishops,[61] opposed to the HML because they believe that 'the compensation to victims has been done; past wounds were closed in the transition'.[62] Not by coincidence, since the late '90s the City Hall of Madrid and the Instituto de Estudios Madrileños sponsored a series of lectures about the Civil War. The speaker chosen by the PP, which controlled both institutions, was always an exponent of historiography linked to the Bishops. Very briefly, 'the religious and political persecution [was] imposed by the Government of the Republic' and the victims were 'killed, in hatred of the faith, in hatred of the Catholic Church, or to belong or work for it'.[63] No wonder then that one of the most important politicians of the PP, the Catholic Mayor Jaime Oreja declared: 'why do I have to condemn Francoism?'[64]

## 4. Looking beyond Spain: Catholic Aletheia vs Democratic Doxa

The expression 'martyrs of the twentieth century' hide between the lines the Bishops' interpretation of the entire century as an age of despair driven by humanity's rejection of God. Clearly the Bishops use an updated version of the fundamentalist post-French Revolution Catholic paradigm in which modernity is understood as an apostasy of the masses and where the Church is presented as a victim of a persecution conducted on a global scale throughout the entire twentieth century and caused by political plans or diabolical ideologies such as Liberalism, Marxism, and National-Socialism. However, the new memory of the Spanish Bishops is not only an involution, but also the product of two opposite phenomena. It is something to be read as a 'reaction' or 'relation' to the socio-political Spanish dynamic, and to the rise of a collective memory as a political issue after the end of the 'Witness Era'.[65] At the same time it is something new, a very modern and flexible reaction to face the post-secular turn which bring a series of complex processes that overlap the religious and the social spheres. To understand the new pastoral of memory we must go back to the problematic relationship between the Catholic Church and democratic modernity. Some sectors of Catholic Bishops, and especially the Spanish ones, perceive political corruption, same sex marriage, divorce, as proof of the crisis of Western Civilization, brought by the extreme consequences of secularization (that marginalizes God from the public sphere) and relativism (which denies an objective fundament for human rights).[66] To give examples of people, martyrs, who testify the Truth to the extreme action, men and women dying for a transcendental absolute, meet the challenge of relativism that cannot possibly conceive of this sacrifice. Paraphrasing the words of *monseñor* Carlos Osoro, former Archbishop of Oviedo, we can say that the Church uses martyrs to 'indicate an authentic social project'.[67] Martyrs are used to convey political positions, a way to criticize abortion (they react to a society 'in which mothers decide about the lives of their unborn children') and to repair the 'degradation of the family' in same sex marriage approved by Zapatero.[68] In 2011 Bishop Alfonso Milián Sorribas, in his pastoral letter *¡Todo un Seminario mártir!* (A Martyr Seminar) wrote that the martyrs should serve as examples 'in this moment, in which many are tempted by fear and insecurity [...] at a time of prevailing greed and sensuality'.[69]

In this sense the new pastoral of memory represents an attempt to reconsider the relationship between citizens and politics, calling for limited sovereignty, limited law-making autonomy. The martyrs witnessed their beliefs until the end, exemplifying a new model of citizenship not founded on opinion (*Doxa*), but on truth (*Aletheia*). It is a transcendental truth defined and preserved by the Church. In *Vosotros sois la luz de el mundo* we can read that martyrs 'testified a supreme Truth that sets us free', this Truth is 'biggest promoter of dignity and freedom of every person'. This means a religious, not rational, foundation of democracy. The characteristics of this new citizen look like those of the martyrs: 'radical following' of Church commandments; austerity and self-discipline. Characteristics very similar to those of the new believer. Martyrs are even a way to face the changes of religion: from the Catholicism *à la carte*, to the crisis of institutional religions. It is due to the depletion of the renewal brought by the Second Vatican Council; the return of the Catholicism of presence (more intransigent) *vis-à-vis* the Catholicism of mediation (more open to dialogue); the impetus given by Church teachings towards emotional religiosity.

However, the model of the Spanish Christian martyr is easily offset by the Muslim suicide bomber, also ready to die for God, but different in that the former does not cause death, and forgives his executioners. I am not saying that the Church encourages 'the clash of civilizations',[70] quite the contrary. This kind of reasoning is used to demonstrate that, on the one hand, religion, even if it proposes the sacrifice, has nothing to do with the murder, and, on the other, that the betrayal of Islam itself is afforded by those who carry out terrorist attacks in the name of Koran. In this respect, the position of Cardinal Rouco Varela is indicative. The pastoral written for the beatification states:

> is said and wants to prove, [...], that faith in God and love in God begets violence. What was the truth for the whole story, and especially in the twentieth century, is the opposite: love to God, [...], produces merciful love, offered with total gratitude to the man. Produce Martyrs![71]

Of course we must not overemphasize the aim of the ecumenical perspective of the prelate. Clearly, the God of reference, the only God of salvation, is the Roman Catholic God. It therefore indicates that one should read more from a socio-cultural than religious perspective, and perhaps unintentionally emphasizes the 'superiority' of Christianity compared to Islam, which easily leads to degeneration. Another way to intercept the electoral strategy of the PP and the growing sense of identity brought about by globalization, migrations dilute the boundaries of the traditional community.

As a special category of victim, the martyrs allow the Church to follow a special path of victimization (martyrdom). That explains why the celebration of the historical memory of the victims of Francoist repression (HML) reopens wounds, while the celebration of the martyrs of persecution Republican helps reconciliation. During the dictatorship, Bishops have spoken about the 'debt to the dead', a debt of the Spanish nation towards the victims of the Republican anticlerical persecution. Their blood allowed the re-establishment of peace and served as the pillar of the (new) Francoist State. For example, in 1948, the Bishop of Solsona, Vicente Enrique y Tarancón, the leader of the Church during the transition, wrote:

> the blood of our martyrs has been [...] the price of our health and
> our peace [...] hand of our iniquity and our mistakes.[72]

Something similar happens again when Bishops speak about the 'heroic forgiveness' as pillar of 'the spirit of reconciliation'.[73] This suggests that the citizens of democracy are now indebted to the martyrs. Their forgiveness has become the base of the democratic present. The references have changed, but the logic has remained the same, namely it strengthens the religious foundation of the common life. In 2007, virtually all of the Bishops issued pastoral letters or gave public talks about the great beatification. Virtually all of them pointed out that new martyrs died forgiving their executioners. The Bishops stated that Spain can construct the reconciliation between its citizens 'over' this forgiveness, as clearly appears in the article written in 2007 by the Archbishop of Valencia, later Cardinal, Agustín García-Gasco. Forgiveness offered by the martyrs to their executioners and beatifications implies:

> the true commitment to reconciliation in relation to conflicts that
> already belong to history and involve a determination to combine
> the forgiveness to the true.[74]

### 5. Conclusions?

The martyrs have become 'agents of memory', a vehicle of meanings and an instrument to fight a struggle for memory, a struggle still in progress, which makes it more difficult to construct a shared vision of the twentieth century traumas. In

2001 an important Catholic newspaper closely linked to the Archbishopric of Madrid stated that:

> after 25 years of parliamentary monarchy, Spain is a real European democracy, where everyone can recognize and honour its [dead], without the others taking this as an offense.[75]

Opinions like this are widespread. Eleven years later, in 2012, another important Catholic weekly review affirmed:

> this autumn the Church has the full right to celebrate the beatification of 300 martyrs from the war [...]. Also, the association of historical memory are seeking the place of their dead to put a written lapel on it.[76]

The comparison does not hold nor do such opinions call for the construction of a shared space of meanings; they lead to atomization which can lead to 'symbolic wars'[77] between 'communities of memory'.[78]

The Spanish society should try to reach a new equilibrium of memory after the dismantling of the accepted memory during the transition, not only because of the HML or of Socialist revanche, but also with the contribution of the same Church. The Spanish society should try to reach a new and real shared collective memory (as much as possible) linked to the new socio-political phase in Spanish democracy. The Church could contribute to the construction of a democratic memory in various ways. To help towards the accuracy of historical research to be accurate, the Bishops could celebrate those personalities that tried to achieve peace between the Spaniards during the conflict.[79] Finally, they could recognize that some chose the Republic and democracy for religious reasons. This would mean celebrating the victims of Francoist 'politicide'.[80] On 28 April 1990, Cardinal Tarancón, then Archbishop Emeritus, wrote an article entitled *Nuevos martires: testigos del evangelio* (New Martyrs: witnesses of the Gospel). Using a theological reading centred on the 'structures of sin' proposed by *Sollecitudo rei socialis*, the Cardinal said that those killed because they 'felt compelled [...] — for religious reasons — to mark firmly the flagrant injustice of the 'powerful'', and also those who 'felt compromised by reasons of faith to take on the cause of the poor and the oppressed, as Jesus did' were already blessed, if not by law, if not by men, at least by God. The prelate, therefore, implicitly recognised the memory of the Catholic world opted by the Republic:

> Not all martyrs are officially declared by the Church. This does not mean they stop being real and authentic holy martyrs.[81]

However, the Church seems to have decided to follow another path. On 29 January 2013, a part of the lower clergy made a public petition to Spanish Prime Minister Mariano Rajoy asking him to abolish the HML, while later, Bishops celebrated in Tarragona 147 new martyrs,[82] none of them killed by the Francoist repression.[83]

## Notes

[1] Asamblea Plenaria de la Conferencia Episcopal Española, *Orientaciones morales antes la situación actual del España* (Madrid: Conferencia Episcopal Española, 2006).

[2] Santos Juliá, 'Echar al olvido. Memoria y amnistía en la transición,' *Claves de Razón Práctica* 129 (2003): 14-24.

[3] Mireno Berrettini, 'La riconciliazione nel pensiero pastorale del Cardinal Tarancón,' *Storia e problemi contemporanei* 47 (2008): 81-90.

[4] Alfonso Botti, 'La riconciliazione in Spagna tra cronaca, politica e storia,' *Storia e problemi contemporanei* 47 (2008): 7-12.

[5] Francisco Sevillano, 'La construcción de la memoria y el olvido en la España democrática,' *Ayer* 52 (2003): 297-319.

[6] Antonio María Rouco Varela, Discurso Inaugural de la XCII Asamblea Plenaria de la CEE, 24 November 2008.

[7] See Mireno Berrettini, 'Spagna e nuovi beati. La Jerarquía tra riconciliazione e combate por la memoria,' *Studi e Ricerche di Storia Contemporanea* 70 (2008): 2-32.

[8] Comisión Permanente de la Conferencia Episcopal Española, *Constructores de la paz* (Madrid: Conferencia Episcopal Española, 1986).

[9] 'Gaudium et Spes. Pastoral Constitution on the Church in the Modern World,' *Church Documents Reference Suite* (Boston: Pauline Books & Media, 2000), 19.

[10] 'Gaudium et Spes,' 36.

[11] John Paul II, *Tertio Millenio Adveniente* (Roma: Libreria Editrice Vaticana, 1994), 33.

[12] John Paul II, *Incarnationis mysterium* (Roma: Libreria Editrice Vaticana, 1994), 11.

[13] International Theological Commission, *Memory and Reconciliation. The Church and the faults of the past* (Roma: Libreria Editrice Vaticana, 2000), 10.

[14] Juan G. Bedoya, 'Los Obispos insisten en que la Iglesia fue "sujeto paciente y victima" de la Guerra Civil,' *El País*, 08 April 2000.

[15] Juan G. Bedoya, 'Rouco dice que en España "sigue habiendo una semilla de guerra". El Cardenal separa la verdad histórica de las valoraciones teológicas,' *El País*, 13 April 2000.

[16] 'Propuesta de la Comisión Especial de Convivencia y Solidaridad Internacional del día 21 de febrero de 2003, sobre el recuerdo, reconocimiento y reparación

moral de las personas fusiladas y represaliadas durante la Guerra Civil en Navarra,'
*Boletín Oficial del Parlamento de Navarra* 37 (2003): 13-14.

[17] Fernando Sebastián Aguilar, 'Acusación injusta,' *Alfa y Omega*, 20 April 2003.

[18] Critical about the event: Manuel Montero, 'Otros "mártires" de la Guerra Civil,'
*El País*, 6 May 2007 and Julián Casanova, 'Franco, la Iglesia católica y sus
mártires,' *El País*, 26 June 2007.

[19] See Miquel Alberola, 'Una iglesia para los "mártires" del 36,' *El País*, 2 July
2007.

[20] 'La CRMH de A Coruña invita a Rouco Varela a visitar las fosas comunes de
Galicia,' *La Voz de Galicia*, 6 January 2011.

[21] Comisión pola Recuperación da Memoria Histórica, "Carta aberta ao Sr. D.
Antonio María Rouco Varela, presidente da Conferencia Episcopal Española,"
Memoriadaconuna (Blog), 7 January 2011. Viewed 29 march 2014.

[22] Asamblea Plenaria de la Conferencia Episcopal Española, *La fidelidad de Dios
dura siempre. Mirada de fe al siglo XX* (Madrid: Conferencia Episcopal Española,
1999).

[23] Asamblea Plenaria de la Conferencia Episcopal Española, *Vosotros sois la luz del
mundo (Mt 5,14). Mensaje con motivo de la beatificación de 498 mártires del siglo
XX en España* (Madrid: Conferencia Episcopal Española, 2007).

[24] Ricardo Blázquez Pérez, Discurso Inaugural del Excmo. y Rvmo. Sr. D. Ricardo
Blázquez Pérez, Obispo de Bilbao Presidente de la Conferencia Episcopal
Española, Viewed 29 March 2014.

[25] 'Mons. Martinez Camino: 'No pueden sacarse de contexto las palabras de
perdón' de Mons. Blázquez,' *Aciprensa*, 24 November 2007.

[26] 'Amigo afirma que el discurso del Blázquez no representa a la Iglesia,' *El País*,
21 November 2007.

[27] José Sánchez González, *Beatificaciones en Roma el 28 de Octubre de 2007*
(Sigüenza-Guadalajara: Obispado de Sigüenza-Guadalajara 2007).

[28] Demetrio Fernández, 'Mártires de nuestro tiempo,' *Zenit*, 3 November 2011.

[29] Braulio Rodríguez Plaza, *Mártires* (Valladolid: Arzobispado de Valladolid,
2007).

[30] Antonio María Rouco Varela, 'San Rafael Arnáiz Barón: un santo de nuestro
tiempo, Homilía en la Eucaristía de Acción de Gracias en honor de San Rafael
Arnáiz Barón con motivo de su Canonización,' *Archimadrid*, 12 October 2009.

[31] Oficina de Información de la Conferencia Episcopal Española, *Beatificación de
498 mártires del siglo XX en España* (Madrid: Conferencia Episcopal Española,
2007).

[32] 'Purificar la memoria, servir a la verdad, pedir perdón,' *Boletín Oficial del
Obispado de Vitoria* 10 (2009): 646-648.

[33] See Mireno Berrettini, 'A settant'anni dalla Carta Collettiva dell'Episcopato

spagnolo: Jerarquía, martirio, memoria collettiva,' *Un conflitto che non passa. Storia, memoria e rimozioni della guerra civile spagnola*, ed. Enrico Acciai and Giulia Quaggio (Pistoia: ISRPT, 2012), 42-65.

[34] It has been criticized by some sectors of catholics. See Herria 2000 Eliza and Comunidades Cristianas Populares and Coordinadora de Sacerdotes de Euskal Herria, *Memoria y Justicia* (Bilbao: CCP, 2009).

[35] Laura Sierra, 'Aparece un religioso entre los restos de 50 fusilados en una fosa de Gumiel de Izán,' *El Norte de Castilla*, 6 July 2011.

[36] See the consideration about space and memory in Castile done by Emina Hadziosmanovic and Nigel Hunt, 'Towards narrating trauma: the impact of the civil war in former Yugoslavia,' in this book. They affirm that 'a traumatic event took place has historical significance for the country itself and the continuation of that history'.

[37] José Núñez López, *Síntesis de la persecución religiosa en España del año 1934 al 1939* (Vigo: Cardeñoso, 2010): 22.

[38] Felipe M. Castro, *Ofrenda martirial de los dominicos de Cantabria en la persecución religiosa de 1936* (Las Caldas de Besaya: Cantabria PP. Dominicos, 1996): 7.

[39] Pedro García Hernández, *Crónica martirial. 271 misioneros claretianos mártires 1936-39* (Madrid: Publicaciones claretianas, 2000): 23.

[40] Manuel Nieto Cumplido and Luis Enrique Sánchez García, *La persecución religiosa en Córdoba 1931-1939* (Córdoba: Deán y Cabildo de la Santa Iglesia Catedral de Córdoba, 1998): 119.

[41] Ángel David Martín Rubio, *Los mitos de la represión en la Guerra Civil* (Baracaldo: Grafite, 2005): 259.

[42] José Luis Gutiérrez García, *Unidas hasta la muerte. Biografía de las siete beatas mártires del Primer Monasterio de la Visitación de Santa María en Madrid* (Madrid: Edibesa, 1998): 13.

[43] Ángel David Martín Rubio, *La Cruz, el Perdón y la Gloria. La persecución religiosa en España durante la II República y la Guerra Civil* (Madrid: Ciudadela Libros, 2007): 11.

[44] Ángel Garralda García, *La persecución religiosa del clero en Asturias, 1934, 1936 y 1937: Martirios y odiseas* (Avilés: Nieva, 2009): 33 and 21.

[45] Gabino Díaz Merchán, 'Discurso del Presidente a la Conferencia Episcopal,' *Ecclesia*, 9 August 1986.

[46] Vicente Cárcel Ortí, *Persecuciones religiosas y mártires del siglo XX* (Madrid: Palabra, 2001): 138.

[47] Vicente Cárcel Ortí, *Mártires del siglo XX. Cien preguntas y respuestas* (Madrid: Edicep, 2001): 100.

[48] Pío Moa, 'Prólogo,' in Martín Rubio, *Los mitos de la represión en la Guerra*

*Civil*, 18.

[49] Aniceto de Castro Albarran, Guerra Santa. *El sentido católico del Movimiento Nacional* (Burgos: Editorial Española, 1938): 36.

[50] Teodoro Calvo Madrid, *Mártires de Motril y persecución religiosa en la diócesis de Granada (1931-1939)* (Madrid: Edibesa, 2009): 103-104.

[51] Marcos Rincón Cruz, 'Introducción. La persecución religiosa en España (1931-1939),' in José Antonio Martínez Puche, *Mártires dominicos españoles. 92 religiosos, religiosas y seglares de la familia dominicana, mártires de la persecución religiosa de 1936* (Madrid: Edibesa, 2007): 94.

[52] Fernando de la Lama Ruiz-Escajadillo, *Mártires de la Montaña en nuestra cruzada española de liberación 1936-37* (Santander: Sanara, 1994): 12.

[53] Faustino Moreno Villalba, *Los mártires del 36 y Franco* (Sevilla: Apostolado mariano, 1993): 5.

[54] Emilio Sánchez Baeza, *La persecución religiosa en la diócesis de Cartagena-Murcia, 1931-1939* (Madrid: E. Sánchez, 1988): 273.

[55] Antonio Montero Moreno, *Historia de la persecución religiosa en España, 1936-1939* (Madrid: BAC, 1961).

[56] About this period see Alfonso Botti and Massimiliano Guderzo, *L'ultimo franchismo tra repressione e premesse della transizione (1968-75)* (Soveria Mannelli: Rubbettino, 2009).

[57] Alfonso Botti, 'Dalla "guerra giusta" alla "guerra santa". La pubblicistica cattolica spagnola durante la Seconda Repubblica e la Guerra Civile,' *Storia e problemi contemporanei* 42 (2006): 61-91

[58] Pablo González, 'Camino: 'Los marxistas idearon en los años 30 un plan para exterminar a la Iglesia', *La Nueva España*, 20 December 2011.

[59] Lousi Lougen, 'El cardenal Amato beatifica en Madrid a 23 mártires de la persecución religiosa en España,' *Agencia SIC*, 18 November 2011.

[60] Asamblea Plenaria de la Conferencia Episcopal Española, *La fidelidad de Dios dura siempre. Mirada de fe al siglo XX* (Madrid: Conferencia Episcopal Española, 1999).

[61] See Pedro Carlos González Cuevas, 'El retorno de la "tradición" liberal-conservadora. El "discurso" histórico-político de la nueva derecha española,' *Ayer* 22 (1996): 71-87; Xosé Manoel Núñez Seixas, 'Sobre la memoria historia reciente y el "discurso patriótico" español del siglo XXI,' *Historia del Presente* 3 (2004): 137-155.

[62] These are the words of a PP politician, Manuel Atencia, see 'Ley de Memoria Histórica ¿Insuficiente o innecesaria? Los rescoldos de la guerra aún queman,' *El siglo de Europa*, 18 December 2006.

[63] Alfonso Carlos Peña, *Persecución religiosa en Madrid durante la guerra* (Madrid: Ayuntamiento de Madrid, 2001): 21.

[64] Enrique Clemente, '"¿Por qué voy a tener que condenar yo el franquismo?" Entrevista a Jaime Mayor Oreja,' *La Voz de Galicia*, 13 October 2007.

[65] The expression and the concept is taken from Annette Wieviorka, *L'Ère du témoin* (Paris: Hachette, 2002).

[66] The complex relationship between catholic Church and human rights is described in Daniele Menozzi, *Chiesa e diritti umani. Legge naturale e modernità politica dalla Rivoluzione francese ai nostri giorni* (Bologna: il Mulino, 2012).

[67] Carlos Osoro, 'Homilía en el 75° aniversario de los Mártires de Turón. Parroquia de San Martín de Turón, 9 de octubre de 2009,' *Boletín Oficial del Arzobispado de Oviedo*, 11 (2009): 607.

[68] A balance of relations between the Church and the Socialist Government in Mireno Berrettini, 'The Spanish Catholic Church from the Zapatero Era to the Rajoy Government,' in *Politics and Society in Contemporary Spain: From Zapatero to Rajoy*, ed. Bonnie N. Field and Alfonso Botti (New York: Palgrave, 2013): 161-178.

[69] Alfonso Milián Sorribas, '¡Todo un Seminario mártir!,' *Iglesia en Barbastro-Monzón*, 6 Noviembre 2011.

[70] The famous formula is taken by Samuel P. Huntington, *The Clash of Civilizations and the Remaking of World Order* (New York: Simon & Schuster 1996).

[71] Antonio María Rouco Varela, *Los nuevos Mártires de Madrid* (Madrid: Arzobispado de Madrid, 2007). See also Julián López Martín, *Carta pastoral con ocasión de la Beatificación de 34 Siervos de Dios relacionados con nuestra Diócesis* (León: Obispado de León, 2007); Antonio Algora Hernando, *La llamada de Dios. Los pobres y la pobreza* (Ciudad Real: Obispado de Ciudad Real 2007); Juan del Río Martín, *Martirio y reconciliación* (Jerez de la Frontera: Obispado de Jerez de la Frontera, 2007).

[72] Vicente Enrique y Tarancón, 'Nuestros mártires,' *Boletín Oficial Eclesiástico del Obispado de Solsona*, 105 (1948): 1-12.

[73] *Beatificación de 498 mártires del siglo XX en España*, Madrid, 2007.

[74] Agustín García-Gasco, 'Reconciliación,' *Paraula. Iglesia en Valencia*, 25 March 2007.

[75] Ramón Armengod, 'La honra de los mártires,' *Alfa y Omega*, 22 June 2001.

[76] Juan Rubio, 'Mártires una vez más. La sangre sigue fresca,' *Iglesia Viva*, 12 November 2012.

[77] The concept is taken from Anna Lisa Tota, 'Le città della memoria. Introduzione,' in *La memoria contesa. Studi sulla comunicazione sociale del passato* (Milano: Franco Angeli, 2001): 17-30.

[78] The concept is taken from Micheal Richards, 'El régimen de Franco y la política de memoria de la Guerra Civil española,' *Guerra Civil. Mito y memoria*, ed. Julio Arostegui (Madrid: Marcial Pons, 2006): 167-200.

[79] See Alfonso Botti, 'Católicos para la paz en la Guerra Civil española. Prehistoria de los Comités pour la paix civile et religieuse en Espagne', *La Iglesia y el franquismo. Homenaje a Aita Onaindia* (Gernika: Publicaciones del Museo de la Paz de Gernika 2007): 185-199.

[80] The expression in taken from Javier Rodrigo, *Hasta la raíz. Violencia durante la Guerra civil y la dictadura franquista* (Madrid: Alianza 2008): 81.

[81] Vicente Enrique y Tarancón, 'Nuevos martires: testigos del evangelio,' *Vida Nueva*, 28 April 1990. The article was inspired by the tragic story of Archbishop Oscar Romero, Bishop of San Salvador, killed in 1980 for denouncing the atrocities of the military.

[82] Oficina de Información de la Conferencia Episcopal Española, *Nota de prensa final de la C Asamblea Plenaria de la Conferencia Episcopal Española* (Madrid: Conferencia Episcopal Española 2012). Same thesis in Asamblea Plenaria de la Conferencia Episcopal Española, *Los mártires del siglo XX en España, firmes y valientes testigos de la fe. Mensaje con motivo de la Beatificación del Año de la fe, en Tarragona, el 13 de Octubre de 2013* (Madrid: Conferencia Episcopal Español 2013).

[83] The document has been published by Tomás de la Torre Lendínez, 'Recogida de firmas para abolir la ley de memoria histórica,' *Infocatólica*, 29 January 2013.

# Bibliography

Alberola, Miquel. 'Una iglesia para los "mártires" del 36'. *El País* 02 July 2007.

Algora Hernando, Antonio. *La llamada de Dios. Los pobres y la pobreza*. Ciudad Real: Obispado de Ciudad Real 2007.

Armengod, Ramón. 'La honra de los mártires'. *Alfa y Omega* 22 June 2001.

Asamblea Plenaria de la Conferencia Episcopal Española, *La fidelidad de Dios dura siempre. Mirada de fe al siglo XX*. Madrid: Conferencia Episcopal Española, 1999.

Asamblea Plenaria de la Conferencia Episcopal Española, *Los mártires del siglo XX en España, firmes y valientes testigos de la fe. Mensaje con motivo de la Beatificación del Año de la fe, en Tarragona, el 13 de Octubre de 2013*. Madrid: Conferencia Episcopal Español 2013.

————.*Orientaciones morales antes la situacion actual del España*. Madrid: Conferencia Episcopal Española, 2006.

————. *La fidelidad de Dios dura siempre. Mirada de fe al siglo XX*. Madrid: Conferencia Episcopal Española, 1999.

————.*Vosotros sois la luz del mundo (Mt 5,14). Mensaje con motivo de la beatificación de 498 mártires del siglo XX en España*. Madrid: Conferencia Episcopal Española, 2007.

Bedoya, Juan G. 'Los Obipos insisten en que la Iglesia fue "sujeto paciente y victima" de la Guerra Civil'. *El País* 08 April 2000.

————. 'Rouco dice que en España "sigue habiendo una semilla de guerra". El Cardenal separa la verdad histórica de las valoraciones teológicas'. *El País* 13 April 2000.

Berrettini, Mireno. 'A settant'anni dalla Carta Collettiva dell'Episcopato spagnolo: Jerarquía, martirio, memoria collettiva'. *Un conflitto che non passa. Storia, memoria e rimozioni della guerra civile spagnola*, ed. Enrico Acciai and Giulia Quaggio, Pistoia: ISRPT, 2012: 42-65.

————. 'La riconciliazione nel pensiero pastorale del Cardinal Tarancón'. *Storia e problemi contemporanei* 47 (2008): 81-90.

————. 'Spagna e nuovi beati. La Jerarquía tra riconciliazione e *combate por la memoria*'. *Studi e Ricerche di Storia Contemporanea* 70 (2008): 2-32

————. 'The Spanish Catholic Church from the Zapatero Era to the Rajoy Government'. *Politics and Society in Contemporary Spain: From Zapatero to Rajoy*, ed. Bonnie N. Field and Alfonso Botti, New York: Palgrave, 2013: 161-178.

Botti, Alfonso and Massimiliano Guerzo, *L'ultimo franchismo tra repressione e premesse della transizione (1968-75)*. Soveria Mannelli: Rubbettino, 2009.

Botti, Alfonso. 'Católicos para la paz en la Guerra Civil española. Prehistoria de los Comités pour la paix civile et religieuse en Espagne', *La Iglesia y el franquismo. Homenaje a Aita Onaindia*. Gernika: Publicaciones del Museo de la Paz de Gernika 2007: 185-199.

————. 'Dalla "guerra giusta" alla "guerra santa". La pubblicistica cattolica spagnola durante la Seconda Repubblica e la Guerra Civile'. *Storia e problemi contemporanei* 42 (2006): 61-91

————. 'La riconciliazione in Spagna tra cronaca, politica e storia'. *Storia e problemi contemporanei* 47 (2008): 7-12.

Calvo Madrid, Teodoro. *Mártires de Motril y persecución religiosa en la diocesis de Granada (1931-1939)*. Madrid: Edibesa, 2009.

Cárcel Ortí, Vicente. *Mártires del siglo XX. Cien preguntas y respuestas*. Madrid: Edicep, 2001.

————. *Persecuciones religiosas y mártires del siglo XX*. Madrid: Palabra, 2001.

Carlos Peña, Alfonso. *Persecución religiosa en Madrid durante la guerr*a. Madrid: Ayuntamento de Madrid, 2001.

Casanova, Julián. 'Franco, la Iglesia católica y sus mártires'. *El País* 26 June 2007.

Castro, Felipe M. *Ofrenda martirial de los dominicos de Cantabria en la persecución religiosa de 1936*. Las Caldas de Besaya: Cantabria PP. Dominicos, 1996.

*Church Documents Reference Suite*. Boston: Pauline Books & Media, 2000.

Clemente, Enrique. '"¿Por qué voy a tener que condenar yo el franquismo?'. Entrevista a Jaime Mayor Oreja'. *La Voz de Galicia* 13 October 2007.

Comisión Permanente de la Conferencia Episcopal Española. *Contructores de la paz*. Madrid: Conferencia Episcopal Española, 1986.

Cumplido, Manuel Nieto and Luis Enrique Sánchez García, *La persecución religiosa en Córdoba 1931-1939*. Córdoba: Deán y Cabildo de la Santa Iglesia Catedral de Córdoba, 1998.

De Castro Albarran, Aniceto. *Guerra Santa. El sentido católico del Movimiento Nacional*. Burgos: Editorial Española, 1938.

De la Lama Ruiz-Escajadillo, Fernando. *Mártires de la Montaña en nuestra cruzada española de liberación 1936-37.* Santander: Sanara, 1994.

De la Torre Lendínez, Tomás. 'Recogida de firmas para abolir la ley de memoria histórica'. *Infocatólica* 29 January 2013.

Del Río Martín, Juan. *Martirio y reconciliación.* Jerez de la Frontera: Obispado de Jerez de la Frontera, 2007.

Díaz Merchán, Gabino. 'Discurso del Presidente a la Conferencia Episcopal'. *Ecclesia* 9 August 1986.

Enrique y Tarancón, Vicente. 'Nuestros mártires'. *Boletín Oficial Eclesiástico del Obispado de Solsona* 105 (1948): 1-12.

Enrique y Tarancón, Vicente. 'Nuevos martires: testigos del evangelio'. *Vida Nueva* 28 April 1990.

Fernández, Demetrio. 'Mártires de nuestro tiempo'. *Zenit,* 3 November 2011.

García Hernández, Pedro. *Crónica martirial. 271 misioneros claretianos mártires 1936-39.* Madrid: Publicaciones claretianas, 2000.

García-Gasco, Agustín. 'Reconciliación'. *Paraula. Iglesia en Valencia* 25 March 2007.

Garralda García, Ángel. *La persecución religiosa del clero en Asturias, 1934, 1936 y 1937: Martirios y odiseas.* Avilés: Nieva, 2009.

González Cuevas, Pedro Carlos. 'El retorno de la "tradición" liberal-conservadora. El "discurso" histórico-político de la nueva derecha española'. *Ayer* 22 (1996): 71-87.

González, Pablo. 'Camino: "Los marxistas idearon en los años 30 un plan para exterminar a la Iglesia"'. *La Nueva España* 20 December 2011.

Gutiérrez García, José Luis. *Unidas hasta la muerte. Biografía de las siete beatas mártires del Primer Monasterio de la Visitación de Santa María en Madrid.* Madrid: Edibesa, 1998.

Herria 2000 Eliza and Comunidades Cristianas Populares and Coordinadora de Sacerdotes de Euskal Herria, *Memoria y Justicia*. Bilbao: CCP, 2009.

Huntington, Samuel P. *The Clash of Civilizations and the Remaking of World Order*. New York: Simon & Schuster 1996.

International Theological Commission. *Memory and Reconciliation. The Church and the faults of the past*. Roma: Libreria Editrice Vaticana, 2000.

John Paul II. *Incarnationis mysterium*. Roma: Libreria Editrice Vaticana, 1994.

John Paul II. *Tertio Millenio Adveniente*. Roma: Libreria Editrice Vaticana, 1994.

Juliá, Santos. 'Echar al olvido. Memoria y amnistía en la transición'. *Claves de Razón Práctica* 129 (2003): 14-24.

López Martín, Julián. *Carta pastoral con ocasión de la Beatificación de 34 Siervos de Dios relacionados con nuestra Diócesis*. León: Obispado de León, 2007.

Lougen, Lousi. 'El cardenal Amato beatifica en Madrid a 23 mártires de la persecución religiosa en España'. *Agencia SIC* 18 Noviembre 2011.

Martín Rubio, Ángel David. *La Cruz, el Perdón y la Gloria. La persecución religiosa en España durante la II República y la Guerra Civil*. Madrid: Ciudadela Libros, 2007.

———. *Los mitos de la represión en la Guerra Civil*. Baracaldo: Grafite, 2005.

Martínez Puche, José Antonio. *Mártires dominicos españoles. 92 religiosos, religiosas y seglares de la familia dominicana, mártires de la persecución religiosa de 1936*. Madrid: Edibesa, 2007.

Menozzi, Daniele. *Chiesa e diritti umani. Legge naturale e modernità politica dalla Rivoluzione francese ai nostri giorni*. Bologna: il Mulino 2012.

Milián Sorribas, Alfonso. '¡Todo un Seminario mártir!,' *Iglesia en Barbastro-Monzón* 6 November 2011.

Montero Moreno, Antonio. *Historia de la persecución religiosa en España, 1936-1939*. Madrid: BAC, 1961.

Montero, Manuel. 'Otros "mártires" de la Guerra Civil'. *El País* 6 May 2007.

Moreno Villalba, Faustino. *Los mártires del 36 y Franco*. Sevilla: Apostolado mariano, 1993.

Núñez López, José. *Síntesis de la persecución religiosa en España del año 1934 al 1939*. Vigo: Cardeñoso, 2010.

Núñez Seixas, Xosé Manoel. 'Sobre la memoria historia reciente y el "discurso patriotico" espanol del siglo XXI'. *Historia del Presente* 3 (2004): 137-155.

Oficina de Información de la Conferencia Episcopal Española. *Beatificación de 498 mártires del siglo XX en España*. Madrid: Conferencia Episcopal Española, 2007.

―――. *Nota de prensa final de la C Asamblea Plenaria de la Conferencia Episcopal Española*. Madrid: Conferencia Episcopal Española 2012.

Osoro, Carlos. 'Homilía en el 75° aniversario de los Mártires de Turón. Parroquia de San Martín de Turón. 9 de octubre de 2009'. Boletín Oficial del Arzobispado de Oviedo 11 (2009): 607.

Richards, Micheal. 'El régimen de Franco y la política de memoria de la Guerra Civil española', *Guerra Civil. Mito y memoria*, ed. Julio Arostegui, Madrid: Marcial Pons, 2006: 167-200.

Rodrigo, Javier. *Hasta la raíz. Violencia durante la Guerra civil y la dictadura franquista*. Madrid: Alianza 2008.

Rodríguez Plaza, Braulio. *Mártires*. Valladolid: Arzobispado de Valladolid, 2007.

Rouco Varela, Antonio María. 'San Rafael Arnáiz Barón: un santo de nuestro tiempo, Homilía en la Eucaristía de Acción de Gracias en honor de San Rafael Arnáiz Barón con motivo de su Canonización'. *Archimadrid* 12 October 2009.

―――. *Los nuevos Mártires de Madrid*. Madrid: Arzobispado de Madrid, 2007.

Rubio, Juan. 'Mártires una vez más. La sangre sigue fresca'. *Iglesia Viva* 12 November 2012.

Sánchez Baeza, Emilio. *La persecución religiosa en la diócesis de Cartagena-Murcia, 1931-1939*. Madrid: E. Sánchez, 1988.

Sánchez González, José. *Beatificaciones en Roma el 28 de Octubre de 2007*. Sigüenza-Guadalajara: Obispado de Sigüenza-Guadalajara 2007.

Sebastián Aguilar, Fernando. 'Acusación injusta'. *Alfa y Omega* 20 April 2003.

Sevillano, Francisco. 'La construcción de la memoria y el olvido en la España democrática'. *Ayer* 52 (2003): 297-319.

Sierra, Laura. 'Aparece un religioso entre los restos de 50 fusilados en una fosa de Gumiel de Izán'. *El Norte de Castilla* 6 July 2011.

Tota, Anna Lisa. 'Le città della memoria. Introduzione,' in *La memoria contesa. Studi sulla comunicazione sociale del passato*. Milano: Franco Angeli, 2001: 17-30.

Wieviorka, Annette. *L'Ère du témoin*. Paris: Hachette, 2002.

**Mireno Berrettini** (PhD in Political Science) is currently a postdoctoral fellow at the Università Cattolica del Sacro Cuore. He collaborates with the journals *Spagna Contemporanea* and *Panorama*. His research focuses on issues related to the Catholic Church and Catholicism. His latest publication 'The Spanish Catholic Church from the Zapatero Era to the Rajoy Government' has appeared in *Politics and Society in Contemporary Spain: From Zapatero to Rajoy* (Palgrave 2013), edited by B.N. Field and A. Botti.

# Part 4

# Post-Traumatic Recovery and Growth

# Developing Trauma-Informed Pedagogy in a Classroom with 6-8 Year Old Children

*Elspeth McInnes, Alexandra Diamond and Victoria Whitington*

**Abstract**
Trauma exposure has immediate and potentially enduring adverse effects, which vary with the age of onset, the frequency and severity of the experience. The most common context of trauma for children living in Western democracies – family violence and child abuse – affects between a quarter and a third of all children. In such contexts exposure to trauma and toxic stress often begins early, and happens frequently and severely. Children living with chronic stress or trauma run the risk of becoming hyper-vigilant or dissociative and withdrawn. In school such children find it hard to achieve a learning state receptive to new information. In 2012 a project was initiated to support a teacher to create a safe learning environment for each student in a class that included several chronically stressed and traumatized 6 to 8 year-old children. The project provided ongoing teacher professional learning about brain development and the emotional and behavioural impacts of chronic stress and trauma to build understanding that would result in improvements in practice. With the support of a community outreach worker, changes made improved behaviour management and teacher-child interaction approaches, class routines aimed to promote social and emotional development, and opportunities for supported teacher reflection on practice were provided. Data collected included teacher and outreach worker interview responses, children's academic literacy scores, school attendance, recall of feeling words, and the pattern of class peer relationships across the school year. By the end of the year, the teacher identified his capacity to support children's social emotional development had improved; the number of feelings words in children's vocabulary had increased significantly; and children had many more mutual friendships. These findings indicate the high effectiveness of the project to create positive changes in the children's ability to identify emotions and make friends.

**Key Words:** Trauma, stress, well-being, learning, pedagogy, children, school, early years, social development, emotional development.

*****

## 1. Introduction

Young children's environments shape their life trajectories for health, learning and behaviour.[1] After family environments, children over five spend most time at school so that early school experiences affect children's life trajectories significantly. Concerns grew in 2009 when Salisbury Communities for Children (SC4C) that provides services for families in Salisbury East, in urban South

Australia indicated vulnerability in one or more developmental domains for 28.8% of 5-year olds, 6.8% above the state average. The same data set established that 11.2% of children were vulnerable in the Emotional Maturity domain, seldom showing pro-social and helping behaviour, and frequently exhibiting anxious, fearful or aggressive behaviour, hyperactivity and inattention.[2] In 2012, SC4C outreach to schools included a project in a class of 6-to 8-year-old children to better support stressed or traumatised children in the class. Two key resources used had a serious impact on children: Play is the Way, 'a cooperative physical games programme', requires children 'to work together towards positive collective outcomes'[3] while *Kimochis*, plush characters that come with interactive storybooks relating feelings to storyline events, aim to 'teach children to identify and express feelings in positive ways'.[4] The project tracked class relationships with sociometric techniques, developed by Jacob Moreno,[5] that detail group inter-relations.[6] A brief review of relevant research literature will precede the detailed project methods and results.

## 2. Chronic Stress, Trauma and Learning

'Chronic stress' relates to continuing high levels of cortisol and other stress hormones in the body while 'Trauma' refers to reaction to events that threaten survival. Common sources of chronic stress or traumatization include child neglect,[7] family violence, or witnessing injury or death.[8] Traumatizing exposures prove particularly harmful to children with unavailable comforting responses.[9]

Chronically stressed or traumatized children have difficulties integrating new information,[10] as their reactive states impede cognition, language, reflection and abstraction,[11] creating poor attention[12] and memory loss.[13] Behaviours include withdrawal, pessimism and anxiety, avoidance and explosive outbursts.[14] Trauma-affected children can alter 'the experience of the whole class group'.[15] At school, as emotional self-management plays an important role in making friends,[16] children identified as socially and emotionally vulnerable risk rejection by peers and its consequences.[17] Peer acceptance in primary school indeed results in further healthy psychological adjustment[18] and successful learning.[19]

Children who succeed despite severe stress are considered 'resilient'.[20] Their resilience stems from supportive relationships with adults,[21] and/or competent peers.[22] Positive interactions with trusted others help repair stress and trauma-associated difficulties.[23] Masten et al. highlight the role of schools in supporting children's resilience.[24] Bray argues for a concept of post-traumatic growth as part of a continuum with pain and distress at one end, and thriving self-actualisation at the other, which he links to experiences, capacities and agency through time.[25] Individuals with good pre-trauma functioning and social support tend to have positive recovery trajectories, whilst those with poor function and social support carry increased risks of negative outcomes. The cumulative and interdependent impacts of exposure to chronic stress and trauma underscore the importance of providing children with optimal social environments for development and learning. As a result, the project implemented by the SC4C outreach worker and teacher to improve the well-being of children in the class underwent evaluation to identify whether the children's emotional literacy and social relationships improved.

### 3. Research Design

The class comprised 27 children, aged 6 to 8 years. Nine children came from families with English as a second language and one child was Aboriginal. Nine children had a chronic illness or disability. Eleven lived in low-income families. All children participated in class activities and the relevant school staff as well as the parents of 19 children gave consent to collect data. Six strategies were implemented during the 2012 school year:

- teacher in-service development regarding stress and trauma as well as the *Kimochis*[26] and *Play is the Way*[27] resources;
- using the resources to shape classroom interactions;
- sharing class activities with parents;
- teacher modelling emotional self-regulation;
- teacher reflective interviews, and
- ongoing SC4C outreach worker support.

In Term 1 the outreach worker and teacher engaged with research resources to develop their expertise in chronic stress and trauma without interventions with students. In Term 2, they introduced *Play is the Way* in the class and across the school. Late in Term 2, class parents attended an evening barbecue to share the games with their children, the teacher and the SC4C outreach worker.

In Terms 2, 3 and 4, the teacher asked children, 'Name three people in the class who are important to you'. At the end of Term 2 the teacher asked each child to list words naming feelings. In Term 3 he introduced *Kimochis*, and invited the parents again to share the activities. In Term 4 the teacher again asked each child to list all the feelings words they knew as well as: 'What is important to you at school?'

The teacher participated in four interviews reflecting on the project, one per term. The outreach worker provided a project journal and participated in an interview at the end of the year. A teaching student also reflected on her involvement in implementing *Play is the Way*.

This paper reports on and discusses results from teacher interviews and the teaching student's reflections, as well as interview data from the SC4C Outreach worker. It also presents and discusses results from children's data gathered by sociometrics, the lists of feelings words, and children's responses about what mattered to them at school. During the year, the teacher collated children's scores in standardised spelling and reading tests, as well as data on class attendance. We undertook a thematic analysis of interview data, and analysed quantitative data using descriptive statistics.

## 4. Results and Discussion
A. Teacher Interviews

Nine key themes emerged from the teacher interviews about his reflections on the project at the end of each term. Presented below, they come along with illustrative quotes.

1. Teacher actively builds positive, caring relationships with/between children and engages in relationship repair:

   I have gone to students and ... sat them down one-on-one and ...asked them why, but if you don't have a ...relationship at the start where they trust, they're not going to say it, so it is about getting to know the students individually.

   So I ... tend to think while I can't sit down and talk to a student like I would as a counsellor one-on-one, that's where I do try and take in more of what they say, in those little incidental conversations, to try and learn as much as I can about them in the time I've got and with what I've got, so I often sit with the kids when they're eating their lunch and ...talk to a few of them. When I do have to discipline I'm really mindful of repairing the relationship as well afterwards.[28]

2. Teacher interprets behaviour as communication about the child's state, rather than the child's innate nature:

   I know I've definitely shifted my thinking as a teacher. Instead of handing out consequences for poor behaviour, I ask them a lot more now about their choices and making good and bad choices, and understanding that a child who has or is experiencing trauma doesn't have the ability to ... always line up the consequences about behaviour.

   Definitely there was a period in my teaching where 'I've asked you to do something, I expect you to do it. We don't need this cool down, calm down, you just need to do it', and I've really changed my way of thinking since that time. It still comes down to picking a battle, choosing what's important and what's not, but definitely giving those kids time to cool down and calm down is very important.[29]

3. Teacher takes a holistic approach to children and expresses concern about aspects of their development and learning, includes families, and sees his role as much broader than curriculum 'delivery':

Definitely those who are experiencing difficulty in learning, my focus is instilling confidence in them that they can do it because, I'm a strong believer …that positive thoughts often lead to positive results; negative thoughts, negative results, and … I believe it carries over into other areas of your life as well, so definitely if the child can believe they can do it, more than likely they'll try. If they can't at the moment they're giving up, but really trying to push them in a direction that if it is hard, well what can you do to get through it, and that comes down to that 'Be brave, give it a go, don't be scared if it's too hard.'

That's the big thing that we've talked about all year that if you run away from it, it will never get solved. If you confront it, be brave and talk about it, try and work through the solution, I can't promise it won't stop, but you at least know what's causing it and how to maybe deal with it, rather than just running away and having it build up.[30]

It was great to hear families say 'I've heard my son or daughter talk about this at home', they come home and do talk about it. So all those nights where I think, is this working, are they getting it? it was sort of nice to hear that. Oh yeah, my son's come home … he's told my other son about this, and how we work through problems and stuff, so it was really positive'.[31]

4. Teacher sees the class as a community, and acknowledges his role in leading the creation of that community, with himself as a positive role model:

The thing that this group is good at is tolerance and understanding. They're very empathetic towards others if you explain to them what the problem is, and I guess that's … the teaching side of it.... If they don't know what the problem is, they don't understand it, therefore they're not empathetic, but if I can voice what some people are feeling and understanding, they're very good at coming up with solutions on how we can help other people. When I have challenged them to work with different people they've been fantastic every time. I guess it is just about teaching them those parts of society that makes us like get along and work together.[32]

I've had to become more of a role model of the behaviour, like good and bad - being able to be honest enough with this stuff, to acknowledge your mistakes. I guess it comes down to being brave yourself, putting yourself out there.[33]

5. Teacher sees the school as a community. Teacher emphasises the importance of a general school approach so that as they progress through the school, children experience consistency with a common language expressing shared understandings:

[*Play is the Way* is] definitely better with the whole school. I've noticed out in the yard, particularly with a lot of the younger students, I can ask them "Do you know the golden rule?" and because they've seen the posters around the school they say "Oh yeah, yeah, what is it?" and if they don't know it, somebody else does. So it helps with that language to solve problems out in the yard. That is a pretty big bonus to having a whole-school approach to it.[34]

6. Teacher provides a social and emotional development learning program, including empathy, tolerance, perspective-taking.

It's got to be something that's taught. It's a big thing, and I guess as I've matured as a teacher as well I do understand that it is something that needs to be taught. I remember when I first started I just expected that kids would know that, it was like the students will follow because I expect it. But now I've sort of learned … you do have to teach it and model it and you can't assume that every child comes from a background where it will be taught.[35]

7.  Teacher builds his own knowledge about stress and trauma and its ongoing effects on children:

    I did a *Minds and Matters* [course] where they did talk a lot about trauma and how that affects people's ability to concentrate and function, and therefore learn.

    And then in [School Y], ... we did a whole professional development day particularly on trauma. ... I know [trauma has a] sustained, prolonged effect, ... where the mind sort of can't switch off from that; they're still in that heightened state. So ... without knowing all the jargon and everything behind it, I do believe I've got a pretty good basic understanding of what [trauma] is and how it affects people, which then does help me ... day to day.[36]

8.  Teacher values outside support to implement Social and Emotional Learning program:

    Well definitely number one on that list is [Outreach Worker] and he has played a huge supporting role, particularly talking with [child A] and [child B]. He's been able to supplement a lot of the content we've talked in the classroom and deliver it to them one-on-one or, you know, intensify it for those kids. Yeah, [Outreach Worker] has really helped support the learning in the classroom. He also came in and did the introduction for the *Kimochis* to give me a chance to look at it and see it as well, so he's been huge, organising the nights. He was the one that organised the meals and got the food.

    [The student] really helped get *Play is the Way* started, set up. I've talked a number of times about how it would have fallen in a hole if she wasn't there, just the fact to have an extra pair of hands in the room where [she] could deliver the content and I could sort of translate that and support those who weren't ready to deal with it. We had quite a few runners at that stage and [she] was vital.[37]

9.  Teacher reflects on program, on individual children's progress, and on his own professional learning:

A lot of the students, particularly the ones we've talked about being those potential trauma cases, they're moving greatly from that, I guess what we call the egocentric point of view to considering others. They still don't always do it and in the moments of anger and the emotions taking over, they often forget it, but definitely in those calmer moments I'm seeing a lot more understanding and empathising with other people than what I was seeing at the start of the year. That would be the biggest change I've seen in the kids, and I'm not sure if that's just simply through just them getting older and developing, but definitely the language we're using and all of the talk has been around making sure you think about how the other person would feel in that situation, and that has definitely become a lot more automatic at this stage of the year.[38]

... I don't consider myself to be overly emotionally literate myself. I've been a person who guards themselves pretty heavily and doesn't really share too much emotion. I still feel like I am that sort of person to a point, but it has definitely forced me to open myself up to the children a bit more and develop even closer relationships with the students than what I possibly would normally do. I found that a challenge with younger kids as well, like how do I relate to them on their level? Having taught older students for quite a while, it's been a huge step for me, and this *Kimochis* and *Play is the Way* has helped me take that step to open myself up and speak to the kids on their level. That's been the biggest thing for me personally this year, forcing me to reflect on myself a bit more. I think for me it has been about that building of myself and being able to share with other people, and giving names to different emotions and things like that too.[39]

The interviews affirmed the value of the selected resources; however the teacher's commitment was essential to sustained, thorough implementation. The four teacher interviews with a researcher across the year provided a reflective tool which supported the teacher's understanding of the changes made in the classroom, but also stimulated self-reflection on his own professional and personal development from his involvement in the project. Engagement in building relationships in the classroom required the teacher's willingness to reveal his feelings to the class and to model 'making good choices'. By sharing his feelings, the teacher positioned himself as a member of the class community, understanding the critical value of a relationships based approach to successful change. He engaged with the children as individuals he appreciated and cared for. The teacher shifted from simply handing out punishments for 'bad' behaviour, to inviting children to make choices about who they wanted to take charge of their behaviour – themselves or the teacher. He coached them towards greater social and emotional competence. Creating a community in the classroom required participants to become mindful of their own and others' feelings.

B.  University Student's Reflection

A 4th year pre-service educator assisted with initial implementation of *Play is the Way* games in Term 2, attending on two mornings for five weeks. The student reflected on children's behaviour:

> Children's behaviour became easier to control and they seemed to be connecting my instructions with the effectiveness of the game and the choices they were making. By the end of Week 5, I was able to see a dramatic change in the children. Some children who would not participate in the beginning at all, went from being involved for 10 minutes, to participating in the whole session. It was quite a feeling of accomplishment as this is something the teacher and counsellor thought would not be possible for some of the children in the class.[40]

C.  Outreach Worker Interview

The interview with the Outreach Worker identified 4 key themes regarding the building of a classroom climate that supported children's wellbeing.

1.  Supporting change takes time and continuity. The Outreach Worker had a clear vision for change based on values, reflection and a 'big picture' approach:

> ...deciding what are we wanting to see as a result of our kids going through 13 years of education. Are we wanting to see them come out, you know, get a job, or are we wanting them to come out as meaningful citizens who can actually play a role ...that contributes to a greater range of things?....What I want to be different, ... rather than lots of other projects that... work for six months or work for a year, or whatever, what I want to see is something that's more systemic in change... and making an ongoing, deeper difference.[41]

The Outreach Worker ensured he took advantage of opportunities to learn more about how best to support primary school children's wellbeing:

> For the first probably six months, I can't count the number of different training sessions I went to, to look at all the different programs that schools were running. The guidance role to [the teacher] was pivotal. That made the difference in what he did in the classroom. [An essential role was] challenging the thinking of that teacher, and helping him to grow throughout the year ... getting him to try new things at his pace .... When I was able to come alongside of him ... he then tried something new and moved in that new direction.[42]

> It needed a lot of sensitivity around where [the teacher] was at, where was his learning at, where was his thinking at, what was he ready to look at, what was he ready to change, what was he ready to think about, so I knew very carefully that if I pushed him too much I was going to push him away. He'd struggled and he would fall back to the behaviour work of just maintaining the classroom, and I think...there has been a growth there over time. ..generally I would spend a good four to five hours a week with that class, so actually, sometimes it would be just sitting in on the class and just being there, and letting the teacher try new things, and therefore he had the confidence to do that. Sometimes it was actually being there at the start of the day or the end of the day and just talking to parents and building those relationships, which we found were pivotal when we came to the family nights.[43]

> 2. The Outreach Worker saw that sustainable change required a community focus involving parents:

> > I'm realising that my role very much is more of a community development role ... trying to build capacity in the community, to actually to get them to support themselves again...we've moved into the people-centric model of support, and we have just unknowingly taken away all the community support or the family support, and what we need to do is move that more community-centric model. And I think that's probably what I'm seeing my role ... being.... If we have that community around that classroom, amazing things can happen.... if we recognise that and use the school

> as that pivot, we can engage parents, we can engage kids, we can engage adults, we can engage the whole community. [44]

As a result, parents willingly engaged in positive school activities with their child:

> [The teacher] thought we won't get parents, we might get two or three, and then we had over 70 people... In the optional teacher interviews at the end of Term 3, the rest of the school getting one or two parents and the teacher is getting over 15... [The teacher] said one of the things this has done for him is re-ignited his faith in parents wanting to be involved with their child's learning and he was starting to see that if we provide a learning environment the kids enjoy, where the kids flourish, then they'll share it with their parents and the kids acted as peer educators for their parents. [45]

This classroom-community approach meant that the Outreach Worker moved away from simply intervening with individual children:

> The strategies that worked best were relating them back to the classroom, so again it wasn't me as a professional coming alongside of a child, setting something up, and then when I'm not there it fails. When it was linked back into the classroom, linked back into what was happening with their relationship with [X], the class teacher, that's when it was most successful. [46]

The Outreach Worker saw schools as "community central":

> One of the biggest challenges [for] interdisciplinary work is that outside agencies have a reluctance to go to schools. They expect everybody to come to them, and I can say this being from an agency myself, they expect that things will come to them, that's where they'll meet parents and that's where they'll see the children, and they're constantly frustrated [when] families don't turn up, children don't turn up, and so what I constantly do is try to encourage services to work in the schools.....At the same time there are some schools that don't like letting services in, so it's a bit of a both-way change, but it's about changing the policies, about changing the way agencies work. [47]

3. The Outreach Worker saw good relationships as keys to better outcomes:

The pivotal core here was the sense of relationships created in that classroom, the relationship between [the teacher] and the students, between the students and myself, and between parents and the class as well. That meant that there was a significant level of trust, and so the children were willing to engage with the program fully, the parents were willing to engage with it, and we got the greater outcome. ... if that community sense can be there, then any program has the potential to have a great effect, but often I think what I see is these programs are often used in isolation from those things.[48]

[Child T] started (at another) school, he was constantly suspended, constantly excluded, and when you look through his file one of the biggest things he's never been able to do is form a relationship with someone at school, so he's had no one to contact and want to go back to. What I highlighted to the teacher only last week was, you know, [child T] has now been in the school three terms and this is the first time in his whole schooling life he's not even been suspended, so something is happening right for him, and one of the things I did very early on, probably about Term 2 with the teacher, was I initiated the idea of him spending time with [child T] one-on-one, doing some models up in the Tech Room, and the profound effect that had on building a relationship between the teacher and [child T]. [Child T] has Oppositional Defiance Disorder, his issues are not going to go away, but certainly we saw a great reduction in his defiance in the classroom, purely because he had that relationship with the teacher.[49]

4. The Outreach Worker saw that structured resources enabled children to build better relationship skills:

[Child S] for example, ... high on the autism spectrum, she came at the start of this year, she's in Year 3, had not been able to engage more than five minutes in her schooling life since she started, constantly leaving the classroom, constantly not wanting to be involved, would always say nobody wants to spend time to play with her, and we did the *Play is the Way* program. For the first week [child S] was really confronted by the idea that she had to become uncomfortable and try to solve a situation with her class, but by the third week [child S] was choosing to engage, and we weren't having to sit on top of her, she was actually freely engaging. By the fifth week she'd chosen some people she could now play with and she was reporting that she was having friends play at recess and lunch, and then we looked at her sociogram. You'll see that she went from Term 1 where she couldn't identify anybody at all, to Term 4 where she was writing extra numbers to add extra kids on the list.[50]

The Outreach Worker's contribution crucially established and sustained the project. The Outreach Worker provided leadership and advocacy for positive change through relationship building. His tasks encompassed researching and selecting suitable pedagogical resources, providing training in the use of these resources, supporting and encouraging the teacher in the use of the resources in the classroom, engaging with individual children and their families and supporting parents to engage more deeply with the school and their children's relationship to school.

The significance of the Outreach Worker's contribution to the implementation of the project provides an indication of the unseen barriers to wider changes in school practices across the primary school system. A first hurdle concerns the high level of demand on teachers to deliver the curriculum, to prepare children for standardised testing and to meet children's diverse needs and abilities. Placing additional demands on teachers risks rising stress levels and an understandable reluctance to take on new, extra work. The teacher in this project needed to accept taking on professional learning about trauma and chronic stress, implementing new class activities and ways of interacting in the classroom. The school and the teacher needed to accept the presence and engagement of 'an outsider' with the children and families of their school community. This acceptance itself relied on the establishment of a trust relationship between the Outreach Worker, the school and the teacher. The Outreach Worker extended those trust relationships into the classroom and engaged with children on a regular basis at the school, as well as making connections with parents at drop-off and pick-up times. Such connections then further developed through the parent events showcasing the children's activities using *Play is the Way* and *Kimochis*.

As the Outreach Worker noted, services often wait for families to come to them in preference to going where children and families are. As a compulsory universal service, schools offer a unique opportunity to make connections with families who may otherwise never engage with community services.  Services would need to move to a greater outreach focus and schools to move further towards inviting community services and parents into school environs.

D. Children's Sociometric Data

In Term 2, 18 participants were chosen 35 times by other classmates, rising to 50 times for 19 participants by Term 4. Across the whole class, the number of mutual relationships increased threefold from 8 to 25. Peer acceptance is critical to children's adjustment at school[51], so the considerable increase shown in mutual friendships over the year indicated a more supportive social and emotional climate may have developed in response to the interventions.

E. Children's Emotional Literacy and *Kimochis*

Before *Kimochis*, the children recalled between 4 and 11 feeling words ($M =$ 6.75, $SD = 2.22$). After the intervention they recalled between 5 and 22 feeling words ($M = 11.33$, $SD = 4.94$). A paired samples t-test identified a significant increase in feeling words, $t(11) = -3.298$, $p = .004$ (one tailed). The teacher noted in interviews that over the same period children became more able to discuss their feelings and resolve conflict. Emotion knowledge, research establishes, predicts positive and negative social behaviour[52], children's peer-nominated sociometric status and child self-reports of peer victimization and rejection[53]. Social emotional learning programs, such as the *Promoting Alternative Thinking Strategies* curriculum (PATHS) for preschool-age children, have found that parents and teachers rate children with improved emotion knowledge skills as more socially competent than peers and less socially withdrawn at the end of the school year.[54]

F. What Mattered to the Children at School

In Term 4 when asked, 'What is important to you at school?' Eight children nominated class activities, seven named sport and play. Six children said 'friends'. Two children said school made them 'feel brave'. This last comment reflects a word prominent in project activities providing some evidence of children adopting the vocabulary of the *Play is the Way* program. The reference to a feeling, rather than people, places or activities, also provides some evidence of children's ability to identify valued feelings in themselves.

G. Children's Attendance

Children's school attendance was logged, with principal-approved exemptions included as attendances. The percentages of days each child attended school in Term 1 and in Term 4 proved that children's attendance improved between Terms 1 and 4. However without comparing the averages for Year 3/4 classes in the state, this result cannot count as an outcome of the intervention. However improved attendance, along with emotional readiness to learn, would set the stage for learning over the next years.

H. Children's Academic Achievements

Reading and spelling level data provided by the teacher over the school year indicated that children's academic literacy improved across the school year. Individual children's reading and spelling ages in Term 1 strongly positively related to reading and spelling ages in Term 4, and followed individual achievement trajectories. No evidence emerged that the interventions improved children's academic outcomes, but also no evidence that the intervention affected children's reading and spelling achievements.

## 5. Conclusion

All children need to feel part of their school communities. Chronically stressed or traumatized children can find this difficult. Withdrawal, low trust and inability to identify feelings commonly result from chronic stress and trauma.[55]

The data provide promising indicators of positive change in participating children's social relationships at school and their ability to identify their own and others' feelings. Given that social withdrawal, lack of trust and inability to identify feelings usually connects with chronic stress and trauma, these positive changes can indicate increasing well-being for children in the classroom.

The selected resources, *Play is the Way* and *Kimochis*, provided effective tools to promoting improved social relationships and a wider vocabulary of feelings words which children used to relate to their own and others' experiences. A generalised school approach and assistance with implementation of the resources proved important to successfully embedding the programs in classroom activities.

The gradual implementation of the activities through the school year allowed all participants to practise working with the selected resources and to become more confident in their use over time. The gradual implementation of activities also allowed time for children to develop new relationships with others in their class community.

The teacher's strategies of forming and sustaining individual relationships with children in the class, of leading and modelling a sense of community and revealing and modelling his own management of his feelings, enabled children to develop a sense of trust, of being valued and able to contribute to their classroom community. Again these strategies addressed some of the negative consequences of chronic stress and trauma, which include difficulty trusting others, low self-esteem and a sense of loss of control.

The Outreach worker played a key role in identifying resources, providing training in their use and assisting with their implementation. The role included one-on-one interaction with children experiencing difficulties as well as follow-up with families. The strategy of inviting parents to two barbecues to share the games with their children allowed parents and the teacher to make connections between school and home activities and for parents to discuss and, in some cases, adopt some of the concepts and language which their children were learning through the class activities. Staff observed that parents were using children's learned vocabulary from the games. Coming to school for food and fun activities with their children allowed parents to positively engage with the school environment.

This project's findings of positive changes in children's relationships at school and emotional literacy demonstrate that targeted strategies can create inclusive educational environments. Inclusive classroom environments offer an effective avenue for supporting children's recovery from chronic stress or trauma. Benefits flow to individual children and their families, school staff and the wider community as children change from being isolated and 'in trouble' to being valued members and citizens of the communities they help to create.

## Notes

[1] Fraser Mustard, *Investing in the Early Years: Closing the Gap between What We Know and What We Do* (Adelaide: Department of Premier and Cabinet, 2008), 2.

[2] Australian Early Development Index, *Community Profile 2011 Salisbury, South Australia* (Parkville, Victoria: Centre for Community Child Health, 2011), viewed 27 August 2013.

[3] Helen Street, et al., 'The Game Factory: Using Cooperative Games to Promote Pro-social Behaviour among Children', *Australian Journal of Educational and Developmental Psychology* 4 (2004): 97.

[4] Kimochis, *Kimochis Teacher's Curriculum* (Queensland: Spectronixinoz, 2011).

[5] Jonathan D. Moreno, ed., 'The Autobiography of J. L. Moreno', *MD Journal of Group Psychotherapy, Psychodrama & Sociometry* 42.1(1989): 52.

[6] Lawrence Sherman, *Sociometry in the Classroom: How to Do It* (Ohio: Miami University n.d.).

[7] Karen Seccombe, '"Beating the Odds" Versus "Changing the Odds": Poverty, Resilience, and Family Policy', *Journal of Marriage and the Family* 64.2 (2002): 384.

[8] Phyllis T. Stien and Joshua C. Kendall, *Psychological Trauma and the Developing Brain: Neurologically Based Interventions for Troubled Children* (Binghamton: Haworth Press, 2004), 16.

[9] National Scientific Council on the Developing Child, *Excessive Stress Disrupts the Architecture of the Developing Brain* (Boston: Harvard University, 2005).

[10] Australian Childhood Foundation, *Making Space for Learning: Trauma Informed Practice in Schools* (Victoria: Australian Childhood Foundation, 2010), 3.

[11] Annette Streeck-Fischer and Bessel A. van der Kolk, 'Down Will Come Baby, Cradle and All: Diagnostic and Therapeutic Implications of Chronic Trauma on Child Development', *Australian and New Zealand Journal of Psychiatry* 34 (2000): 916.

[12] Bessel A. van der Kolk, 'Developmental Trauma Disorder', *Psychiatric Annals* 35 (2005): 401.

[13] Heather C. Abercrombie, et al., 'Cortisol Variation in Humans Affects Memory for Emotionally Laden and Neutral Information', *Behavioural Neuroscience* 117.3 (2003): 505-516.

[14] Phyllis T. Stein and Joshua C. Kendall, *Psychological Trauma and the Developing Brain: Neurologically Based Interventions for Troubled Children* (Binghamton: Haworth Press, 2004), 86.

[15] Australian Childhood Foundation, *Making Space for Learning,* 64.

[16] Antonius H. N. Cillessen and Amy D. Bellmore, 'Social Skills and Interpersonal Perception in Early and Middle Childhood', in *Blackwell Handbook of Childhood Social Development*, eds. Peter K. Smith and Craig H. Hart (Malden: Blackwell, 2004), 356.

[17] Robert D. Laird, et al., 'Peer Rejection in Childhood, Involvement with Anti-Social Peers in Early Adolescence, and the Development of Externalizing Behaviour Problems', *Development and Psychopathology* 13.2 (2001): 337.

[18] Sara Pederson, et al., 'The Timing of Middle Childhood Peer Rejection and Friendship: Linking early Behaviour to early Adolescent Adjustment', *Child Development* 78.4 (2007): 1037.

[19] Laird, et al. 'Peer Rejection in Childhood, 351.

[20] Jack A. Naglieri and Paul A. LeBuffe, 'Measuring Resilience in Children,' in *Handbook of Resilience in Children*, eds. Sam Goldstein and Robert Brooks (USA: Springer-Verlag New York Inc., 2005), 107.

[21] Ann S. Masten and Marie-Gabrielle J. Reed, 'Resilience in Development,' in *Handbook of Positive Psychology*, eds. C. R. Snyder and Shane J. Lopez (New York: Oxford University Press, 2002), 74.

[22] Emmy E. Werner, 'What We Can Learn about Resilience from Large Scale Longitudinal Studies,' in *Handbook of Resilience in Children*, eds. Sam Goldstein and Robert Brooks, (USA: Springer-Verlag New York Inc., 2005), 105.

[23] Bruce D. Perry and Chris R. Ludy-Dobson 'The Role of Healthy Relational Interactions in Buffering the Impact of Childhood Trauma,' in *Working with Children to Heal Interpersonal Trauma: The Power of Play*, ed. Eliana Gill (New York: Guildford, 2010), 42.

[24] Ann S. Masten, et al., 'Promoting Competence and Resilience in the School Context', *Professional School Counselling*, 1 December 2008 (Huntingdon Valley PA: Farlex, 2008).

[25] Peter Bray, in this volume.

[26] Kimochis, *Kimochis* (Moorabbin: Plushy Feely Corp, 2008).

[27] Wilson McCaskill, *Play is the Way* (Greenwood WA: The Game Factory, 2007).

[28] Teacher Interview One, 6 March 2012, 13.

[29] Ibid., 9.

[30] Ibid., 13.
[31] Teacher Interview Two, 20 June 2012, 17.
[32] Teacher Interview One, 6.
[33] Teacher Interview Two, 9.
[34] Teacher Interview One, 12.
[35] Ibid., 3.
[36] Ibid., 7-8.
[37] Teacher Interview Four, 6 December 2012, 9-10.
[38] Ibid., 1.
[39] Ibid., 3.
[40] Pre-Service Teacher Reflection, 29 October 2012.
[41] Outreach Worker Interview, 6 December 2012, 15.
[42] Ibid., 1.
[43] Ibid., 5.
[44] Ibid., 4.
[45] Ibid., 4.
[46] Ibid., 9.
[47] Ibid., 15.
[48] Ibid., 9.
[49] Ibid., 6.
[50] Ibid., 7.
[51] Laird, et al. 'Peer Rejection in Childhood', 351.
[52] Carroll Izard et al., 'Emotion Knowledge as a Predictor of Social Behavior and Academic Competence in Children at Risk.' *Psychological Science* 12.1 (2001): 18-23.
[53] Alison L. Miller et al., 'Emotion Knowledge Skills in Low-Income Elementary School Children: Associations with Social Status and Peer Experiences,' *Social Development* 14.4 (2005): 637-51.
[54] Celene E. Domitrovich, Rebecca C. Cortes, and Mark T. Greenberg, 'Improving Young Children's Social and Emotional Competence: A Randomized Trial of the Preschool "Paths" Curriculum', *The Journal of Primary Prevention* 28.2 (2007): 67-91.
[55] Streeck-Fischer and van der Kolk, 'Down Will Come Baby', 905.

# Bibliography

Abercrombie, Heather C., Ned H. Kalin, Marchell E. Thurow, Melissa A. Rosenkranz and Richard J. Davidson. 'Cortisol Variation in Humans Affects Memory for Emotionally Laden and Neutral Information'. *Behavioural Neuroscience* 117.3 (2003): 505-516.

Australian Childhood Foundation. *Making Space for Learning: Trauma Informed Practice in Schools.* Victoria: Australian Childhood Foundation, 2010.

Australian Early Development Index. *Community Profile 2011 Salisbury, South Australia, Australian Early Development Index.* Parkville, Victoria: Centre for Community Child Health, 2011.

Cillessen, Antonius H. N., and Amy D. Bellmore. 'Social Skills and Interpersonal Perception in Early and Middle Childhood'. *Blackwell Handbook of Childhood Social Development,* edited by Peter K. Smith and Craig H. Hart, 355-374. Malden: Blackwell, 2004.

Domitrovich, Celene E., Rebecca C. Cortes, and Mark T. Greenberg. 'Improving Young Children's Social and Emotional Competence: A Randomized Trial of the Preschool "Paths" Curriculum.' *The Journal of Primary Prevention* 28.2 (2007): 67-91.

Izard, Carroll, Sarah Fine, David Schultz, Allison Mostow, Brian Ackerman, and Eric Youngstrom. 'Emotion Knowledge as a Predictor of Social Behavior and Academic Competence in Children at Risk'. *Psychological Science* 12.1 (2001): 18-23.

Kimochis. *Kimochis.* Moorabbin: Plushy Feely Corp, 2008.

Kimochis. *Kimochis Teacher's Curriculum.* Queensland: Spectronicsinoz, 2011.

Laird, Robert D., Kristi Y. Jordan, Kenneth A. Dodge , Gregory S. Pettit, and John E. Bates. 'Peer Rejection in Childhood, Involvement with Anti-Social Peers in Early Adolescence, and the Development of Externalizing Behaviour Problems'. *Development and Psychopathology* 13.2 (2001): 337-354.

Masten, Ann S., Janette E. Herbers, J. J. Cutuli, and Theresa L. Lafavor. 'Promoting Competence and Resilience in the School Context'. *Professional School Counselling,* 1 December 2008, Huntingdon Valley, PA: Farlex.

Masten, Ann S., and Marie-Gabrielle J. Reed. 'Resilience in Development'. *Handbook of Positive Psychology,* edited by C. R Snyder and Shane J. Lopez, 74-88. New York: Oxford University Press, 2002.

McCaskill, Wilson. *Play is the Way.* Greenwood WA: The Game Factory, 2007.

Miller, Alison L., Kathleen Kiely Gouley, Ronald Seifer, Audrey Zakriski, Maria Eguia, and Michael Vergnani. 'Emotion Knowledge Skills in Low-Income Elementary School Children: Associations with Social Status and Peer Experiences'. *Social Development* 14.4 (2005): 637-51.

Moreno, Jonathan D. ed., 'The Autobiography of J. L. Moreno'. *MD Journal of Group Psychotherapy, Psychodrama & Sociometry* 42.1 (1989): 52.

Mustard, Fraser. *Investing in the Early Years: Closing the Gap Between What We Know and What We Do.* Adelaide: Department of Premier and Cabinet, 2008.

Naglieri, Jack A., and Paul A. LeBuffe, 'Measuring Resilience in Children'. *Handbook of Resilience in Children*, edited by Sam Goldstein and Robert Brooks, 107-124. New York: Springer-Verlag New York Inc., 2005.

National Scientific Council on the Developing Child. Excessive Stress Disrupts the Architecture of the Developing Brain. Boston: Harvard University, 2005.

Pederson, Sara, Frank Vitaro, Edward D. Barker, and Anne I. H. Borge. 'The Timing of Middle Childhood Peer Rejection and Friendship: Linking Early Behaviour to Early Adolescent Adjustment'. *Child Development* 78.4 (2007):1037-1051.

Perry, Bruce D., and Chris R. Ludy-Dobson. 'The Role of Healthy Relational Interactions in Buffering the Impact of Childhood Trauma'. *Working with Children to Heal Interpersonal Trauma: The Power of Play*, edited by Eliana Gill, 26-43. New York: Guildford, 2010.

Seccombe, Karen. '"Beating the Odds" Versus "Changing the Odds": Poverty, Resilience, and Family Policy'. *Journal of Marriage and the Family* 64.2 (2002): 384-394.

Sherman, Lawrence. Sociometry in the Classroom: How To Do It .Ohio: Miami University (n.d.,).

Stein, Phyllis T., and Joshua C. Kendall. *Psychological Trauma and the Developing Brain: Neurologically Based Interventions for Troubled Children.* Binghamton: Haworth Press, 2004.

Streeck-Fischer, Annette, and Bessel A. van der Kolk. 'Down Will Come Baby, Cradle and All: Diagnostic and Therapeutic Implications of Chronic Trauma on Child Development'. *Australian and New Zealand Journal of Psychiatry* 34 (2000): 903-918.

Street, Helen, David Hoppe, David Kingsbury, and Tony Ma. 'The Game Factory: Using Cooperative Games to Promote Pro-social Behaviour among Children'. *Australian Journal of Educational & Developmental Psychology* 4 (2004): 97-109.

van der Kolk, Bessel A. 'Developmental Trauma Disorder'. *Psychiatric Annals* 35 (2005): 401-408.

Werner, Emmy E. 'What We Can Learn about Resilience from Large Scale Longitudinal Studies'. *Handbook of Resilience in Children*, edited by Sam Goldstein and Robert Brooks, 91-105. New York: Springer-Verlag, 2005.

**Elspeth McInnes, Alexandra Diamond and Victoria Whitington** are early childhood researchers in the School of Education at the University of South Australia. Their research interests include child well-being, development and learning, social policy, family services and early childhood workforce professional learning.

# Trauma and Growth: The Psychology of Self-Actualisation and Positive Post-Traumatic Processes

## Peter Bray

**Abstract**

In the aftermath of stressful life events, groups or individuals often report that their devastating experiences have resulted in beneficial changes and positive personal growth outcomes. In the last half century psychology has begun to broadly recognise and understand the potential psychological benefits to individuals who have successfully managed the balance between the painful challenges of trauma, on the one hand, and the emerging effects of flourishing and personal growth, on the other. Counter-intuitively, these life-enhancing outcomes include improved psychological well-being and health; personal and spiritual development; increased coping skills and deepening relationships; enhanced personal resources; and, changes in religious and spiritual assumptions and beliefs. Without denying its earlier interest in trauma as a catalyst of pathology and functional impairment, main stream psychology has become increasingly more catholic in its position concerning the positive potential, incidence, meaning, and outcomes of these post-traumatic growth processes. However, as these outcomes have become measurable, this chapter suggests that psychology's standard Cartesian caution toward trauma as a singularly quantifiable experience is being gently shifted by post-modern perspectives applied to this phenomenon. Presenting a number of key contributions to the field of trauma theory, this chapter considers post-traumatic growth and specifically the role of intuitive intra-psychic processes and transformations in the management and outcomes of trauma. Collectively, the following interdisciplinary strands also capture something of the current optimism and shared understanding about the struggles of post-traumatic experience: Abraham Maslow's theory of peak experience and self-actualisation and Carl Rogers' organismic valuing process; Stanislav Grof's holotropic paradigm and formulation of psycho-spiritual transformation; Lawrence Calhoun and Richard Tedeschi's research on post-traumatic growth; Ronnie Janoff-Bulman's theory of shattered assumptions; and, Martin Seligman and Stephen Joseph's conceptualisations of positive psychology. Rather than trivialising the serious impact of trauma or to deny in some way its suffering, this work suggests that, for some at least, traumatic events might be recognised as opportunities for positive personal growth.

**Key Words:** Growth, pain, peak experience, positive psychology, post-traumatic growth, psycho-spiritual transformation, self-actualisation, shattered assumptions, spiritual emergency, trauma.

*****

## 1. Introduction

The human pain and suffering caused by traumatic events has long been understood to be balanced by the potential for personal growth and has often been interpreted in terms of benefit, a better life, or a spiritual reward. However, not until recently have these commonly held beliefs been recognised and appreciated by the academy as originating in inherently foundational resources that draw upon qualities of self that support thriving. Countering the deficit or sickness model of human experience, which focuses upon negativity, dependence, and accentuates illness and vulnerability, this position has championed the emergence of strength-based responses. Thus, respectfully acknowledging the trauma event as a challenging experience, psychology has become increasingly interested in the phenomena of post-traumatic outcomes related to growth and transformation. Trauma is becoming positively reframed as an opportunity to thrive, rather than decline. Taking into account the shadow side potential of unrealistic professional helper and trauma survivor expectations, a thread of cautious optimism in research and practice suggests that, to paraphrase Nietzsche, what doesn't kill has the capacity to make stronger.[1]

Considering that incidents of post-traumatic growth and psycho-spiritual transformations have been documented throughout recorded history it is perhaps surprising that a deficit model of trauma has endured for so long.[2] From the beginning, mankind has been imprinted by the diurnal cycle, the day's bright promise and the dark fears of the night. Reassured by the indifference of its daily pattern, human beings in their growing mastery have learned to be optimistic about the cycles of the seasons, when to plant, to harvest, and to store. We have understood that the inevitability of death is balanced by the new life that follows. It is axiomatic to all the great cultures of the World that, given appropriate circumstances, the human pain and suffering associated with life threatening events somehow finds its balance in restoration and regeneration. Underpinning these ancient understandings of life, death, and rebirth is the fundamental idea that individuals and groups are likely to undergo psychological transformation through the challenges of difficult journeys. Early examples of the potentially transformative power of suffering can be found in the foundational philosophies and teachings of the ancient Greeks, Hebrews, and early Christians, as well as those of Hindu, Buddhist, and Islamic writings.

Correspondingly, the overly simplified dictum of 'no pain no gain' implies that personal grow comes at a price – a price best left unpaid simply because it creates additional risks that under normal circumstances would be unthinkable. In this safe model the responsibility to embrace one's own destiny is simply avoided because the individual, like Jonah, feels unworthy or cannot trust the self or the world.[3] Certainly, traumatic events create the right conditions to strenuously exercise anxiety and the capacity to both avoid and to embrace pain. Margaret Stroebe and Henk Schut's model of coping with bereavement, for example, describes an oscillation between the inward management of pain and the outward capacity to manage day-to-day living. Similarly, Judith Lewis Herman's describes an oscillation between 'uncontrollable outbursts of anger and the intolerance of rage and the need to desperately seek intimacy and then totally withdrawing from it.'[4] Man's continual pursuit of happiness and his avoidance and fear of pain conceptualised in Jeremy Bentham's utilitarian moral philosophy of 'psychological hedonism', and inversely in Sigmund Freud's self-regulatory 'pleasure-pain principle', correspond to the neurotic compulsion to both fly from and return to the site of pain. By inference, this return confirms that if the medicine tastes bad it must be good.[5] Ronnie Janoff-Bulman sums up this paradox when she states that 'The long-term legacy of trauma involves both losses and gains ... the survivor can focus on one or the other, but both are ever present.'[6]

Prior to a first encounter with a traumatic situation, inexperienced individuals may characterise themselves as happy, whole, invulnerable, non-victims who have assumed up to this point that the world is a safe, relatively just, and controllable place.[7] However, the sudden removal of this familiar sense of agency, together with the very visceral impact of shock, suggests that mental as well as physical damage has occurred that requires some form of treatment to return a person back to pre-trauma levels of functioning. Whilst latterly that may be possible, the expectation that life will return to the same pre-episode functioning is generally erroneous. Successful coping with trauma does not mean a return to the pre-trauma state, to one's earlier assumptions of the world, as one's basic schemas have become fundamentally altered by the event. Coping or recovery must be measured by an ability to incorporate or integrate this new experience, not to deny it. However in spite of subsequently more cautious responses to the world, in the long-term aftermath survivors do acknowledge benefit from their trauma experiences. Nevertheless, coping is never an easy road. A recent meta-analytic review of growth and benefit finding reported a strong correlation to positive well-being and minimal depression but it also noted more intrusive and avoidant thoughts about the stressor.[8] To make a distinction between the virtues of genuine growth outcomes and the perceptions of benefit finding as a coping strategy to manage distress, is interesting but not as productive as understanding that both contribute positively mental health.[9] As Camille Wortman remarks, in a culture that 'champions people who are strong, invulnerable, and independent in the face of adversity' the belief that adversity can be transcended may be the 'only way to maintain psychological comfort.'[10]

The human impetus toward 'self-actualisation', a central principle in the theories and practice of humanist psychologists Abraham Maslow and Carl Rogers, does provide an explanation and a motive force for benefit-finding post-trauma. By appreciating that positive changes can occur in the wake of disaster, survivors of trauma, illness, or other difficult experiences, have noted their own resilience, the strengthening of emotional and relational ties with family and friends, and a greater compassion and altruism. As worldviews and priorities change, so people report an enhanced appreciation of life and a new openness to spiritual experience. More than simply wishful or delusional thinking, benefit finding comes from the knowledge that human beings are inherently adaptable and built to manage change and transformation. Nevertheless, how this growth occurs is still inconclusive.

In truth, how individuals and communities conceive of the positive outcomes of traumatic experiences is highly complex; not only is it to some extent constructed by social and cultural expectations, but the process of psychological and physical growth and its effect on health changes through time. Whilst this suggests a multiple-perspective approach, the psychological measures currently available for the assessment of personal growth and thriving are limited to those that are tangible. Thus an individual's 'religiosity', for example, may be measured by their attendance at church, their prayer life, and their existential concerns, but it is more problematic to measure those private and more esoteric experiences labelled as 'spiritual.'[11] Consequently, discussions about post-traumatic growth would doubtlessly benefit from including areas of human experience, like spirituality, which are often omitted by clinical psychology because they are not easily quantifiable.[12] Nevertheless in the last fifty years transpersonal psychologists, like Stanislav Grof, have explored and experientially mapped those exact dimensions of human experience and do offer ways to identify the role and significance of growthful spiritual experiences in post-traumatic processes.[13]

Counter-intuitively, therefore, traumatic experiences can create opportunities for change dependent upon personal circumstances and a willingness and ability to participate in personal healing work. In this context appalling events may no longer be regarded as personal attacks or the punishment of a malevolent universe but are recognised as random occurrences with little or no connection to people's moral positions or behaviours. Those who have experienced trauma are no longer 'victims', a passive term which diminishes agency and resilience, but are seen as 'survivors' who have actively tackled the challenges presented by difficult life events resourcefully, and who in making sense of their experiences have integrated them.[14] Trauma work actively engages the survivor in activities that go beyond surviving to thriving. For example, as Mark Callaghan and a number of other contributors discuss and describe, it is through memory or memorialising that survivors, actively engaging with the sites of their original trauma, assist themselves to sensibly reinterpret their experiences.[15]

By providing a brief overview of some complementary ideas contributing to the development and application of trauma theory, this chapter traces one humanistic pathway that scholarly work has taken in its development of structural theory and a practical understanding of the positive psychological phenomenon known as post-traumatic or stress-related growth.

## 2. Humanistic Psychology and Self-Actualisation: Kurt Goldstein, Abraham Maslow and Carl Rogers

The humanistic psychology movement was an attempt to redress an imbalance in clinical practice and the perception of pathology. Even before the advent of Freudian analysis, early psychology was primarily concerned to resolve disease and return clients to normal baseline functioning rather than assist them toward improved levels.[16] In the late 1930s neurologist and philosopher Kurt Goldstein, in common with a number of scholars of his time, became interested in investigating the fundamental nature of human existence. His work on pathology suggests that when 'the essence' of the individual is compromised by injury or illness essential and unaccountable changes in the qualities and orientation of the human organism make a return to earlier states impossible. In his practice Goldstein observes that pathology creates and modifies symptoms. These symptoms he explains as 'attempted solutions' that indicate that an organism is engaged in a self-directed process of inner change that results in a new and potentially improved state of ordered functioning. He terms this essentially human organismic capacity to actively seek solutions to 'shock and anxiety' as 'self-actualisation.'[17] With the rider that even a perfect scenario is subject to some potential challenge, Goldstein cautiously ventures that in a normally healthy individual this primal tendency is ideally enacted from within 'out of the joy of conquest'.[18]

Persuaded by Goldstein's ideas Abraham Maslow, the co-founder of humanistic psychology, purposely recommends that academic study focus upon 'the *best* of mankind rather than the *sick* of mankind.'[19] Understanding that in a lifetime people are continually faced with the difficult decision of choosing between safety and growth, Maslow's conceptual hierarchy of needs maps the struggle toward self-actualisation. Unlike Goldstein, however, Maslow regards self-actualisation as only achievable when lower order needs are satisfied first. Ironically, his findings that self-actualisers are more likely to be high achievers were initially quite negatively received and he and his work condemned as elitist. Maslow was particularly interested in the meta-motivational nature and consequences of 'peak experiences', those mystical, transcendent moments of highest happiness and fulfilment reported by many self-actualisers.[20] Impressed by the fullness of their psychological functioning and wholeness, and their spontaneity and openness to experience, he determines that individuals who have received peak experiences have substantially broader universal values and life goals and cease to be motivated by self-interest. Indeed, Maslow discovered that after a period of time 'merely healthy actualisers' could become 'transcendent actualisers', sustaining peak experiences that allowed them to identify their 'highest self with the highest values of the world' and transcend ego because they discriminate less between self and non-self.[21] An acquaintance of Freud, Roberto Assagioli, whose 'psychosynthesis' approach to psychology predates the humanistic, goes even further to suggest that the latter cannot be considered as the 'actualisation of the potentialities latent in the "normal" personality but...the manifestation of...direct experiential awareness of the Transpersonal SELF.'[22]

Maslow presents a list of characteristics, formerly assigned to religious contexts, to encompass all varieties of peak experience. He describes these experiences as unifying, noetic, and ego-transcending, and giving a sense of purpose and integration to the individual. Essentially, peak experiences are ultimately therapeutic in their outcomes as they increase an individual's empathy, free will, self-determination, and creativity. Rather ambitiously Maslow goes on to suggest that peak experiences be studied and cultivated in order to teach and encourage those in our culture who 'have never had them or who repress or suppress them' to find a path to personal fulfilment, integration, and growth.[23] In terms of the protective factors for trauma survivors, however, he notes the obvious benefits derived from a peak experience, 'It is my strong suspicion that even one such [peak] experience might be able to prevent suicide, for instance, and perhaps many varieties of slow self-destruction.'[24] Maslow consistently defends the view that spiritual experience is a higher potentiality of human experience, a potentiality that inherently belongs to us as a biological species. Consequently, in a synthesis of the developmental and the spiritual, Maslow concludes that human developmental realisation is ultimately a spiritual realisation.

Interest in the positive potential of human development through higher consciousness finally inspired Maslow to envision a new kind of 'trans-human' psychology intended to supplant traditional scientific methodology. He posits that it provides a philosophical way of linking religion and science – the sacred with the profane – as well as providing a means of explaining exceptional, self-actualising people.[25] Miles Vich notes that Maslow began using the word 'transpersonal' – meaning 'across or beyond the individual person or psyche' – to describe this new approach to psychology in his correspondence with Stanislav Grof in the mid 1960's.[26] Described as the 'fourth force', transpersonal psychology succeeds behaviourist, psychoanalytic, and humanistic psychologies. Transpersonalists place personal experience before science and authentic spirituality at the heart of healthy functioning and advocate that its practitioners have some skill in personally accessing transpersonal states of consciousness and to be self-actualising.[27]

Whilst Maslow's ideas about human potential are undoubtedly useful, Arthur Janov notes that in redressing the imbalance created by earlier psychologies he caused a new one. Janov sees an inherent weakness in 'skipping over pain to arrive at a peak experience' as it fails to account for the role of pain in blocking or repressing potential.[28] This is useful in terms of perspective because it draws attention to the struggle toward meaning and continuing growth, the part that consciousness has to play in the self-actualisation, and the role of pain in psycho-spiritual crises, such as 'spiritual emergencies'. Lazar further stresses the difficulty to tie down the 'multi-dimensional construct' of the specific 'spirituality' so broadly discussed in Maslow's work.[29] In addition, whilst spiritual and religious experiences may have the capacity to deepen and provide qualitative benefits to individuals recovering from stressful and traumatic life events they are often not differentiated in terms of affect – a distinction yet to be achieved.[30]

Also a founder of humanistic psychology, the emergence in popularity of the therapeutic and educational thinking of Carl Rogers identifies a significant watershed in client work. Turning away from the dominant expert psychoanalytical relationship he espoused a more expansive, non-directive, and person-centred praxis. Central to his theory is the belief in an impulse, an 'actualising tendency', in everyone toward inner growth that leads to better and healthier functioning.[31] This respect for the unique primacy of the person and 'the self', led him to formulate a model of the 'fully functioning person.'[32] Thus, provided with a number of conditions of worth, replicated in the counselling relationship and mediated by the person's direct experiences, the individual develops a 'real self' that is able to achieve his or her potential rather than to persist with an unrealistic 'idealised self' that is incongruent, dissatisfied, and the source of psychological distress and anxiety. Developing Goldstein and Maslow's concepts, Rogers views the self as having the innate capacity to actualise and evolve beyond its current potential. Thus, the fully functioning person is realistic, integrated, and effective because he is fully aware of himself. At a fundamental level therefore, the onus is on the person to trust, value, and accept himself as worthy, to be open to experience, confident, self-directed and to 'become more like the person he wishes to be.'[33] However, Rogers freely admits that there may be any number of 'encrusted psychological defences,' and 'elaborate facades' that need to be removed before this can happen.[34]

Interestingly, Rogers's theory and practice, much like Maslow's, has been criticised for failing to realistically attend to 'people's real suffering.'[35] Jeffrey Masson notes that 'In reading through the many case histories that Rogers provided in his books, I was startled to see an almost total lack of the reporting of genuine traumas.'[36] Typical of the unhelpful comments levelled at humanistic psychology's narcissistic appearance, this criticism overlooks the simple logic that advocates for, and acknowledges, the integrated person moving toward a more expansive and coherent sense of self. It is because of his strong assertion about the uniqueness of all human beings in their management of pain and in the ways that they access their inner resources, that Rogers can fundamentally explain trauma as an internally generated response to real-world stimuli. It also explains why people report perceived growth even in the wake of the most painful of traumas. Unfortunately, this position also prevents a full discussion of the actualising process in terms of stress-related growth. However, Rogers's concept of the 'organismic valuing process' does assume that humans, having evolved to value what will enhance chances of survival and what makes a good life, can innately understand when they are actualising and when they are not.[37] As most people reportedly make reasonable choices, are fairly satisfied and resilient, they can congruently match their explicit choices with their implicit needs and preferences. That most people grow up to manage their emotions and act according to reason, rather than guilt or compulsion, does seem to indicate the presence of a deep process driven by needs for security in both subjective and psychological well-being.[38]

In practice, prizing the uniqueness of the person and the humane development of mind and spirit that produce whole integrated individuals, the person-centred ideal relies upon a worldview that incorporates a 'means of knowing designed to expand a person's hope for him – or herself.'[39] Essentially, Rogers seems to be describing a spirit-centred practice or process in which the application of three conditions – genuineness; unconditional positive regard; and, empathic understanding – permit the 'knowing' of the self through transcendent relationships with each other and, in turn with, part of a larger, if ill-defined, consciousness.[40] Rogers's comment that he has 'underestimated the importance of this mystical, spiritual dimension', tends to support this reading.[41] At their best, the core skills of therapy can be conceived as fundamentally spiritual and the therapeutic relationship as sacred.[42] Indeed, the person-centred approach substantially predicts a fuller integration of transpersonal perspectives into mainstream therapy in the future.[43] Thus taking this transpersonal turn, Rogers suggests that counselling touches 'the cutting edge of our ability to transcend ourselves, to create new and more spiritual directions in human evolution' and, at its core, he regards the therapeutic relationship of counselling as a profound partnership between scientific empiricism and spiritual ways of knowing.[44]

### 3. Transpersonal Psychology and Psycho-Spiritual Transformation – Stanislav and Christina Grof

In their thoughtful analysis of spirituality and trauma, Kenneth Pargament, Kavita Desai, and Kelly McConnell satisfactorily conclude that the literature clearly points to the fact that, as a resource to the self, spirituality 'is part and parcel of the human response to trauma and its resolution' and as such may be implicated in psychological growth and decline.[45] As the transpersonal paradigm continues to influence how we see spiritual experience in the light of a broader 'more holistic model of the self', it enables the fuller observation of the self in transformation.[46] If, as the research suggests, the authentic self is to be discovered through a process of, for example, psycho-spiritual growth, then Stanislav Grof's holotropic paradigm captures this experience as both a quantifiable outcome of trauma and as a dynamic process of consciousness. Based upon the universal concept of organismic self-healing by the arousal of the unconscious, Grof in his unique articulation of post-traumatic growth argues that not only can traumatic events create spiritual crises that lead to self-transformation but that spiritual crises in themselves are traumatic events.[47] Thus transpersonal psychology's explanation of the personal integration of spiritual and transpersonal experiences articulates an alternative process of post-traumatic growth.

Stanislav Grof, co-founder of transpersonal psychology, and Christina Grof contextualise a process of spiritual growth in a cartography of the psyche, first fully realised in *Beyond the Brain*, which emphasises the fundamental reality of a material psyche nested in, and infused by, universal consciousness. Stan Grof has written extensively on the difficulties that accompany the crisis of spiritual awakening, a developmental phenomenon first recognised by Roberto Assagioli, and his conceptual framework describes a traditional, culturally, and experientially rich pathway of growth in which emerging spiritual content can have a positive influence on the achievement of expanding consciousness and maturity.[48] Embracing the concept of the fully functioning and actualising person, he uses a positive 'holotropic' framework to explain the altered open disposition of the psyche. Influenced by traditional and eastern philosophical practices that use meditation and visualisation exercises to discharge or integrate trapped traumatic memory and energy in the psyche, Grof envisages the trauma of highly stressful emotional or physical events and the excessive use of spiritual practice or medication as catalysts to the potential of personal growth. Thus Grof, unlike Rogers, can account for the process of stress-related growth in terms of the experience of spiritual emergence or emergency that he claims can be caused by the psyche's spontaneous rebalancing, or its readiness to be transformed by the external stimulation of traumatic events. He suggests that as material from the unconscious swamps the ego and boundaries between the unconscious and consensus reality dissolves; this emergence is experienced as simultaneously psychologically distressing and disorientating but also as deeply transcendent.

Owing a debt to Carl Jung's collective unconscious and quantum physics, Grof sites his 'holotropic', or 'moving toward wholeness' phenomena, in three broad and accessible interconnected domains of the psyche.[49] Post-trauma individuals draw upon a personal biographical dimension to make meaning and modify their life's narrative. A further spiritual or transpersonal dimension extends the biographical, while permitting the intrusion and mediation of undifferentiated spiritual, mythological, and archetypal experiences. Finally, and uniquely, a fundamental biological and existential perinatal dimension acts as a bridge between the biographical and transpersonal domains, enabling a level of universal consciousness ordinarily beyond an individual's reach.[50] Thus subsumed in a broader typology of non-ordinary states of unitive consciousness that characterise the psycho-spiritual growth process, Maslow's peak experience is extended in a limitless cartography of personal awareness.[51] Fortunately, due to the benign nature and the positive potential of the peak experience, Grof considers this category of spiritual emergency to be the least problematic. He notes that these experiences tend to be 'transient and self limited' with no 'adverse consequences.'[52]

In keeping with Abraham Maslow's observations, Stan and Christina Grof submit that individuals, dependent upon their growing awareness, acceptance and understanding of their transforming levels of consciousness, only gradually experience actualising experiences.[53] They may also experience a strengthening of emotional responses, as well as physical distress and pain. Furthermore, if they attempt to disassociate themselves from difficult emerging memories they can become alienated from themselves. This sudden disorientation makes it hard for individuals to function normally and their exposure to complex inner and outer experiences, representing at a symbolic level the trauma that caused them, may also be experienced as traumatic. Spiritual emergencies can challenge old beliefs; confront ways of existing; alter relationships with reality; bring discomfort with a once familiar world; cause perceptual problems; generate physically forceful energies and spontaneous tremors; and prompt individuals to disclose their experiences and insights.

Generally, in spite of the negative connotation of the term 'emergency', Grof does not regard these psycho-spiritual experiences as pathological because they indicate the organism's natural inclination toward growth. If effectively managed, understood and reconciled, the process of spiritual emergency can birth the same quality of post-traumatic growth outcomes ascribed by Rogers to the actualising authentic self: a greater interest in living; improved health and personal satisfaction; an expanded worldview; and a greater openness to spiritual experience. The successful integration of this personal process, Grof and Grof maintain, can reduce aggression, produce a greater tolerance of racial, political and religious differences, increase ecological awareness, and change values and existential priorities. Importantly, as the psyche contains no boundaries and experiences present as a continuum of many dimensions and levels, a psycho-spiritual transformation will be as uniquely different as the individual experiencing it.[54]

If, as the research suggests, the authentic self is to be discovered in the process of psycho-spiritual growth, then traumatic experiences are seriously implicated in creating the necessary conditions for this to occur. As transpersonal psychology presents a more holistic model of the self it is a useful perspective from which to understand the self in transformation.

### 4. Constructivist Psychology and Post-Traumatic Growth: Lawrence Calhoun and Richard Tedeschi

Inspired by the humanistic position on psychological growth, Lawrence Calhoun and Richard Tedeschi's comprehensive theory of post-traumatic growth (PTG) may be conceptualised as a coping mechanism that has an adaptive function, and may also be described as a process and an outcome. Taking a constructivist turn, Calhoun and Tedeschi indicate that, within the struggle with trauma, rumination – the thinking that resolves incongruence and makes sense of previous goals, the self, and current reality – is the most influential in establishing the new schemas predictive of either adaptive or maladaptive outcomes. The literature indicates that adaptive outcomes can include the recognition of strengths and abilities, more satisfaction with relationships, and a positive change in worldview.[55]

The model of post-traumatic growth, therefore, proposes a systematic approach to the study of the phenomenon of change experienced in the struggle that individuals and groups engage in in the aftermath of a traumatic event. In this context a traumatic event is defined by its capacity to make people rethink their beliefs about how they want to live their lives. According to Ronnie Janoff Bulman's concept of 'psychological preparedness', most individuals pre-trauma are psychologically unprepared for the impact of difficult life events. Individuals, untouched by trauma, hold a personal theory of reality, a fundamental set of workable beliefs confirmed by experience, that confer a degree of agency upon themselves and their assumptions about the world as an essentially benevolent place where 'events are not random, but make sense.'[56] Consequently, the working out through rumination of the challenges presented by the shattering and then remaking of the assumptive world, as well as the achievement of sufficient mastery over them, lies at the heart of Lawrence Calhoun and Richard Tedeschi's model. However, necessarily cautious about outcomes, Calhoun and Tedeschi emphasise the complexity of survivor responses to the psychological processes of growth and assert that whilst some will find benefits in the experience of trauma, others experiences of suffering will outweigh by far any perceived benefits.

Calhoun and Tedeschi's model conceives of an individual, or group, in a sequential process or journey which begins with the 'person pretrauma', continues to the moment that they encounter a 'seismic event' which disrupts their sense of self and their assumptive world, and then precipitates a struggle with three broad 'challenges' to the individual's understanding of their self in the world. These challenges are concerned with personal 'beliefs and goals', 'management of emotional distress', and a restructuring of the life 'narrative.'[57] In this struggle they encounter and employ 'automatic and intrusive' forms of 'cognitive engagement' in a process of 'rumination' which may involve intentional therapeutic acts of 'self disclosure' such as writing and talking that subsequently lead to a 'reduction of emotional distress.' This enables the 'management of automatic rumination' and allows some 'disengagement' from previously significant goals. More deliberate rumination involves a working through leading to 'schema change' and includes significant 'narrative development' that re-views and then repositions a more coherent and realistic self in a more plausible world. In addition, a parallel process concerning two sociocultural categories – 'distal', which represents broad cultural themes; and, 'proximate', which represent smaller social networks and communities with whom the individual interacts – are considered in the context of the fuller process of PTG. Finally, the ideal outcome of the PTG process is a more manageable 'distress and the emergence of a new personal 'narrative' alongside a new understanding and 'wisdom.' Through this sense-making struggle the individual, or group, may begin to view his or her self differently, adopt new priorities, and gain a fresh and 'fuller appreciation of life.'[58]

The model attributes the possibility of post-traumatic growth to five measurable but experientially broad domains. Detailed in Tedeschi and Calhoun's *Posttraumatic Growth Inventory*, they include relating to others; new possibilities; personal strength; spiritual change; and, appreciation of life.[59] All of these domains are of general concern to this chapter, but those to do with 'spiritual change', in which individuals experience a deepening of spiritual life accompanied by significant revisions in worldview and 'appreciation of life', are domains of change that reportedly hold the most post-traumatic growth potential.[60] Nevertheless, Tedeschi and Calhoun's inventory continues to favour quantifiable questions specifically concerned with spiritual and religious knowledge, beliefs, and formal practice rather than actual experiences. Unfortunately, this is not untypical. Findings from a recent review of 12 instruments used to assess post-traumatic change in religiosity and spirituality as a component of growth, overwhelmingly suggested the benefit of adding more items to measure spiritual or religious growth factors and to clarify and revise existing items, in order to sufficiently capture change in these areas.[61] The domain of spirituality also entails the confrontation with existential questions that significantly affects other domains of change. As Stan and Christina Grof have noted, in the process of psycho-spiritual transformation individuals inevitably address existential questions as they confront the death of the self, which suggests that this particular struggle is a 'pivotal part of the transformation process' as well as being 'an integral component of most spiritual emergencies.'[62] Whilst growth outcomes of spiritual change and appreciation of life post-trauma may resemble those of peak experience it is difficult to ascertain if these experiences are in any way the same.

As noted elsewhere, clinical practice might benefit from blending Lawrence Calhoun and Richard Tedeschi's model of PTG with Stan Grof's cartography of the psyche, particularly in their application to processes of spiritual emergency, in order to conceptualise the psycho-spiritual role in post-traumatic growth more clearly.[63] Both perspectives draw upon the traditional writing and teaching of spiritual, religious, and philosophical traditions, and both carry an appreciation of the existential and humanistic philosophies that support the existence of an actualising or self-healing tendency toward positive growth activated by stressful life events. They also assume that personal psychological crises may be precipitated by challenges of unexpected, spontaneous and uncontrollable inner or outer events that leave insufficient time to prepare psychologically. In addition, both positions have stressed the significance of the survivor's open experiential style in their 'struggle' to make meaning of their situation as predictive of a more beneficial outcome. Whilst Tedeschi and Calhoun have noted a minimum threshold of distress that has to be crossed before growth can begin to occur, Grof, like Freud before him, pays attention to the influential balance between internal and external events in the individual's 'readiness' to transform as the ego becomes overwhelmed.[64] Nevertheless, both agree that, given an event with enough 'seismic power to produce the level of subjective disruption that is required', a growth process is possible.[65] Similarly, both approaches consider what can happen when too much distress impairs this natural process of self-healing and how practitioners can assist in getting the process back on track when this occurs.

Finally, whether sought or unsought, the ideal post-traumatic outcome seems to be that the individual has moved beyond his or her previous baseline functioning to a fuller experiencing of their authentic self.[66] At this point survivors are deemed to have entered a 'more expanded way of being', or have achieved a level of 'wisdom', or intellectual knowing that is both experiential and affective.[67] With hindsight, and reframing trauma as an opportunity, the processes of psycho-spiritual and PTG could be regarded as launch platforms for life-long journeys into personal development rather than just short-term goals or outcomes of therapy. Bridging these two positions, therefore, provides a different way to understand their principles, processes, tasks, and outcomes. Similarly, by extending the model of PTG in at least two of its experiential domains might assist in clarifying the complex relationship between spirituality and those growth processes that overwhelm us in the wake of stressful life events.

## 5. Psycho-Social and Transformational Growth: Ronnie Janoff-Bulman

Before moving on to specifically discuss positive psychology's contribution to trauma work, it might help to consider social psychologist Ronnie Janoff-Bulman's ideas on trauma and shattered assumptions. Janoff-Bulman is credited with providing the theoretical scaffolding to support the development of two main theories of positive change that currently influence the positive psychology movement.[68] Her thoughts on trauma have been applied to organismic valuing theory, helping to provide a positive change account of post-traumatic stress as a normal and natural cognitive process that has the potential to generate positive change, and a transformational model of post-traumatic growth.[69] Janoff-Bulman's enthusiastic contributions to theory and discussions concerning assumptions that underpin trauma survivors' schema-change are offered from the perspective of three models of PTG and will assist in qualifying what has been discussed above.[70]

Janoff-Bulman considers the term 'posttraumatic growth' too imprecise in its general description of the potential and benefits to growth in the psychologically difficult context of trauma. According to her, the five factors in Tedeschi and Calhoun's model cannot be assumed sufficiently robust to capture the complex psychological processes that support the pathway to positive change. In her critique, and to provide a clearer explanation of PTG processes, she offers the following explanatory models:

A. Strength through Suffering

This model, embedded in folk lore and 'implicit in the redemptive value of suffering taught in many religions', suggests that exposure to adversity is a personally educative experience that assists survivors to become aware of their previously undiscovered strengths, and develop new resources and coping skills that provide them with new possibilities in life.[71] With respect to the PTG model, 'Knowing that survivors have experienced pain and suffering and have come through their trials is sufficient for understanding their new-found strength.'[72] From this perspective survivors are seen as tempered and strengthened by the challenges of trauma.

B. Psychological Preparedness

This model assumes that most individuals are psychologically unprepared for traumatic events – 'It can't happen to me.' Thus low doses of exposure to traumatic experience can be empowering and create resilience. Survivors who have coped with these experiences are subsequently more likely to manage further stressful experiences and less likely to be affected by subsequent tragedies. Over time they can rebuild, and incorporate into their assumptive world, those positive framed core assumptions that make it structurally and psychologically safer and resistant. Knowing that difficult life events are possible, they rebuild their 'new assumptive world...acknowledging this very real possibility in the future...[to]better withstand the shock of tragedy.'[73]

C. Existential Re-Evaluation

Explicitly meaning-making, and implicitly concerned with the organismic valuing process, this model considers those value-finding responses to the trauma event that are counter-intuitive and therefore harder to make sense of. Examining self-reported benefits about a greater appreciation of life, for example, it tries to understand the nature of the existential struggle toward meaning that occurs for survivors as they try to successfully manage the task of rebuilding their inner worlds. Paradoxically, rather than succumbing to the nihilism of universal meaninglessness, most people touched by tragedy must examine what they most value. Part of that valuing relates to the simple fact of survival. By recognising that life becomes invested with greater meaning, the surviving individual develops a sense of fresh and creative agency and hope. Surviving the awful event supplies the confidence and energy to commit to the creation of new values and worth as well as the ability to make deliberate choices.

In her overview, Janoff-Bulman concludes that, when seen in the context of the pain and distress caused by negative life events, the types of post-traumatic growth outcomes reflected in the first two models are both understood and expected while the third model seems to contradict the experience of trauma itself.

### 6. Positive Psychology: Martin Seligman and Stephen Joseph

Discussing how over the past century psychiatry has perpetuated the 'illness ideology', James Maddux suggests that clinical psychology is socially rather than scientifically constructed. He challenges its assumptions about the nature of psychological adjustment, the 'territory' of clinical psychology and its language, claiming that these affect the ways in which psychologists and others think about the field. He proposes a new vision of clinical psychology that incorporates positive psychological values, which he considers of much more use to the field in the future.[74]

When Martin Seligman formally announced the founding of the positive psychology movement in his Presidential Address to the American Psychological Association in 1999, he was following in the footsteps of previous pioneering presidents Maslow and Rogers in establishing a psychology that acknowledged the human potential toward growth and the changes that follow adversity.[75] Challenging the medical model's assumption that psychological problems have an organic explanation, this emerging orientation of psychology was meant to develop but not diminish what was already known about the human response to suffering, disorder and weakness. Consequently, although its establishment marks a significant move away from clinical psychology's deficit model of the person and from the illness ideology that underpins the medical model it also attempts to reframe pathology positively. Thus, by bridging both domains, post-traumatic stress disorder is gradually reframed as post-traumatic growth. Seligman essentially intended to provide a new way to conceptualise, capture, and examine existing research and to pay more attention to those things that 'make life worth living.'[76] More importantly, perhaps, positive psychology makes the grand assumption that people want and will live meaningful and fulfilled lives, cultivate the best within themselves, and enhance their experiences of love, work, and play.

It might be argued that this paradigm simply gives a further positive twist to the core values and practices of existing models of humanistic and existential psychology. However, Seligman replies that the point of difference is as much philosophical as scientific, that psychology's previous focus on understanding and treating problems from a disease model perspective meant that it had little interest in discussing what makes life worth living. Instead he offers the suggestion that, as suffering and well-being belong to the human condition, psychologists have a responsibility to be equally concerned with both. By asserting that human goodness and excellence are as authentic as distress and disorder, he calls upon the academy to correct this imbalance by focussing on strengths as well as weaknesses, building the best in life, as well as repairing the worst. However, Grant Jewell Rich, arguing for an interdisciplinary approach to the continuing conundrum of what makes people happy, cautiously advances that, in order to gather some future support, positive psychologists must acknowledge the legacy of prior psychologies.

Similarly, he adds, humanistic psychologists must correspondingly pay attention to the emerging work of positive psychology to secure a rapprochement.[77]

In a recent television interview, Seligman realistically accepts that in spite of positive psychology's burgeoning growth, its single prescriptive message may have become distorted by an overemphasis on the centrality of happiness to the achievement of a good life. Echoing Carl Rogers's and Stan Grof's strongly held position that direct experience is the ultimate authority, and the central tenets of humanistic and transpersonal psychologies, he points out that 'well-being is not just the absence of misery; it's the presence of real things' and that society's rather than psychology's present engagement with the elimination of misery ignores the experience of living moment to moment.[78]

No doubt positive psychology's focus on the 'good person', in the globally relativistic 'good life', continues to have its roots firmly fixed in humanistic psychology and reiterates the core work of Maslow and Rogers. However, as Stephen Joseph and Alex Linley suggest in their book *Trauma, Recovery, and Growth*, the study of post-traumatic stress and post-traumatic growth have generally been regarded as separate fields of study.[79] Yet, as they concur, 'growth', broadly 'consistent with the person-centered perspective', metaphorically bridges both literatures and concerns both positions.[80] Thus by integrating humanistic and positive psychologies, they contend that Rogers's intrinsically motivated organismic valuing theory of growth might schematically form the basis of an 'organismic valuing theory of growth following adversity.'[81] In addition, a further synthesis, incorporating social and cognitive perspectives originating in principles of self-actualisation, proposes the incorporation of Ronnie Janoff-Bulman's construct of the assumptive world into a psycho-social framework of post-traumatic stress and growth adjustment.

This model views post-traumatic stress as a process rather than an outcome, linking growth to personality development and psychological well-being. It advances that an event stimulus triggers event cognitions of conscious and non-conscious representations of the experience, linked to distressing and/or positive emotional states, and requires integrative cognitive-emotional processing.[82] Similar to those ruminative functions described in Tedeschi and Calhoun's PTG model, these appraisals can be both automatic and consciously controlled and their frequency indicative of how much cognitive-emotional processing needs to occur, and the corresponding levels of personal coping and adjustment. Altered assumptions about the world, therefore, have the capacity to influence, modify and change personal schemas. Thus, with these assumptions disconfirmed, new trauma-related information is either assimilated into and alter existing models of the world, or existing models of the world simply accommodate the new information without modification. Joseph and Linley contend that schema change and subsequent growth occur at this challenging point of accommodation and not assimilation. With the same caution applied to previous models, which in itself says something about how we assume that processes of change and growth of any sort are intrinsically valuable in themselves, they advise that in the appraisal process 'not all accommodation is positively valued as people can also accommodate the new trauma related information in a negative direction', which may or may not lead to psychopathology.[83] Indeed, Camille Wortman, in her specific consideration of PTG, has questioned if growth under these circumstances is universally good. Furthermore, she suggests that, faced with the expectations of these models, trauma survivors and their professional helpers might 'be disappointed' if they don't 'show personal growth' and 'experience feelings of inadequacy and shame if they are not able to find something good in what has happened'[84]

However, in keeping with all the conceptualisations of growth discussed here so far, as traumatic events cause high levels of affect in the survivor, Joseph and Linley also stress the availability of a richly supportive social context throughout the appraisal process, and re-emphasise that growth is facilitated by an intensely intimate struggle with meaning and not from the event itself. The resulting growth outcomes that they detail are surprisingly similar to those noted by Grof and Grof in their research and congruent with other models of growth; they include self-acceptance; autonomy; environmental mastery; personal growth; positive relationships with others; a purpose in life.[85]

In his later work *What Doesn't Kill Us*, Stephen Joseph develops his approach and reappraises the trauma industry in the light of positive psychologies to present his own model of 'thriving'.[86] He hypothesises that post-traumatic stress can be reframed as 'a natural and normal process of adaption to adversity that marks the beginning of a transformative journey.'[87] In the light of research and the anecdotal accounts of trauma survivors up to the present day he makes a number of proposals that privilege the agency of the survivor. He claims that the medically influenced model of trauma therapy may be outmoded because although unhealable, trauma can be positively managed. Based upon research over the last decade, he suggests that the 'effects of trauma have been overestimated' and that PTSD is not necessarily an inevitable outcome of traumatic events.[88] He goes on to note the erroneous belief that all trauma survivors are damaged and 'destined for a life of unremitting despair.'[89] He observes that research indicates that most survivors are resilient to these difficult and life altering events and have the capacity to resist stressors, often quickly recover, and manage to maintain relatively high levels of functioning. In the vein of Rogers, he concludes that to ignore that 'people are capable of finding pathways to reverse the destructiveness of trauma and turn it to their advantage' is to under-utilize or minimise this potential in their growth. Thus in common with those whose work he builds upon, he admits that recovery consists of finding new meaning, new understanding, and 'reparative methods centred on the sharing of memories.'[90] In reframing PTSD, for example, as a struggle towards growth, he suggests that it might be more readily accessed as a common response to a difficult journey that reviews or revisits the experience in order to make sense and integrate it into a new assumptive view of the world. In his THRIVE model for assisting trauma survivors, he explores the hypothesis that positive change can be consciously organised through an awareness that includes a readiness to make changes to thoughts, behaviour, and emotional states. Conceptualised as a difficult journey the survivor negotiates six stages or 'signposts' that include a personal stock-take or inventory of self; 'harvesting hope' within themselves; positively re-authoring the self-narrative; monitoring changes in self, particularly those that seem positive; intrinsically valuing positive changes; and then expressing these changes in their day to day living. [91]

## 7. Trauma and Growth: Endnote

This chapter conceptualises the post-traumatic experience as a difficult journey toward understanding that oscillates between pain and distress at one end of the spectrum and actualising or thriving at the other. Sufficient trauma provokes a schema change perceived as growth, as well as a struggle, a process, an outcome, and by inference a goal. The challenge of trauma often acts as a pivotal moment in a person's life and for a brief time the individual no longer suffers restraint from other's expectations, and enjoys permission to behave 'out of character.' Individuals have a socially sanctioned permit to explore their genuine selves within a socially acceptable timeframe and for that time to experiment with other persona, with other possible futures, and to plant the seeds of new life experiences. However, how they manage this totally depends upon their experiential capacities and agency through time. In general, good pre-trauma functioning and social support throughout the process predict a positively directed struggle with adversity that will have beneficial outcomes, and the reverse also seems true. Circumscribed by social and cultural expectations, traumatic experiences are unique to the individual and yet capable of being shared in community. In many cases survivors ready and active in their personal processes require minimum assistance as they embark on the terrifying and exciting mission of discovery that will provoke life changes and potentially lead to growth.

This chapter has also advanced the idea that personal growth or thriving can occur as a result of trauma. Indeed, it appears to be a significant and fundamental capacity of the human organism to meet this challenge. Whilst humanistic, existential and transpersonal psychologies provide multiple perspectives and approaches to these stressful and challenging experiences, they are still unable to offer conclusive psychological measures that fully explain or understand post-traumatic growth and thriving. In spite of centuries of anecdotal material proving that growth after trauma is possible, individuals and communities conceptions of this phenomenon will continue to remain contentious until the academy can regard accounts of direct experience as sufficient or quantifiable on their own.

On a cautionary note, although human beings have an innate capacity to value what allows growth, they can still operate against their natures in this regard or fail, for whatever reasons, to engage in self-actualising processes. The central message of this chapter, therefore, is that even though we might have faith in the positive human potential to master and even transcend adversity, it would all be valueless if as human beings we were to senselessly turn our backs on survivors' experiences and cease to work to ameliorate the events or social conditions that continually visit misery and suffering upon them.

Finally, the intuitive processes of the traumatised organism do present some fundamental challenges to psychology. In spite of the burgeoning literature on positive growth, positive psychology's laudable quest to integrate perspectives may only be partially achieved if their work encounters resistance from other psychologies or fails to incorporate or overlooks their earlier work. More significantly, any accommodation or movement forward in this area will remain starkly incomplete if it fails to account for the less quantifiable expressions of human capacity illustrated by peak experience, spiritual emergence, and self-actualisation. Who then will redress the balance between the ideologies of illness and wellness, or begin the careful interdisciplinary bridging required to bring together mainstream psychological sciences and the experiential practices, values and philosophies of the longstanding cultures, and spiritual traditions of the world? The academy's journey into this work has been, and no doubt will continue to be, contentious and inevitably not devoid of its own trauma. However, the achievement and understanding of the mystery of positive growth in the face of adversity does seem a fundamental preoccupation and an important desire of many human beings.

## Notes

[1] Nietzsche coined the phrase 'What doesn't kill me makes me stronger' in his book *Twilight of the Idols*. His existential philosophy powerfully supports the contestable view that, when pushed to one's limits, individuals develop characteristics that make them stronger. Stephen Joseph uses this as a starting point for his book: *What Doesn't Kill Us: The New Psychology of Posttraumatic Growth* (London: Piatkus, 2012).

[2] Much of Stan Grof's writings include examples of the mystery of death and rebirth experiences. See Stanislav Grof, *The Ultimate Journey: Consciousness and the Mystery of Death* (Santa Cruz: MAPS, 2006).

[3] Abraham H. Maslow, 'Theory Z', *Journal of Transpersonal Psychology* 1 (1971): 31-47. Reprinted as *The Farther Reaches of Human Nature* (Harmondsworth: Penguin Books, 1973), 280-95.

[4] Margaret Stroebe and Henk Schut, 'The Dual Process Model of Coping with Bereavement: Rationale and Description', *Death Studies* 23 (1999): 192-224; Judith Lewis Herman, *Trauma and Recovery* (NY: Basic Books, 1992), 56.

[5] Jeremy Bentham, 'The Principles of Utility', *The Principles of Morals and Legislation* (1789); Viewed 5 August 2015,
http://www.econlib.org/library/Bentham/bnthPML1.html#Chapter;
Sigmund Freud, *Beyond the Pleasure Principle,* trans. C. J. M. Hubback, ed. Ernest Jones, Viewed 20 May 2013,
http://www.archive.org/stream/Freud_1922_Beyond_the_Pleasure_Principle_k/Freud_1922_Beyond_the_Pleasure_Principle_k_djvu.txt.
[6] Ronnie Janoff-Bulman, 'Posttraumatic Growth: Three Explanatory Models', *Psychological Inquiry* 15 (2004): 30-34.
[7] Ibid., 34.
[8] Vicki S. Helgeson, Kerry A. Reynolds and Patricia L. Tomich, 'A Meta-Analytic Review of Benefit Finding and Growth', *Journal of Consulting and Clinical Psychology* 74 (2006): 797-816.
[9] For their review of the impact of benefit finding on health outcomes: P. Alex Linley and Stephen S. Joseph, 'Positive Change Following Trauma and Adversity: A Review', *Journal of Traumatic Stress* 17 (2004): 11-21.
[10] Camille Wortman, 'Post-Traumatic Growth: Progress and Problems', *Psychological Inquiry* 15 (2004): 88.
[11] Richard Tedeschi and Lawrence Calhoun, 'The Posttraumatic Growth Inventory: Measuring the Positive Legacy of Trauma', *Journal of Traumatic Stress* 9 (1996): 455-471.
[12] Peter Bray, 'Naming Spirituality in Counsellor Education: A Modest Proposal', *New Zealand Journal of Counselling*, Special Issue on Counsellor Education in Aotearoa New Zealand (2011): 76-97.
[13] Peter Bray, *Hamlet's Crisis of Consciousness: The Deeper Dimensions of Adolescent Loss* (Saarbrucken: VDM Verlag, 2008).
[14] Herman, *Trauma and Recovery.*
[15] Mark Callaghan, in this volume.
[16] Stephen S. Joseph, *What Doesn't Kill Us: The New Psychology of Posttraumatic Growth* (London: Piatkus, 2012), 11.
[17] Kurt Goldstein, *The Organism: A Holistic Approach to Biology Derived from Pathological Data in Man* (Boston: Beacon Press, 1939).
[18] Ibid., 305.
[19] From his chapter 'Grand Delusions: Psychotherapies without Feelings', Arthur Janov, Humanistic Psychotherapy: Proclaiming Potential, Ignoring Pain. Viewed 10 April, 2013. http://www.primaltherapy.com/GrandDelusions/GD11.htm.
[20] Abraham H. Maslow, *Motivation and Personality* (New York: Harper & Row, 1987), 100.
[21] Maslow, 'Theory Z', 327.

[22] Roberto Assagioli, *The Act of Will: A Guide to Self-Actualization through Psychosynthesis* (London: Aquarian/Thorsons, 1994), 119.

[23] Maslow, *Motivation and Personality,* 179.

[24] Ibid., 75.

[25] Mark A. Schroll, et al., 'Reflections on Transpersonal Psychology's 40th Anniversary, Ecopsychology, Transpersonal Science, and Psychedelics: A Conversation Forum', *International Journal of Transpersonal Studies* 28 (2009): 39-52.

[26] Miles A. Vich, 'Some Historical Sources of the Term "Transpersonal"', *Journal of Transpersonal Psychology* 20 (1988): 107-110.

[27] Schroll et al., 'Reflections on Transpersonal Psychology's 40th Anniversary', *International Journal of Transpersonal Studies* 28 (2009): 39-52.

[28] Janov, 'Grand Delusions'.

[29] Aryeh Lazar, 'The Relation Between a Multidimensional Measure of Spirituality and Measures of Psychological Functioning Among Secular Israeli Jews', *Journal of Transpersonal Psychology* 41 (2009):4.

[30] Annick Shaw, Stephen S. Joseph and Alex P. Linley, 'Religion, Spirituality, and Posttraumatic Growth: A Systematic Review', *Mental Health, Religion & Culture* 8 (2005): 1-11.

[31] For more on 'self- actualisation' see Carl Rogers, *Client-Centered Therapy: Its Current Practice, Implications and Theory* (London: Constable, 1951).

[32] For more on the 'fully functioning person' see Carl Rogers, *On Becoming a Person: A Therapist's View of Psychotherapy* (London: Constable, 1961).

[33] Ibid., 36.

[34] Carl Rogers, 'A Client-Centered/Person-Centered Approach to Therapy', in *The Carl Rogers Reader*, eds. Howard Kirschenbaum and Valerie Land Henderson (Boston: Houghton Mifflin, 1989), 135-156.

[35] Arthur Janov cites Jeffrey Masson, in *Against Therapy: Emotional Tyranny and the Myth of Psychological Healing* (New York: Athenaeum, 1988), 201-202.

[36] Ibid.

[37] Carl Rogers, 'A Theory of Therapy, Personality and Interpersonal Relationships as Developed in the Client-Centered Framework'. *Psychology: A Study of a Science. Vol. 3: Formulations of the Person and the Social Context*, ed. Sigmund Koch (New York: McGraw Hill, 1959), 184-256.

[38] Kennon M. Sheldon, Jamie Arndt and Linda Houser-Marko, 'In Search of the Organismic Valuing Process: The Human Tendency to Move Towards Beneficial Goal Choices', *Journal of Personality* 71 (2003): 835-869.

[39] 'Center for Studies of the Person-Purpose of the Center'. Viewed 14 September, 2012. http://centerfortheperson.org/.

[40] Carl Rogers, *A Way of Being* (New York: Houghton Mifflin, 1995).

[41] Ibid., 130.

[42] Tangi Hepi and Elizabeth Denton, 'Secular Science Meets Sacred Art: The Bi-Cultural Work of Tangi Hepi, *New Zealand Journal of Counselling* 30 (2010): 13-22.

[43] Keith Morgen, Oliver J. Morgan, Craig Cashwell and Geri G. Miller, 'Strategies for the Competent Integration of Spirituality into Addictions Counseling Training and Supervision'. Viewed 18 May 2013.
http://counselingoutfitters.com/vistas/vistas10/Article_84.pdf.

[44] Rogers, *On Becoming a Person*, 134.

[45] Kenneth Pargament, Kavita Desai and Kelly McConnell, 'Spirituality: A Pathway to Posttraumatic Growth or Decline?', in *Handbook of Posttraumatic Growth: Research and Practice*, eds. Lawrence Calhoun and Richard Tedeschi (Mahway: Lawrence Erlbaum, 2006),121-132.

[46] Brian L. Lancaster and Jason T. Palframan, 'Coping with Major Life Events: The Role of Spirituality and Self-Transformation', *Mental Health, Religion & Culture* 12 (2009): 260.

[47] Originating in Grof's 'holotropic' model of the psyche, and first detailed in *Beyond the Brain* (New York: State University New York Press, 1985), 'spiritual emergence' and 'spiritual emergency' are the subject of, Stanislav Grof and Christina Grof, *Spiritual Emergency* (New York: G. P. Putnam, 1989), and, *The Stormy Search for Self* (Los Angeles: J. P. Tarcher, 1990).

[48] Roberto Assagioli, *Psychosynthesis: The Definitive Guide to the Principles and Techniques of Psychosynthesis* (London: Thorsons, 1993).

[49] Carl G. Jung, 'The Archetypes and the Collective Unconscious', *Collected Works*, Vol 9i.1. (Princeton: Princeton University Press, 1959/1981).

[50] Stanislav Grof, *The Holotropic Mind: The Three Levels of Human Consciousness and How They Shape Our Lives* (New York: Harper Collins, 1993).

[51] Grof and Grof, *Spiritual Emergency.*

[52] Stanislav Grof, *Psychology of the Future: Lessons from Modern Consciousness Research* (Albany: State University of New York Press, 2000), 158.

[53] Grof and Grof, *The Stormy Search for Self.*

[54] Peter Bray, 'A Broader Framework for Exploring the Influence of Spiritual Experience in the Wake of Stressful Life Events: Examining Connections Between Posttraumatic Growth and Psycho-Spiritual Transformation', *Mental Health, Religion and Culture* 13 (2010): 293-30.

[55] Other significant works on this subject by Lawrence Calhoun and Richard Tedeschi, were published in 1995, 1996, 2004, 2006, and in 2008.

[56] Ronnie Janoff-Bulman, 'Posttraumatic Growth', 33.

[57] Lawrence Calhoun and Richard Tedeschi Calhoun, eds., *Handbook of Posttraumatic Growth: Research and Practice* (London: Lawrence Erlbaum Associates, 2006).

[58] Bray, 'A Broader Framework', 293-295.

[59] Tedeschi and Calhoun, 'The Posttraumatic Growth Inventory', 455-471.

[60] Lancaster and Palframan, 'Coping with Major Life Events', 257-276.

[61] Justin J. F. O'Rourke, Benjamin A. Tallman and Elizabeth M. Altmaier, 'Measuring Post-Traumatic Changes in Spirituality/Religiosity', *Mental Health, Religion & Culture* 11 (2008): 719-728.

[62] Grof and Grof, *The Stormy Search for Self*, 57.

[63] Bray, 'A Broader Framework', 293-295.

[64] Sigmund Freud, *Inhibitions, Symptoms, and Anxiety* (London: The Hogarth Press, 1926), 87-172.

[65] Richard Tedeschi, Crystal Park and Lawrence Calhoun, eds., *Posttraumatic Growth: Positive Changes in the Aftermath of Crisis* (London: Lawrence Erlbaum Associates, 1998), 215–216; Grof, *Psychology of the Future.*

[66] Calhoun and Tedeschi, *Handbook of Posttraumatic Growth*, 308.

[67] Grof and Grof, *The Stormy Search for Self*, 34.

[68] Stephen S. Joseph and Lisa D. Butler. 'Positive Changes following Adversity', *PTSD Research Quarterly* 21 (2010): 1-3. See also, Ronnie Janoff-Bulman's seminal work *Shattered Assumptions: Towards a New Psychology of Trauma* (New York: Free Press, 1992).

[69] Stephen Joseph and P. Alex Linley, 'Positive Psychological Perspectives on Posttraumatic Stress: An Integrative Psychosocial Framework', in *Trauma, Recovery and Growth: Positive Psychological Perspectives on Posttraumatic Stress*, eds. Stephen Joseph and P. Alex Linley (Hoboken: John Wiley and Sons, 2008), 3-20.

[70] Ronnie Janoff-Bulman, 'Schema-Change Perspectives on Posttraumatic Growth', in *Handbook of Posttraumatic Growth: Research and Practice*, eds. Lawrence Calhoun and Richard Tedeschi (Mahway: Lawrence Erlbaum, 2006), 81-99.

[71] Ronnie Janoff-Bulman, 'Posttraumatic Growth', 31.

[72] Ibid.

[73] Ibid., 32.

[74] James E. Maddux, 'Positive Psychology and the Illness Ideology: Toward a Positive Clinical Psychology', *Applied Psychology: An International Review* 57 (2008): 54-70.

[75] Stephen Joseph and P. Alex Linley, 'Positive Psychological Perspectives on Posttraumatic Stress', in *Trauma, Recovery and Growth: Positive Psychological*

*Perspectives on Posttraumatic Stress,* eds. Stephen Joseph and P. Alex Linley (Hoboken: John Wiley and Sons, 2008).
[76] Martin E. Seligman and Jane Gilham, eds., *The Science of Optimism and Hope: Research Essays in Honor of Martin E. Seligman* (Philadelphia: Templeton Foundation Press, 2000). 415.
[77] Grant Jewell Rich, 'Positive Psychology: An Introduction', *Journal of Humanistic Psychology* 41(2001): 8-12.
[78] 'Martin Seligman on Newsnight'. Viewed 13 April 2013.
http://www.youtube.com/watch?v=Q-Vhjmdp4nI.
[79] Stephen Joseph and P. Alex Linley, 'Positive Psychological Perspectives on Posttraumatic Stress', 3-20.
[80] Stephen Joseph, 'Growth Following Adversity: Positive Psychological Perspectives on Posttraumatic Stress', *Psychological Topics* 18 (2009): 335-343.
[81] Ibid., 339.
[82] Ibid., 335-343.
[83] Ibid., 339.
[84] Camille Wortman, 'Post-Traumatic Growth: Progress and Problems', 81.
[85] Stephen Joseph and P. Alex Linley, 'Positive Psychological Perspectives on Posttraumatic Stress', 11.
[86] Stephen Joseph, *What Doesn't Kill Us.*
[87] Stephen Joseph, *What Doesn't Kill Us,* xvii.
[88] Ibid., xvi.
[89] In this radio interview Stephen Joseph suggests that traumatic events can become a self-fulfilling prophesy in which PTSD is the expected outcome. 'Life Matters'. BBC National Radio. Viewed 26 April 2013.
http://www.abc.net.au/radionational/programs/lifematters/thursday-26-april-2012/3973020.
[90] Stephen Joseph, *What Doesn't Kill Us,* xvii.
[91] Ibid., 181-222.

## Bibliography

Assagioli, Roberto. *The Act of Will: A Guide to Self-Actualization through Psychosynthesis.* London: Aquarian/Thorsons, 1994.

———. *Psychosynthesis: The Definitive Guide to the Principles and Techniques of Psychosynthesis.* London: Thorsons, 1993.

Bentham, Jeremy 'The Principles of Utility', *The Principles of Morals and Legislation* (1789). Viewed 20 May 2013. http://www.econlib.org/library/Bentham/bnthPML1.html#ChapterIOfthePrinciple of Utility.

Bray, Peter. *Hamlet's Crisis of Consciousness: The Deeper Dimensions of Adolescent Loss.* Saarbrucken: VDM Verlag, 2008.

———. 'A Broader Framework for Exploring the Influence of Spiritual Experience in the Wake of Stressful Life Events: Examining Connections between Posttraumatic Growth and Psycho-Spiritual Transformation'. *Mental Health, Religion and Culture* 13 (2010): 293-30.

———. 'Naming Spirituality in Counsellor Education: A Modest Proposal'. *New Zealand Journal of Counselling*, Special Issue on Counsellor Education in Aotearoa New Zealand (2011): 76-97.

Calhoun, Lawrence and Richard Tedeschi, eds. *Handbook of Posttraumatic Growth: Research and Practice.* London: Lawrence Erlbaum Associates, 2006.

Freud, Sigmund. *Beyond the Pleasure Principle.* Translated by C. J. M. Hubback, edited by Ernest Jones. Viewed 20 May 2013.

———. *Inhibitions, Symptoms, and Anxiety.* London: The Hogarth Press, 1926.

Goldstein, Kurt. *The Organism: A Holistic Approach to Biology Derived from Pathological Data in Man.* Boston: Beacon Press, 1939.

Grof, Stanislav. *Beyond the Brain: Birth, Death and Transcendence in Psychotherapy.* Albany: State University New York Press, 1985.

———. *The Holotropic Mind: The Three Levels of Human Consciousness and How They Shape Our Lives.* New York: Harper Collins, 1993.

———. *Psychology of the Future: Lessons from Modern Consciousness Research.* Albany: State University of New York Press, 2000.

———. *The Ultimate Journey: Consciousness and the Mystery of Death.* Santa Cruz: MAPS, 2006.

Grof, Stanislav and Christina Grof, eds. *Spiritual Emergency: When Personal Transformation Becomes a Crisis.* New York: G. P. Putnam's Sons, 1989.

———. *The Stormy Search for Self.* Los Angeles: J. P. Tarcher, 1990.

Helgeson, Vicki S., Kerry A. Reynolds and Patricia L. Tomich. 'A Meta-Analytic Review of Benefit Finding and Growth'. *Journal of Consulting and Clinical Psychology* 74 (2006): 797-816.

Hepi, Tangi and Elizabeth Denton. 'Secular Science Meets Sacred Art: The Bi-Cultural Work of Tangi Hepi'. *New Zealand Journal of Counselling* 30 (2010): 13-22.

Herman, Judith Lewis. *Trauma and Recovery.* New York: Basic Books, 1992.

Janoff-Bulman, Ronnie. *Shattered Assumptions: Towards a New Psychology of Trauma.* New York: Free Press, 1992.

———. 'Posttraumatic Growth: Three Explanatory Models'. *Psychological Inquiry* 15 (2004): 30-34.

———. 'Schema-Change Perspectives on Posttraumatic Growth'. *Handbook of Posttraumatic Growth: Research and Practice*, edited by Lawrence Calhoun and Richard Tedeschi, 81-99. Mahway: Lawrence Erlbaum, 2006.

Janov, Arthur. *Humanistic Psychotherapy: Proclaiming Potential, Ignoring Pain.* Posted June 2005. Viewed 10 October 2012. http://www.primaltherapy.com/GrandDelusions/GD11.htm

Joseph, Stephen S. *What Doesn't Kill Us: The New Psychology of Posttraumatic Growth.* London: Piatkus, 2012.

———. Life Matters. BBC National Radio. Viewed 26 April 2012.

Joseph, Stephen S. and Lisa D. Butler. 'Positive Changes Following Adversity'. *PTSD Research Quarterly* 21 (2010): 1-3.

Joseph, Stephen S. and P. Alex Linley, eds. *Trauma, Recovery and Growth: Positive Psychological Perspectives on Posttraumatic Stress.* Hoboken: John Wiley and Sons, 2008.

Jung, Carl G. 'The Archetypes and the Collective Unconscious'. *Collected Works,* Vol. 9.1. Princeton: Princeton University Press, 1959/1981.

Lancaster, Brian L. and Jason T. Palframan. 'Coping with Major Life Events: The Role of Spirituality and Self-Transformation'. *Mental Health, Religion & Culture* 12 (2009): 257-276.

Lazar, Aryeh. 'The Relation Between a Multidimensional Measure of Spirituality and Measures of Psychological Functioning Among Secular Israeli Jews' *Journal of Transpersonal Psychology* 41 (2009): 4.

Linley, P. Alex and Stephen S. Joseph. 'Positive Change Following Trauma and Adversity: A Review'. *Journal of Traumatic Stress* 17 (2004): 11-21.

Maddux, James E. 'Positive Psychology and the Illness Ideology: Toward a Positive Clinical Psychology'. *Applied Psychology: An International Review* 57 (2008): 54-70.

Maslow, Abraham H. *The Farther Reaches of Human Nature.* Harmondsworth: Penguin Books, 1973.

———. *Motivation and Personality.* New York: Harper Row, 1970.

O'Rourke, Justin J. F., Benjamin A. Tallman and Elizabeth M. Altmaier. 'Measuring Post-Traumatic Changes in Spirituality/Religiosity'. *Mental Health, Religion & Culture* 11 (2008): 719-728.

Pargament, Kenneth, Kavita Desai and Kelly McConnell. 'Spirituality: A Pathway to Posttraumatic Growth or Decline?' *Handbook of Posttraumatic Growth: Research and Practice,* edited by Lawrence Calhoun and Richard Tedeschi, 121-132. Mahway: Lawrence Erlbaum, 2006.

Rich, Grant Jewell. 'Positive Psychology: An Introduction'. *Journal of Humanistic Psychology* 41 (2001): 8-12.

Rogers, Carl. *Client-Centered Therapy: Its Current Practice, Implications and Theory.* London: Constable, 1951.

————. 'A Theory of Therapy, Personality and Interpersonal Relationships as Developed in the Client-Centered Framework'. *Psychology: A Study of a Science. Vol. 3: Formulations of the Person and the Social Context*, edited by Sigmund Koch, 184-256. New York: McGraw Hill, 1959.

————. *On Becoming a Person: A Therapist's View of Psychotherapy.* London: Constable, 1961.

————. 'A Client-Centered/Person-Centered Approach to Therapy'. *The Carl Rogers Reader*, edited by Howard Kirschenbaum and Valerie Land Henderson, 135-156. Boston: Houghton Mifflin, 1989.

————. *A Way of Being.* New York: Houghton Mifflin, 1995.

Seligman, Martin. *Newsnight.* Viewed 13 July 2012.
http://www.youtube.com/watch?v=Q-Vhjmdp4nI

Seligman, Martin E. and Jane Gilham, eds. *The Science of Optimism and Hope: Research Essays in Honor of Martin E. Seligman.* Philadelphia: Templeton Foundation Press, 2000.

Schroll, Mark A., Stanley Krippner, Miles A. Vich, James Fadiman and Valerie Mojeiko. 'Reflections on Transpersonal Psychology's 40th Anniversary, Ecopsychology, Transpersonal Science, and Psychedelics: A Conversation Forum'. *International Journal of Transpersonal Studies* 28 (2009): 39-52.

Shaw, Annick, Stephen S. Joseph and Alex P. Linley, 'Religion, Spirituality, and Posttraumatic Growth: A Systematic Review. *Mental Health, Religion & Culture* 8 (2005): 1-11.

Sheldon, Kennon M., Jamie Arndt and Linda Houser-Marko. 'In Search of the Organismic Valuing Process: The Human Tendency to Move Towards Beneficial Goal Choices'. *Journal of Personality* 71 (2003): 835-869.

Stroebe, Margaret and Henk Schut. 'The Dual Process Model of Coping with Bereavement: Rationale and Description'. *Death Studies* 23 (1999): 192-224.

Tedeschi, Richard and Lawrence Calhoun. 'The Posttraumatic Growth Inventory: Measuring the Positive Legacy of Trauma'. *Journal of Traumatic Stress* 9.3 (1996): 455-471.

Tedeschi, Richard, Crystal Park and Lawrence Calhoun, eds. *Posttraumatic Growth: Positive Changes in the Aftermath of Crisis.* London: Lawrence Erlbaum Associates, 1998.

Vich, Miles A. 'Some Historical Sources of the Term "Transpersonal"'. *Journal of Transpersonal Psychology* 20 (1988): 107-110.

Wortman, Camille. 'Post-Traumatic Growth: Progress and Problems'. *Psychological Inquiry* 15 (2004): 81-90.

**Peter Bray** is an Associate Professor in The Faculty of Humanities, Arts and Trades at the Eastern Institute of Technology in Hawke's Bay, NZ. Widely published in scholarly peer-reviewed journals, he has recently edited two collections of work which reflect his developing interest in trauma, *Voicing Trauma and Truth: Narratives of Disruption and Transformation* (2013) with his son Oliver Bray, and '*The Strangled Cry': The Communication and Experience of Trauma* (2013), with Apara Nanda. Currently, his research and writing in counselling and psychology concern themselves with exploring the position of individuals challenged by crises, and the roles that spiritual dimensions of experience play in their post-traumatic growth. Peter Bray is the author of *Hamlet's Crisis of Consciousness: The Deeper Dimensions of Adolescent Loss* (2008).